Contents

Chapter One 1
Chapter Two 11
Chapter Three 17
Chapter Four 28
Chapter Five 38
Chapter Six 49
Chapter Seven 62
Chapter Eight 75
Chapter Nine 90
Chapter Ten 102
Chapter Eleven 112
Chapter Twelve 125
Chapter Thirteen 139
Chapter Fourteen 151
Chapter Fifteen 163
Chapter Sixteen 174
Chapter Seventeen 190
Chapter Eighteen 201
Chapter Nineteen 213
Chapter Twenty 226
Chapter Twenty-One 237

JOHN CHAPTER ONE

"In the beginning was the word, and the word was with God, and the word was God &c."—John 1, v. 1, 2, 3.

1. The Word, the uncreated Son,
When finite things began to be,
Existing, God with God alone,
Thou wast from all eternity!
God in thy Father's bosom laid,
Ineffably begot by Him,
Thou wast, before the worlds were made,
God independent and supreme.

2. All-wise, all-good, almighty Lord,
God over all Thou always art,
Jehovah's everlasting Word,
Spoken into thy creature's heart:
With God essentially the same,
Distinct in personality,
Thou art the absolute I AM,
And all things made were made by Thee.

"In him was life, and the life was the light of men."—John 1, v. 4.

Fountain of life to all that live,
Thyself, th' essential Life divine,
Thou didst to our first parents give,
And in their sinless nature shine:
The Life was Light, and happiness,
And wisdom pure with Thee bestow'd:
In all thy works they saw thy face,
While all thy works were fill'd with God.

"The light shineth in darkness, and the darkness comprehended it not."—John 1, v. 5.

Still on the fallen soul of man
Thou dost a beam of glory shed,
A ray of grace, an hidden grain,
A spark of life, an heavenly seed:
He wakes, and thinks by slow degrees,
Nor yet the Principle perceives,
Or knows the Light by which he sees,
Or feels the Life by which he lives.

"John came to bear witness of the Light, that all men through It might believe."—John 1, v. 7.

1. The first Apostle of the Lamb,
First witness to the Light he came,
First confessor of thine;
Jesus, thy honour'd minister
He came, thy coming to declare,
Eternal Word Divine.

2. But shining in the faithless heart,
Thou only dost the power impart
His record to receive,
"That every fallen child of man
"Thro' Thee the saving grace may gain,

"And in Thyself believe."

"That was the true light, which lighteth every man that cometh into the world."—John 1, v. 9.

1. True Light of the whole world, appear,
Answer in us thy character,
Thou uncreated Sun;
Jesus, thy beams on all are shed,
That all may by thy beams be led
To that eternal throne.

2. Lighten'd by thy interior ray,
Thee every child of Adam may
His unknown God adore,
And following close thy secret grace,
Emerge into that glorious place
Where darkness is no more.

3. The universal Light Thou art,
And turn'd to Thee the darkest heart
A glimmering spark may find:
Let man reject it, or embrace,
Thou offer'st once thy saving grace
To me, and all mankind.

4. Light of my soul, I follow Thee,
In humble faith on earth to see
Thy perfect day of love,
And then with all thy saints in light,
To gain that beatific Sight,
Which makes our heaven above.

"He was in the world, and the world was made by him, and the world knew him not."—John 1, v. 10.

1. Jesus, the world was made by Thee,
That men in all thy works might see
Thy wisdom, love, and power,
But thro' their own false wisdom blind,
Their present God they cannot find,
Or worthily adore.

2. In pity for our helpless race,
Thou cam'st the shades of sin to chase,
The manifested Word,
Yet still the world lie wrapt in night,
And shut their eyes against the Light,
And will not know their Lord.

"He came unto his own, and his own received him not."—John 1, v. 11.

1. Thyself Thou would'st to sinners give,
But Thee thine own will not receive
With all thy proffer'd love,
Thy subjects they refuse to be,
Disdaining to be led by Thee
To endless joys above.

2. Thee if they finally deny,
And harden'd unbelievers die,

Yet, by themselves undone,
Thy creatures, and redeem'd they are,
Invited, and design'd to share
Thine everlasting throne.

"As many as received him, to them gave he power to become the sons of God, even to them that believe on his name."—John 1, v. 12.

1. Thee, Jesus, full of truth and grace,
My God, my Saviour I embrace,
To all thy creatures given,
My Prophet, Priest, and King receive,
And in thine only name believe,
For pardon, grace, and heaven.

2. Sole, self-existing God, I own
The merit of thy death alone
Hath ransom'd all mankind,
And every dying slave in Thee
With peace, and perfect liberty,
May life eternal find.

3. I use the power by Thee bestow'd
T' accept thee as my Lord my God,
The privilege divine
Assur'd thou wilt on me bestow,
That born of God my soul may know,
Whate'er Thou art, is mine.

4. Not differing from a servant now,
I wait in humble faith, till Thou
Art in my heart reveal'd:
Then shall I Abba Father cry,
An heir of all in earth and sky,
An heir of glory seal'd.

"The Word was made flesh, and dwelt among us (and we beheld his glory, the glory as of the only begotten of the Father) full of grace and truth."—John 1, v. 14.

1. What angel can the grace explain!
The very God is very man,
By Love Paternal given!
Begins the uncreated Word,
Born is the everlasting Lord,
Who made both earth and heaven.

2. Behold him high above all height,
Him God of God, and Light of Light,
In a mean earthy shrine;
Jehovah's Glory dwelt with men,
The Person in our flesh is seen,
The Character Divine!

3. Not with these eyes of flesh and blood;
Yet lo, we still behold the God
Replete with truth and grace,
The truth of holiness we see,
The truth of full felicity
In our Redeemer's face.

4. Transform'd by the extatic Sight,
Our souls o'reflow with pure

delight,
And every moment own
The Lord our whole Perfection is,
The Lord is our immortal bliss,
And Christ and heaven are one.

"Of his fulness have we all received, and grace for grace."—John 1, v. 16.

1. Him in whom all fulness dwells
Every true believer feels,
Every soul by Christ restor'd
Shines a copy of his Lord;
Father of his church and Head,
All the heaven-begotten seed
Cry, We have receiv'd from Him,
Grace for grace, as limb for limb.

2. O that with the faithful I
Could thy fulness testify!
Jesus, is there not in Thee
Grace, sufficient grace for me?
Let me now with thee receive
All thou dost to sinners give,
All thou hast, and all thou art
Dwell forever in my heart!

"The law was given by Moses, but grace and truth came by Jesus Christ."—John 1, v. 17.

1. The fiery law by Moses given
Was thunder'd in a voice from heaven;
In shadowy types and victims slain,
Which could not purge our sinful stain;
It only pointed at the Lamb:
But grace and truth by Jesus came.

2. He in our mortal flesh reveal'd,
The types substantially fulfil'd,
By one sufficient sacrifice,
Forever smoking thro' the skies,
He answer'd the demand of God,
And quench'd the wrath with all his blood.

"No man hath seen God at any time; the only begotten Son, which is in the bosom of the Father, he hath declared him."—John 1, v. 18.

1. Thee, Son of the Most-high,
Jesus we glorify,
In thy Father's bosom laid,
Thou dost all his secrets know,
Partner of our nature made
Dost declare his name below.

2. With eyes of faith we see
Th' Invisible in Thee,
When thou dost thy Sire reveal,
Then I know thee who thou art,
Find the great Unsearchable,
God residing in my heart.

3. Thou dost the Spirit confer,
The heavenly Comforter:
Thus the tri-une God of love
God of glory we receive,
Antedate the joys above,
Here the life eternal live.

"He confessed, and denied not; but confessed, I am not the Christ."—John 1, v. 20.

1. The saint indeed, the humble man
Such as he is delights t' appear,
In words distinct, and strong, and plain
Disowns his Saviour's character,
Renounces man's misplac'd esteem,
As what belongs to God, not him.

2. He doth not in their error leave
The men who foolishly extol,
Too highly of his grace conceive,
Him holy, pure, or perfect call,
But all their fond conceits removes,
And still the lowest place he loves.

"And they asked him, What then? Art thou Elias? And he saith, I am not. Art thou that prophet? And he answered, No."—John 1, v. 21.

1. In unambiguous words and few,
Which just suffice his mind t' express,
He disavows the praise undue;
The truth they urge him to confess
Simply declares, from falsehood free,
Nor wounds his own humility.

2. His own advantages of grace,
If known, yet he regards them, not;
The good he truly doth possess
O'relooks, as slighted and forgot:
Yet while he seeks himself to hide,
He hates the modest veil of pride.

"Then said they unto him, Who art thou? what sayest thou of thyself?"—John 1, v. 22.

The humble man by Jesus sent,
If just authority constrain,
As mercy's meanest instrument
Speaks of himself with irksom pain,
And chusing to remain unknown,
Fixes our thoughts on Christ alone.

"He said, I am the voice of one crying in the wilderness."—John 1, v. 23.

1. More than a prophet sent by God,
Forerunner of the Lord most-high,
With all Elijah's spirit endued,
Himself he doth not magnify,
But while Messiah he proclaims,
Himself a voice, a nothing names.

2. Full of the greatness of his Lord
Himself he studies to abase,
Let Jesus be alone ador'd,
Object of universal praise,

Proprietor of all esteem
Bow all in earth and heaven to Him!

"Behold the Lamb of God, which taketh away the sin of the world."—John 1, v. 29.

1. Did Jesus for the world atone?
"Yes; for the world of the elect."
Love could not die for some alone,
And all the wretched rest reject:
For the whole helpless world that lay
In desperate wickedness, he died,
And all who dare believe it, may
With me be freely justified.

2. Charg'd with the universal load,
The sins of every soul, and mine,
By faith I see the Lamb of God,
The bleeding sacrifice Divine!
My sins, transfer'd from me to Him,
Shall never be by justice found,
All carried down that purple stream,
All in that open fountain drown'd!

"I saw the Spirit descending from heaven, like a dove, and it abode upon him."—John 1, v. 32.

1. Spotless, meek, and holy Lamb,
Why didst Thou the Spirit receive?
From thy throne on Thee He came,
That Thou might'st to sinners give,
Might'st communicate to me
The divine pacific Dove,
Fill my heart with purity,
Innocence, and fruitful love.

2. Let him, Lord, my heart inspire,
All thy gracious mind reveal,
Kindle the baptismal fire,
Now the heir of glory seal;
Let the Comforter come down,
Take possession of my breast,
Make the heavenly nature known,
On my soul forever rest.

"Upon whom thou shalt see the Spirit descending and remaining on him, the same is he which baptizeth with the holy Ghost."—John 1, v. 33.

By this celestial sign
We the Baptizer know,
And all baptiz'd with love Divine
The self-same token show:
On them the Spirit of grace
Descends, and still abides,
And fills with fruits of righteousness,
And to his glory guides.

"Behold the Lamb of God!"—John 1, v. 36.

1. God supreme, who died'st for me

In that atoning Lamb,
Weary of not loving Thee,
Griev'd at my heart I am:
Thee I never yet beheld
In bleeding majesty Divine,
Never felt thy love reveal'd,
Or that had kindled mine.

2. Suffering in the sinner's place,
Transfixt on Calvary,
Give me eyes thy mournful face
Thy mangled form to see;
Lovely in thy garments dyed,
Crush'd with the universal load,
Shew me now thy hands and side,
And conquer by thy blood.

3. Help, O help mine unbelief,
Or thou hast died in vain,
Come, and heal my sin and grief,
And purge my nature's stain;
Saviour of the world, bestow
The precious gift of faith divine,
Then my Ransomer I know,
I feel that thou art mine.

"They followed Jesus."—John 1, v. 37.

1. Naked is my heart to Thee;
Would I not thy follower be,
Tread the path which Thou hast trod,
Track thee, Saviour, by thy blood,
Meekly thine afflictions share,
Every day thy burthen bear,
Drink thy passion's sacred cup,
Fill thy mournful measure up?

2. Thou didst once for sin atone,
Tread the winepress quite alone,
Yet I may thy grief partake,
Suffer for my Master's sake,
Thro' the strength thy cross supplies
Mingle with thy sacrifice,
Bow my head on yonder tree,
Die for one who died for me.

"Jesus turned, and saw them following, and saith unto them, What seek ye? They said unto him, Master, where dwellest thou?"—John 1, v. 38.

1. We seek the Saviour of mankind,
If He infuse the good desire,
But Jesus we can never find,
Unless we of himself inquire,
Leave every ministerial John,
And ask for Christ of Christ alone.

2. The law points out the Victim slain,
And tow'ard him a few steps we go,
But never can to Christ attain,
Till He the power of faith bestow,
Turning to us, himself impart,
And speak in mercy to the heart.

3. Master (as such Thyself I own)
My Master and Director be,
Instruct me in the way unknown,
Which leads to happiness and Thee,
And by the lessons of thy love
Conduct me to thy house above.

"He saith unto them, Come and see &c."—John 1, v. 39.

1. Inspir'd with faith, we come and see,
The place of thy abode we know,
And tarry in thy house with Thee;
Where two or three are met below,
Thee, Jesus, in the midst we meet,
Whose presence makes the church compleat.

2. Come all, and see our Saviour here!
He still doth in his house abide,
Assembled with his church appear
Diffus'd thro' earth and scatter'd wide:
And here we all with Christ may sup,
Till to his throne He takes us up.

"He first findeth his own brother Simon, and saith unto him, We have found the Messiah."—John 1, v. 41.

The man who hath his Saviour found,
And knows where He vouchsafes to dwell,
Should never bury in the ground
His treasure, or his faith conceal,
But testify the gospel-word,
And others urge to seek their Lord.

"And he brought him to Jesus."—John 1, v. 42.

'Tis not enough to speak for God:
If God our faithful labours speed,
We minister the grace bestow'd,
And precious souls to Jesus lead,
Point them to the Messiah nigh,
And place beneath his pitying eye.

"When Jesus beheld him, he said, Thou art Simon &c."—John 1, v. 42.

Happy whome'er the God of grace
Beholds with looks of tender love!
His look is saving to our race,
Our miseries and sins remove,
His looks immortal strength impart,
And reach the poor, expecting heart.

"Jesus findeth Philip, and saith unto him, Follow me."—John 1, v. 43.

1. O the riches of thy grace!
Grace surpassing all our thought,
Grace transcending all our praise,
Finding those who sought thee not!
Grace doth more than sin abound,
For a world of sinners free:
Me their guilty chief it found,
Me it drew to follow Thee.

2. Master of my heart and will,
Both are in thy gracious hand,
Seek, and call, and draw me still
Subject to thy mild command:
Then I after Thee shall run,
Fly on wings of faith and love,
Find thee, Saviour, on thy throne,
Glorify thy grace above.

"Philip findeth Nathanael, and saith unto him, We have found him of whom Moses in the law, and the prophets did write Jesus of Nazareth, the son of Joseph."—John 1, v. 45.

1. While all his holy angels
With hymns of praise surround him,
We sing below, Who Jesus know,
And in our hearts have found him:
Whom Moses and the prophets
Foretold by inspiration,
We now embrace, Our Lord confess,
Our Saviour, and Salvation.

2. To all our guilty brethren
We the good news discover,
Believe, and you Shall find Him too,
The universal Lover;
Receive the true Messias
Whom God to man hath given,
And when you see, And know tis He,
You know the joys of heaven.

"Nathanael said unto him, Can there any good thing come out of Nazareth?"—John 1, v. 46.

An Israelite indeed,
A foe to worldly art,
May be by prejudice misled,
Yet never err in heart:
God will not leave him long
Without distincter light,
Or let a soul continue wrong
Whose life is in the right.

"Philip saith unto him, Come and see."—John 1, v. 46.

By tasting Him we know,
By faith we come and see
Th' Invisible reveal'd below,
Th' incarnate Deity:
We search the written word,
We weigh, and all things prove,
And wait the leizure of our Lord
To manifest his love.

"Behold an Israelite indeed, in whom is no guile."—John 1, v. 47.

O were I like him sincere,
Blest with Jacob's character,
Artless, innocent, and plain,
Upright both to God and man!
True to all which I profess,
In simplicity of grace,
Lord, I would thy follower be,
Seek the praise that comes from Thee.

"Before that Philip called thee, when thou wast under the fig-tree, I saw thee."—John 1, v. 48.

1. Me, I know, thine eye beheld
From the eye of man conceal'd,
Where I ignorantly pray'd
In the solitary shade:
Conscious of my nakedness,
Cover'd with my leafy dress,
There I heard thy secret call,
There began to feel my fall.

2. Drawn I was and taught by thee
From my earliest infancy,
In the lessons of thy grace
I my heavenly Master trace:
Searcher of my simple heart,
God's omniscient Son thou art,
Israel's King I worship thee;
Come, and fix thy throne in me.

"Rabbi, thou art the Son of God, thou art the King of Israel."—John 1, v. 49.

Jesus, thou our Rabbi art,
Thy sayings we receive
With docility of heart,
And joyfully believe;
Thee, the Son of God confess,
Co-equal with thy Father own,
Israel's King, thy sway we bless,
And hail thee on thy throne.

"Thou shalt see greater things than these."—John 1, v. 50.

Yes, my gracious God and Lord,
If I believe in thee,
I shall prove thine utmost word,
And greater wonders see,
I shall in thy will delight,
And comprehend with saints above
All the length, and bredth, and height,
And depth of perfect love.

"Hereafter you shall see heaven open, and the angels of God ascending and descending upon the Son of man."—John 1, v. 51.

1. Greater things Nathanael view'd,
When heaven he saw thrown wide,
Saw the Son of man and God
On wings of Cherubs ride,
Israel's car and steeds of fire
For Israel's glorious King sent down,
Christ with all th' angelic quire
Returning to his throne.

2. These the greater things which I,
Ev'n I expect to see,
Christ descending from the sky
In beauteous majesty,
With his bright angelic train,
While all his saints behold him near,
I shall see my Lord again,
And in his sight appear.

3. Israel spiritual, renew'd
In love, and pure in heart,

We shall meet and clasp our God,
And never never part,
Midst th' acclaiming hosts ascend,
With all the clarions of the sky,
Rapt to bliss which cannot end,
To life which cannot die.

JOHN CHAPTER TWO

"There was a marriage in Cana of Galilee; and the Mother of Jesus was there."—John 2, v. 1.

Mother of Purity Divine,
The Virgin grac'd a nuptial feast:
But who in Jesus' Spirit join,
They entertain a nobler Guest,
Who meet and marry in the Lord,
Blest as the first unspotted pair,
They find their paradise restor'd,
And Purity himself is there.

"And both Jesus was called, and his disciples to the marriage."—John 2, v. 2.

1. They, only they the Lord invite
Their hallow'd nuptials to attend,
Who seek in Him their chief delight,
Their Bridegroom and celestial Friend,
Who ask his love their feast to crown,
In wrestling faith their wants declare,
And bring the blisful Spirit down
By all the powers of humble prayer.

2. They bid the Lord's disciples too,
Who marry as his saints approve,
Expose their hearts to open view,
Set on th' eternal things above,
Who not with flesh and blood confer,
But counsel with the faithful take,
And call the church their bliss to share,
And love them all for Jesus sake.

3. How fatal, and unlike to these
The world's alliances profane,
Where sinners match, themselves to please,
And lust and foul intemperance reign,
By avarice, or ambition join'd,
They banish God from all their thought,
And madly cast his fear behind,
While Mammon ties the hellish knot.

"When they wanted wine, the mother of Jesus saith unto him, They have no wine. Jesus saith unto her, Woman, what have I to do with thee? mine hour is not yet come."—John 2, v. 4.

I.

1. Our real want of needful food
We still may represent to God,
With true simplicity:
Saviour, thou dost with smiles approve
Our humble confidence of love

Which all expects from Thee.

2. Yet must we not presume to know,
Or tell thee when thy grace to show,
Thy benefits to give,
But trusting in thy mercy's power,
The manner and appointed hour
Unto thy wisdom leave.

3. Then let us urge our meek request,
Nature's anticipating haste
With patient faith forego,
Assur'd, thou wilt thy people feed,
And outward and immortal bread
In thy own time bestow.

"When they wanted wine, the mother of Jesus saith unto him, They have no wine. Jesus saith unto her, Woman, what have I to do with thee? mine hour is not yet come."—John 2, v. 4.

II.

1. Loos'd from the ties of flesh and blood,
Jesus, in all the things of God
Thy messenger should be,
Deaf to the voice of nature's now,
To Thee for his instructions bow,
And singly look to Thee.

2. Harshly Thou dost thy mother treat,
Least pious parents should forget
Their sons are not their own,
Or plead a right to interfere
In matters where thy minister
Is taught of God alone.

"His mother saith unto the servants, Whatsoever he saith unto you, do it."—John 2, v. 5.

Reprov'd she answers not a word,
But waiting on her heavenly Lord
Her confidence holds fast,
With faith increas'd the check receives,
He will, she fully now believes,
Do his own work at last.

"Jesus saith, Fill the water pots with water. And they filled them up to the brim."—John 2, v. 7.

1. When wine they want, th' Almighty Lord
Water in stead of wine demands:
He both created by his word,
Nothing his sovereign will withstands;
And every year in every vine
He changes water into wine.

2. Annext to means improbable
Thy blessing, Lord, we oft perceive,
Who, when thou dost thy mind reveal,
Thy word implicitly believe,
And do what Thou art pleas'd t'

ordain,
And thus a farther grace obtain.

"When the ruler of the feast had tasted the water that was made wine &c."—John 2, v. 9.

1. Jesus, to Thee our wants we tell
(But need no Advocate with Thee)
Fountain of life, Salvation's Well,
Divine, imparadizing Tree,
Thou are the true immortal Vine,
Which chears thy saints with heavenly wine.

2. Our thirsty souls the wine require,
Which from thy wounded body flow'd,
The ben'fits of thy death desire,
The virtues of thy precious blood;
The Spirit from thy throne above,
The full effusion of thy love.

3. Convert our nature into grace,
Our heart to things of earth inclin'd
To objects spiritual upraise,
To heavenly good our groveling mind,
And give our new-born souls a taste
Of joys which shall forever last.

4. The Vessels of thy mercy fill
(Till our glad hearts with thanks o'reflow,)
With power to do thy utmost will,
And perfect holiness below,
Fill up our soul's capacity
With all the love which is in Thee.

"Thou hast kept the good wine until now."—John 2, v. 10.

1. Call'd to the marriage of the Lamb,
Jehovah in our flesh we see;
T' espouse his church, from heaven He came,
The great stupendous mystery
Made by his incarnation known,
And join'd our nature to his own.

2. Under thy shade, O Christ, we sing,
Partakers of thy nuptial feast;
Thou hast reserv'd the better thing,
To chear thy every welcome guest,
To gladden all the faithful race
With the good wine of gospel-grace.

3. Now in the end of time reveal'd
Thy choicest, sweetest grace we prove,
And fill'd with Thee, our souls are fill'd
With purity of perfect love,
Of love unknown in ages past,
Kept in thy heart to crown the last.

4. Thou dost in closest bonds unite
Our souls incorporate with Thee;
We antedate the full delight
The saints supreme felicity,
Flesh of thy flesh, bone of thy bone,
With Thee inexplicably one.

5. Thy saints in holiness compleat,
Consummated by rapturous love
Shall at thy side triumphant sit,
And keep the marriage-feast above:
And when thy blisful face we view,
We drink the wine forever new.

"This beginning of miracles did Jesus, and manifested forth his glory; and his disciples believed on him."—John 2, v. 11.

I.

1. To change the soul's ignoble taste,
T' inspire the hope of things divine,
Of pleasures pure which always last,
And change our water into wine,
Jesus at first his grace exerts,
And heav'nward turns our earthly hearts.

2. Chang'd the strong bent of nature's will
With joy and wonder we confess,
New hopes, desires, sensations feel,
Hunger and thirst for righteousness,
And worship that Incarnate Word,
And see that Glory of the Lord.

"This beginning of miracles did Jesus, and manifested forth his glory; and his disciples believed on him."—John 2, v. 11.

II.

1. Not the desires of men to please,
Thou dost thy first of wonders show,
But sent from heaven our earth to bless,
Jehovah manifest below,
Thou dost thy peerless power display,
And faith's eternal basis lay.

2. This demonstration of thy grace,
This proof of thy Divinity,
Saviour, in every age and place
Convinc'd thy true disciples see,
Built on the rock that cannot move,
The truth of thine almighty love.

3. Who changes water into wine,
Can sinners into saints convert:
Thy grace omnipotent divine
I trust to make me as Thou art,
To form my heart averse from

sin,
And bid mine inmost soul be clean.

4. The virtue of thy perfect love
This soul shall to the utmost save,
And when my hidden Life above
Appears, my Ransom from the grave,
This body vile shall mount thy throne,
And shine immortal, as thine own.

"The Jews passover was at hand, and Jesus went up to Jerusalem."—John 2, v. 13.

Thou dost the forms commend
Of outward righteousness,
And teach us constantly t' attend
The channels of thy grace:
Thy practise as our law
We gladly, Lord, receive,
And keep thy feasts with sacred awe,
And to thy statutes cleave.

"He drove them all out of the temple."—John 2, v. 15.

If all who holy things profane
Out of the Christian Church were driven,
Alas, how few would there remain
T' adore the Majesty of heaven!

"Take these things hence: make not my Father's house an house of merchandise."—John 2, v. 16.

More odious than the birds and beasts,
Creatures design'd for sacrifice,
Are careless crouds and worldly priests,
Who now provoke thy glorious eyes,
Profane the temple of the Lord,
Their venial ministry disgrace,
And sell the prayer, the psalm, the word,
And buy in hell the hottest place.

"The zeal of thine house hath eaten me up."—John 2, v. 17.

1. Our fervent zeal for God to show,
We must not with our meekness part,
Or lukewarm and indifferent grow,
To prove our gentleness of heart:
Meekness and zeal in Jesus join'd,
In saints begotten from above,
Compose, and fill the Christian mind
With purest flames of perfect love.

2. Saviour, I want that ardent zeal
Which in thy heavenly bosom glow'd,
That strong desire to do the will,
And serve the family of God:

Into my heart thy Spirit of grace,
Of love, and true devotion pour,
To fill the consecrated place,
And all my ravish'd soul devour.

"What sign shewest thou unto us, seeing thou dost these things?"—John 2, v. 18.

No right the house of God to cleanse
Has he, whose heart remains impure;
But if he chase the creature thence,
His ministerial call is sure:
A life of apostolic love,
This is the standing miracle,
This only can his mission prove
And justify the pastor's zeal.

"But this spake he of the temple of his body."—John 2, v. 21.

1. Jesus' soul and body are
The true Temple of the Lord,
Come we then and worship there
God in the incarnate Word!
There the pure religion lies,
Dwells the Father in his Son
God who reigns above the skies,
God is found in Christ alone.

2. Very Man of very man,
Temple of the Deity,
Whom the heavens cannot contain,
Bow our inmost souls to Thee:
Exiles while on earth we mourn,
Captives in a world of care,
All our thoughts to Thee we turn,
Every wish and every prayer.

3. Prostrate now the Shrine before
Join we in thy Spirit's cry,
Thine humanity adore,
Wait thy coming from the sky:
Come, and fix the Temple here,
All thy majesty reveal,
With thy blushing scars appear
Heaven and earth with glory fill.

"Many believed in his name: but Jesus did not commit himself unto them."—John 2, v. 23, 24.

1. Jesus, thou know'st what is in man,
So false and changeable, and vain:
If now we in thy name believe,
If thee this moment we receive,
The next we cast our faith away,
And basely our dear Lord betray.

2. Thou canst not to our keeping trust
Thy grace, no sooner gain'd than lost:
But that we may in Thee confide,
With us continually abide,
A people for thyself prepare,
And keep our hearts by reigning there.

JOHN CHAPTER THREE

"The same came to Jesus by night."—John 3, v. 2.

Shall we discourage or repel
The men who their own weakness feel,
And come to Christ by night?
Or cherish the first dawn of grace,
And teach them Jesus to confess
With all the sons of light!

"Rabbi, we know that thou art a teacher come from God, for no man can do these miracles that thou dost, except God be with him."—John 3, v. 2.

1. A Teacher come from God, and more,
In Thee we God himself adore,
While in our inward parts
Thou dost thy kind instructions write,
And make them the supreme delight
Of true believing hearts.

2. Master, instruct us thus to know
Th' eternal God reveal'd below,
By miracles of grace
Of thy divinity convince,
For only God can cancel sins,
And save a ruin'd race.

3. God over all unless Thou art,
Thou canst not change the evil heart,
Our soul-diseases heal;
But of thy Spirit born, we prove
Thou art th' Almighty God of love
By proofs infallible.

"Except a man be born again, he cannot see the kingdom of God."—John 3, v. 3.

The truth, and blessedness, and need
Of this great change I know,
But do I witness it indeed,
Do I the tokens show?
Marks of this birth, they all are vain
Without thy Spirit's power,
Then only am I born again,
When I can sin no more.

"How can a man be born when he is old?"—John 3, v. 4.

Saviour of men, I ask no more
How can the wonder be,
But trusting in thy gracious power,
I leave it all to Thee;
That heavenly birth I wait to prove,
I look to be restor'd,
In age, to the new life of love,
The image of my Lord.

"Except a man be born of water and of the Spirit, he cannot enter into the kingdom of God."—John 3, v. 5.

1. The water and the Spirit join,

The inward grace and outward sign
In that great mystery
Thro' which our souls are born again,
Thy kingdom first on earth obtain,
And then thy glory see.

2. Who the baptismal rite receive,
And by and in thy Spirit live
The sinless life unknown,
Children of God they reign in love,
Joint-heirs with Thee, O Christ, remove,
To share thy heavenly throne.

"That which is born of the flesh, is flesh &c."—John 3, v. 6.

1. The sinful father of mankind
Could only sinful men beget,
Hence our whole race to ill inclin'd
Th' offence original repeat,
In Adam's fallen likeness born
We eat the interdicted tree,
Our will from our Creator turn,
And all thro' pride as Gods would be.

2. Born of the flesh, to flesh alone
Our vile, corrupt affections cleave,
Our reason sensualiz'd we own,
To the desires of men we live;
Carnal alike in heart and mind,
Flesh, only flesh, ourselves we know,
And no good thing in us we find,
Till Thou, O Christ, thy Spirit bestow.

"Marvel not that I said unto thee, Ye must be born again."—John 3, v. 7.

1. Adam descended from above,
Thou only canst that Spirit impart,
That Principle of heavenly love
Regenerate in the sinful heart:
O might He now from Thee proceed,
Fountain of life and purity,
Implant the nature of our Head,
And work the mighty change in me!

2. The seed infus'd, the good desire,
Into a tree immortal raise,
With all thy sanctity inspire,
With all thy plenitude of grace;
Spotless, and spiritual, and good
My heart and life shall then be thine,
And in my Lord's similitude
Renew'd, I shall forever shine.

"The wind bloweth where it listeth &c."—John 3, v. 8.

1. Strangers to nature's mystery,
We hear its sound, but cannot see
The vague, impetuous wind:
The Spirit's course we cannot trace,

The secret motions of that grace
Whose plain effects we find.

2. The ways of God are dark to man,
In vain we would describe, explain,
Delineate, or define,
The manner still remains unknown,
The sure reality we own,
And feel that birth Divine.

3. Just as He lists, the Spirit blows,
But whence he comes, and whither goes
No mortal comprehends;
How he begins his power t' exert,
By what degrees renews the heart,
Or when his progress ends.

4. The soul in which his work is done,
Alike to worldly minds unknown
To all that know not God;
The spiritual regenerate man
Others discerns, but never can
Himself be understood.

5. His life a daily death they see,
A riddle of absurdity,
And quite unlike their own,
While sav'd from low terrestrial views
He things invisible pursues,
And pants for God alone.

6. The heavenly principle within,
The spring of all his acts, unseen
And unsuspected lies,
His end they cannot understand
Who seeks some undiscover'd land,
A kingdom in the skies!

"How can these things be?"—John 3, v. 9.

1. The change we all may feel and show,
And born of God, his kingdom see;
In vain we would the manner know,
And still inquire, how can it be?
Or boldly ignorant explode
Th' inexplicable truths of God.

2. Who first by reason's scanty line
Can the immense Creator mete,
Fathom the depths of love divine,
Of power, and wisdom infinite,
May then the miracle explore
How saints can live, and sin no more.

"Art thou a master of Israel, and knowest not these things?"—John 3, v. 10.

1. The masters of our Israel may
The fact by sure experience prove,
May know the Truth, the Life, the Way,
Born of his Spirit from above,
In real holiness renew'd,
By faith the genuine sons of God.

2. But few th' incarnate Word receive,
Author of that mysterious birth,
They will not in his name believe,
Or quit for heaven the things of earth,
But on the outward sign rely
Till Christ-less in their sins they die.

"We speak that we do know, and testify that we have seen; and ye receive not our witness."—John 3, v. 11.

1. Our Maker and redeeming Lord,
Whom all thy heavens cannot contain,
The real Light, th' eternal Word,
The Truth itself, Thou speak'st to man;
Who only dost the Father know,
Thou dost his mysteries reveal,
The wisdom of his conduct show,
And teach the ways unsearchable.

2. Yet none of all our fallen race
By his own proper power receives
The record of thy heavenly grace,
Or in thy faithful word believes;
Unless Thou take the bar away,
Our helpless unbelief remove,
Thy life into our souls convey,
And teach our hearts that God is Love.

3. The truth thy witnesses have known,
And seen, and felt, they all confess,
Yet still the Christian world disown
That second birth to righteousness:
Jesus, the Spirit's power exert,
The stubborn infidels convince,
The humbled infidels convert,
And truly save from all their sins.

"If I have told you earthly things and ye believe not, how shall ye believe, if I tell you of heavenly things?"—John 3, v. 12.

Who will not now the word believe,
And feel that wondrous birth below,
How shall their carnal hearts conceive
The joys which in thy presence flow,
The rivers of unmixt delight,
The pleasures of thy house above,
The soul-beatifying sight,
The extasies of glorious love!

"No man hath ascended up to heaven, but he that came down from heaven, even the Son of man which is in heaven."—John 3, v. 13.

Jesus, Son of God and man,
To the regenerate given,
Thou dost to their hearts explain

The mysteries of heaven;
With Thyself in Spirit one
The members in their Head ascend,
Taste the raptures of thy throne,
The joys which never end.

"As Moses lifted up the serpent in the wilderness, even so must the Son of man be lifted up."—John 3, v. 14.

He hath been lifted up for me,
For me when weltring in my blood:
I saw him hanging on the tree,
And virtue from his body flow'd,
The poison of my sins expel'd,
And all my wounds that moment heal'd.

"That whosoever believeth in him, should not perish, but have eternal life."—John 3, v. 15.

1. O Thou who hast our sorrows took,
My God for sinners crucified,
To Thee I for salvation look,
And while I in thy cross confide,
Thy passion's fruit with faith receive,
And quicken'd by thy death I live.

2. Sav'd from the death of sin and hell
Thro' thine atoning sacrifice,
I wait, till Thou the life reveal,
Reserv'd for me above the skies,

Purchas'd with all thy precious blood,
The rapturous, endless life of God.

"God so loved the world, that he gave his only begotten Son, that whosoever believeth in him, should not perish, but have everlasting life."—John 3, v. 16.

I.

1. How hath He lov'd us? how?
Can man or angel tell?
While prostrate at that cross we bow,
His love's effects we feel:
The virtue of that sign
Our gasping souls receive,
And ransom'd by the death Divine
We shall forever live.

2. No angel from his throne
He sent the world to save,
But God his one, beloved Son
To desperate sinners gave:
Who in his bosom lay
He on his foes bestow'd,
The Lamb that bore our sins away,
And wash'd us in his blood.

3. Jehovah's name is Love,
And love his heart inclin'd
To send his Fellow from above,
A Victim for mankind:
'Twas found in Him alone,
Salvation's wondrous cause,

Who freely gave his only Son
To save us by his cross.

"God so loved the world, that he gave his only begotten Son, that whosoever believeth in him, should not perish, but have everlasting life."—John 3, v. 16.

II.

1. Thee, Lord, who on the tree
Didst buy the general peace,
Author of our salvation, we
Author of faith confess:
Thou dost the faith bestow
Thy blessed Self t' embrace,
The faith from which our virtues grow,
And all our fruits of grace.

2. Our souls are born again
Thro' faith inspir'd by Thee,
Thro' faith thy nature we obtain,
Thine immortality;
It doth thy mind reveal,
Thy hallowing blood applies,
And shuts the gates of death and hell,
And opens paradise.

"God sent not his Son into the world to condemn the world: but that the world through him might be saved."—John 3, v. 17.

1. Thou didst not send thy Son
To aggravate our guilt,
But for the sins of all t' atone
His precious blood was spilt:
Not as our Judge he came,
But our Redeemer kind,
That all believing in his name,
May life and pardon find.

2. Thou didst thy Son bestow,
Thy truth of grace to prove,
And Jesus did by dying show
Sincerity of love:
He suffer'd in our place,
By mercy's sole decree:
Know every child of Adam's race,
Thy Saviour died for thee!

"He that believeth on Him is not condemned."—John 3, v. 18.

Lord, I believe, and stand secure
In all I speak, and do, and feel;
My conscience finds an answer sure
To every charge of earth, or hell:
Nigh to the Judge I boldly draw;
My Surety all his anger bore,
My Lord fulfill'd the fiery law,
And God the just can ask no more.

"He that believeth not is condemned already, because he hath not believed in the name of the only begotten Son of God."—John 3, v. 18.

1. Who doth not in the Son believe
Condemn'd he in his sins remains,

But death-devoted, a reprieve
Thro' Jesus intercession gains:
Yet O, the sentence must take place,
If still his Saviour he denies,
And scorning all his proffer'd grace
A wilful unbeliever dies.

2. Shut up by unbelief, within
The tempter's power a while he dwells,
Under the guilt of reigning sin
Its cruel tyranny he feels;
He might thro' Jesus name receive
The power which all believers know,
But will not come to Christ, and live,
But will not lose his place below.

"This is the condemnation, that light is come into the world, and men loved darkness rather than light, because their deeds were evil."—John 3, v. 19.

1. Poor sinful souls, diseas'd, and blind,
Who will not thy salvation see,
Their merciful Physician find,
Or come for light, O Lord, to thee,
Because they madly hug their chain,
And with their sins refuse to part,
Their sins and unbelief remain,
And still the vail is on their heart.

2. All in their wretched selves alone
The cause of their damnation lies,
Lovers of sin they hate and shun
The Light that pains their guilty eyes,
Who the dire deeds of darkness do
Abhorrence of the light they feel,
And the broad dreary path pursue
Which leads to the profoundest hell.

"He that doeth truth cometh to the light, that his deeds may be manifest, that they are wrought in God."—John 3, v. 21.

The truth who from their heart obey
Rejoice as children of the light,
To stand confess'd in open day
And blameless walk before thy sight:
Their lives with scrutiny severe
They by thy word and Spirit prove,
That all their actions may appear
Wrought in the light and power of love.

"John was baptizing; for John was not cast into prison."—John 3, v. 23, 24.

Happy those who labour on
For God with all their power,
Labour till their course is run,
And they can work no more:
Happier, when their toils are past,
If liberty they sacrifice,

Offering up their lives at last
To win the martyr's prize.

"Rabbi, he that was with thee ... baptizeth, and all men come to him &c."—John 3, v. 26, 27.

1. It is mine own infirmity!
I would have all prefer,
And zealously caress, like me,
My favourite minister:
I grudge alas, at their success,
And secretly repine,
If other instruments of grace
Are follow'd more than mine.

2. Ah, Lord, inlarge my selfish heart,
And I shall gladly own
The Giver of all good Thou art,
And dost the help alone;
To Thee I shall the glory give,
Thine only choice approve,
And all thy messengers receive
With pure, impartial love.

"John said, A man can receive nothing, except it be given him from heaven."—John 3, v. 27.

Lord, if Thou hast sent forth me
Us'd a sinner's ministry,
All the glory I disclaim,
Feel I worse than nothing am,
For my talents, gifts, or grace
Thee let thy disciples praise,
God the heavenly Fountain own,
Magnify my God alone.

"I am not the Christ, but I am sent before him."—John 3, v. 28.

1. Th' ambassador of the Most-high,
Forerunner of his heavenly Lord
Himself can never magnify,
But trembles to dispense the word,
Savour of life or death to deal,
And thus his awful charge fulfil.

2. He dares not arrogate or share
The praise which all to God should pay,
Sent by instructions to prepare
By penitence the Saviour's way,
And in himself the pattern give
How sinners should their Lord receive.

"He that hath the bride is the Bridegroom: but the friend of the bridegroom rejoiceth greatly, because of the Bridegroom's voice: &c."—John 3, v. 29.

I.

1. Jesus is of his church possest
And clasps her to his loving breast,
He will not with his purchase part,
He holds his consort in his heart:
Who in Jesus' heart abide,
Faithful souls are all his bride.

2. My spirit doth in God rejoice

Attentive to the Bridegroom's voice,
He brings his kingdom from above,
He fills me with the life of love,
"Rise, my love, without delay,
"Rise, my fair, and come away!"

"He that hath the bride is the Bridegroom: but the friend of the bridegroom rejoiceth greatly because of the Bridegroom's voice: &c."—John 3, v. 29.

II.

1. No greater joy the servant knows,
Than when the Master's voice he hears,
And Jesus on his church bestows
The peace that chases all their fears;
The servant is the Bridegroom's friend,
Delighted with his only praise,
When Christ he doth to souls commend,
And shares with them the gospel-grace.

2. This happiness, O Lord, is mine,
I taste the bliss thy word imparts,
The word of righteousness divine
Spoken into thy people's hearts:
Thou hast betroth'd thy church to Thee,
United to the faithful soul,
And now the happy day I see,
And now my holy joy is full.

"He must increase, but I must decrease."—John 3, v. 30.

1. I would be less and less
That Jesus may increase,
Would myself renounce, despise,
Till on earth no longer seen,
Least of all in my own eyes,
Least of all esteem'd by men.

2. A voice, and nothing more,
I only go before;
Jesus' poorest instrument,
Jesus' harbinger I am,
Live to spend and to be spent,
Live to glorify his name.

3. My life is not my own,
Bestow'd for Him alone;
Ready at the Master's call
Every blessing I resign,
Fame, and strength, and life, and all,
Die, to serve the cause Divine.

"He that cometh from above is above all: he that is of the earth is earthy, and speaketh of the earth."—John 3, v. 31.

Meer man of earthly origin,
Is all infirmity and sin,
The meaness of his native place
His spirit and his speech bewrays:
Jesus, the Lord, and God most high
Reveals the secrets of the sky,
And speaks in blessings from

above
The language pure of heavenly love.

"And what he hath seen and heard, that he testifieth; and no man receiveth his testimony."—John 3, v. 32.

1. The everlasting God is He,
And was from all eternity,
Who in his Father's bosom lay,
And doth on earth his form display;
The things He saw, and heard, and knew
Of these he bears a record true,
Discovers the redeeming plan,
And shews the heart of God to man.

2. Freely he left his throne above,
To tell the world that God is Love;
Yet few the saving truth receive,
Or dare on Jesus' word believe:
Not one of our unfaithful race
Doth of himself his Lord embrace,
We all reject whom God hath given,
The Witness, and the Man from heaven.

"He that hath received his testimony, hath set to his seal, that God is true."—John 3, v. 33.

Jesus, thy record we receive,
And by a power from Thee believe,
By faith divine our seal set to,
That Thou art God, that Thou art true,
By faith thy promises we gain,
Thy strict fidelity maintain,
And sav'd from sin, exult to prove
The truth of thy redeeming love.

"He whom God hath sent, speaketh the words of God: for God giveth not the Spirit by measure unto him."—John 3, v. 34.

1. Sent from the heavenly Father down,
Thou cam'st to make the Godhead known,
The mysteries divine t' impart,
And speak his words into my heart:
That Spirit I in measure feel
Who doth the things of God reveal,
Fathoms the depths of Deity,
And dwells with all his grace in Thee.

2. The words Thou dost from God declare
Pure life, and quickning spirit are,
Their own divinity they prove,
Th' eternal Truth, and Power, and Love:
Our penetrated hearts agree
Never was man that spake like Thee,
God over all the Speaker own,

And seat thee on thy fav'rite throne.

"The Father loveth the Son, and hath given all things into his hand."—John 3, v. 35.

1. God made his mind to prophets known,
But Thou art his beloved Son,
Vested with plenitude of power
To Teach, and Expiate, and Restore:
I see thee full of truth and grace,
My Prophet, Priest, and King confess:
Exert thy threefold energy,
Instruct, Forgive, and Reign in me.

2. Thou workest all the works Divine,
Fulfillest all his love's design:
Thy Church's Head, and great High-priest,
In Thee thy Father shines confest,
Dispenser of his every grace,
Saviour of the peculiar race,
The Way, where all may walk forgiven
The Truth of bliss, the Life of heaven!

3. Salvation is in Jesus name,
I every other hope disclaim
My soul into thy hands commend,
On Thee my only God depend;
Observant of thy just commands,
I rest in thine almighty hands,
And trust Thee for my place above,
So dearly bought by dying Love.

"He that believeth on the Son, hath everlasting life: but he that believeth not the Son, shall not see life: but the wrath of God abideth on him."—John 3, v. 36.

1. Jesus, believing on thy name
Rais'd from the dead in sin I am,
My true, eternal Life Thou art
By faith residing in my heart;
Thy nature, Lord, in Love I know,
Imparted to thy saints below,
Anticipate th' immortal prize
And live the life of Paradise.

2. But born in sin and misery
He still is dead, who knows not Thee,
Who still thy gospel disobeys,
A stranger to the life of grace,
True happiness he cannot prove,
Or see the blisful life above,
Under the curse his wretched breath
He yields, and dies the second death.

JOHN CHAPTER FOUR

"When the Lord knew how the Pharisees had heard that Jesus baptized more disciples than John; He left Judea, and departed again into Galilee."—John 4, v. 1, 3.

1. Teach me, Saviour, by thy grace
To answer thy design,
When the threatning world to face,
And when their rage decline;
Far from rashness as from fear
I would not, Lord, myself expose,
Would not shrink from danger near,
Or dare, or dread my foes.

2. Thou by thy example guide
And certify my heart
When I should the storm abide,
And when I should depart:
Let me till thy time is come,
From place to place thy follower fly,
Fly, till thou recall me home
And then stand still, and die.

"He must needs go through Samaria."—John 4, v. 4.

See the heavenly Shepherd's zeal,
Saviour of the sinful kind,
Pity doth his heart compel
A lost sheep to seek and find!
Love constrains him to draw near
To the soul redeem'd of old,
Claims the thoughtless wanderer,
Brings her back into his fold.

"Jesus being wearied with his journey, sat thus on the well."—John 4, v. 6.

I.

1. Wandring souls, lift up your eyes
Mark Him fainting on the road,
Him who made both earth and skies,
Wonder at the wearied God!
God descending from above
Takes your flesh, and frailties too,
Wearied in the toil of love,
Wearied in pursuing you.

2. Jesus, we thy mercy bless,
Gladly in our service tir'd,
By thy toil and weariness
Rest thou hast for us acquir'd;
Thy fatigue our souls relieves
Long with Satan's yoke opprest,
Rest from sin and fear it gives,
Present, and eternal rest.

"Jesus being wearied with his journey, sat thus on the well."—John 4, v. 6.

II.

1. Weary on the well reclin'd,
Mercy in thy weariness
Mercy in thy rest we find;
Then thou stay'st to grant thy

peace,
Waitest there to seize thy stray,
Rest and pardon to bestow,
Wearied with her sinful way
That she may her Saviour know.

2. Welcome weariness and pain!
Servant of thy church and Thee,
Saviour shall I not sustain
That thou didst sustain for me?
Let my toil advance thy praise,
My repose resemble thine,
Tend to minister thy grace,
Serve the blessed cause divine.

"Give me to drink."—John 4, v. 7.

He asks, that he may give,
His creature's wants relieve,
Drink he earnestly desires,
Water he vouchsafes to crave,
Souls, his vehement spirit requires,
Thirsts expiring souls to save.

"The Jews have no dealings with the Samaritans."—John 4, v. 9.

1. Contrary sects we see
In this alone agree,
Sects that bear the Christian name,
Each from each in heart remov'd,
Mutual intercourse disclaim,
Hate the souls whom God hath lov'd.

2. As hereticks and foes
Each other they oppose,
Every church the chosen race,
Every party is the bride,
Strangers, enemies to grace,
Heathens all the world beside.

"If thou knewest the gift of God ... thou wouldst have asked of him, and he would have given thee living water."—John 4, v. 10 &c.

1. Jesus, the Gift divine I know,
The gift divine I ask of thee;
The living water now bestow,
Thy Spirit and thyself on me:
Thou, Lord, of life the Fountain art,
O could I find thee in my heart!

2. Thee let me drink, and thirst no more
For drops of finite happiness:
Spring up, O Well, in heavenly power,
In streams of pure perennial peace,
In joy which none can take away,
In life which shall forever stay.

"Art thou greater than our father Jacob, which gave us the well, and drank thereof himself, and his children, and his cattle."—John 4, v. 12.

Fulness of the Deity
Resides in Christ the Lord:
Greater far than Jacob, Thee
The patriarch ador'd:
Well of life, divinely deep,
Out of thy plenitude of grace

Water now thy lambs and sheep,
And all the heavenborn race.

"Whosoever drinketh of this water shall thirst again."—John 4, v. 13.

1. Joy in our enjoyments here
Cannot alas be found,
Tir'd the gazing eye, the ear
Is glutted with the sound,
Passions with their food increase,
And higher by indulgence rise,
Every creature promises,
But nothing satisfies.

2. Drinking cannot quench, or cool
The fever of desire,
Thus inflam'd the thirsty soul
Doth more and more require,
Tortur'd thus by gnawing pains,
And scorch'd with fire unquenchable,
Here the restless sinner gains
An antepast of hell.

"Whosoever drinketh of the water that I shall give him, shall never thirst."—John 4, v. 14.

1. The living water of thy grace,
On me, indulgent Lord, bestow,
To quench my thirst of happiness,
Vouchsafe that taste of heaven below:
When of thy love I freely take,
My wants are all in one supplied,
When in thy likeness I awake,
My soul is fill'd, and satisfied.

2. My eager thirst of creature-bliss,
My earthly vain pursuits are o're,
The Lord my peace and Portion is,
Injoying Christ, I ask no more;
I drink the river from above,
The Spirit's pure, pellucid stream,
The Fount himself, the Life, the Love,
And all the joys of heaven in Him.

"But the water that I shall give him, shall be in him a well of water springing up into everlasting life."—John 4, v. 14.

I.

1. Thou promisest thyself t' impart
To all who ask thyself of thee:
Open the fountain in my heart,
Spring up, O Well of life, in me!
The Root and Principle of grace,
In me let thy good Spirit abide,
Renew in perfect holiness,
And add me to the glorified.

2. Not like a sudden, transient flood,
But fixt, and permanent, and sure,
The grace Thou hast on me bestow'd
Deep let it in my soul endure,

Swift to its Source celestial move,
Freely fulfil thy whole design,
With all th' activity of love,
With all the powers of life Divine.

"But the water that I shall give him, shall be in him a well of water springing up into everlasting life."—John 4, v. 14.

II.

Religion true to visit earth
In pure divinity descends,
But mindful of its heavenly birth,
To heaven in all its motions tends;
Returning to its blest abode,
It mingles with the chrystal Sea,
It bears my spirit back to God,
My God thro' all eternity.

"Sir, give me this water, that I thirst not, neither come hither to draw."—John 4, v. 15.

1. Thee Saviour, that I may
Thro' thy own Spirit know,
The willingness to pray,
The thirst of grace bestow,
The first imperfect wish inspire,
And then fulfil thine own desire.

2. Prevented by thy love,
Lord, if I now begin
To seek the things above,
The grace that saves from sin,
Do Thou the living water give,
Which makes my soul forever live.

3. The streams of holiness
Into my spirit pour,
And kept in perfect peace
I then shall thirst no more,
But seek my whole felicity,
But find it all compriz'd in Thee.

"Thou hast had five husbands, and he whom thou now hast is not thy husband."—John 4, v. 18.

1. Prince, and Saviour of mankind,
Giver of repentance true,
Bring my secret sins to mind,
Drag them into open view,
Shew me that I dread to know,
To himself the sinner shew.

2. What I cannot hide from Thee,
From myself I hide in vain:
Give me, Lord, myself to see,
Break my heart with grief and pain,
Then my guilty load remove,
Then reveal thy pardoning love.

"I perceive that Thou art a prophet."—John 4, v. 19.

1. Lighten'd by a ray of grace,
Christ, and sin I now perceive,
Conscious of my wickedness,
Jesus I my God believe;
God supreme Thou surely art,
God alone can search the heart.

2. Thee descended from the sky
More than Prophet I embrace:
Thine atoning blood apply;
Then I shall my Priest confess:
Fill me with thy Spirit's power,
Then I shall my King adore.

"Ye shall neither in this mountain, nor yet at Jerusalem worship the Father."—John 4, v. 21.

To no single sect confin'd,
Or place, as heretofore,
God the Father of mankind,
We every where adore,
Coming to his gracious throne
Thro' Christ we all have free access,
In the Spirit of his Son,
The truth of holiness.

"Ye worship ye know not what."—John 4, v. 22.

God who out of Christ adore,
Adore they know not what,
Serve him without faith or power
For yet they know him not;
Blind, and void of filial fear,
Till Christ their unbelief remove,
Then they see, confess, revere,
And praise the God they love.

"We know what we worship: for salvation is of the Jews."—John 4, v. 22.

Sprinkled with th' atoning blood
By faith divine applied,
Knowingly we worship God
In Jesus pacified,
Inward Jews our Lord confess,
(Whose temples pure our bodies are)
In the Spirit of fervent praise,
And sacrificial prayer.

"The hour cometh, and now is, when the true worshippers shall worship the Father in spirit and in truth: for the Father seeketh such to worship him."—John 4, v. 23.

1. Ritual services are past,
The shadows fled away,
God is manifest at last,
And brings the gospel-day;
Worship spiritual and true
The God of holiness ordains,
Works in man to will and do;
And pure religion reigns.

2. God's accepted worshipper
Begotten from above
Breathes the Spirit of grace and prayer
Of humble faith and love,
All his saints the law fulfil
Ingraven on their inward parts,
Sanctified by Jesus will,
They give him all their hearts.

3. Such the Father seeks, and owns
His worshippers indeed,
Such he calls his genuin sons,
Who in his footsteps tread:
Such on earth he cannot find,
Unless he forms us by his grace,
Makes us one in heart and mind

With Christ our Righteousness.

"God is a Spirit, and they that worship him, must worship him in spirit and in truth."— John 4, v. 24.

1. Thou, O God, a Spirit art,
Whose glory fills the sky,
Breathe within my childlike heart,
And there "my Father" cry!
Come in Christ, and fill the place
With Wisdom, and effectual Power,
Thee I then shall truly praise,
And worthily adore.

2. All my powers shall then be brought
Into captivity,
Every passion, every thought
Shall bow, and worship Thee,
Thee mine inmost soul shall bless,
Like angels worshipping above,
Silent at thy feet confess
Th' o'rewhelming force of Love!

"I know that Messias cometh: when he is come, he will teach us all things."—John 4, v. 25.

1. Come, thou Prophet of the Lord,
Mighty both in deed and word,
Prophet by thy Father seal'd,
With his hallowing Spirit fill'd,
Sent, anointed to proclaim
His unutterable name,
Come, Divine Interpreter,
All his will to man declare.

2. Visible thro' faith, I know,
God thou dost to sinners show;
Show us in thy Spirit's light
How to worship Him aright;
By the unction of thy grace
Lead us into all thy ways:
All our unbelief remove,
Teach us every thing in love.

"Jesus saith unto her, I that speak unto thee, am He."— John 4, v. 26.

Jesus, Lord, for Thee I stay,
Come, and take my sins away,
Manifest the Deity,
"I who speak to souls, am He!"
Speak, eternal God, to mine,
Light of life, in darkness shine:
Thou the true Messias art,
Teach, by living in my heart.

"His disciples marvelled that he talked with the woman."— John 4, v. 27.

1. A wonder of grace To angels and men!
The Ancient of days With mortals is seen,
With sinners converses, His Spirit imparts,
His numberless mercies Makes known to our hearts.

2. No matter how vile, The sinner has been;
His word and his smile Redeems us from sin,

With kind conversation He comforts the worst,
And shews his salvation To profligates first.

"The woman then left her water-pot, and went her way into the city, and saith to the men, Come, see a man which told me &c."—John 4, v. 28, 29.

1. See a soul with pardon blest,
Freely sav'd by grace alone!
Knowing Christ, she cannot rest,
Till she makes her Saviour known:
Chang'd by one almighty word,
Earthly things she leaves behind,
Flies th' Apostle of the Lord,
Lord of her and all mankind.

2. Sinners, come by faith, and see
A celestial Man unknown,
One who hath reveal'd to me
All I have in secret done:
Virtue doth from Him proceed;
All my life and heart he shew'd:
Is not this the Christ indeed?
Is not this th' omniscient God?

"His disciples prayed him, saying, Master eat &c."—John 4, v. 31.

1. Jesus keeps the soul in view,
His converted messenger,
Doth in mind and heart pursue,
Fills with zeal, and acts in her,
Acts on those to whom he sends,
Those he for his Father seeks;
Still upon her tongue attends,
Blesses every word she speaks.

2. Souls to win is Jesus' meat;
Jesus thus instructs his own
Nature's cravings to forget,
Living not by bread alone:
Preachers by the gospel live,
Feed on that themselves dispense,
Strength and nourishment receive,
More than life derive from thence.

"I have meat to eat that ye know not of."—John 4, v. 32.

But if thou the Father show,
Manifest to me his love,
I that hidden meat shall know,
I my Master's joy shall prove,
Gladly in thy labours share,
Feast with thee on heavenly food,
Servant of thy church, declare
"Heaven on earth is Serving God."

"My meat is to do the will of him that sent me, and to finish his work."—John 4, v. 34.

Sent of God to do his will
Every gospel-minister
Should his Father's work fulfil,
Serve the heirs of glory here,
All his business and delight
Souls to win thro' Jesus' love,
Till he joins the saints in light,
Banquets with his Lord above.

"Lift up your eyes, and look on the fields; for they are white already to harvest."—John 4, v. 35.

1. Jesus, we now with pure delight
Lift up our eyes and see
The gospel fields to harvest white,
The crouds that flock to thee;
Call'd by thy ministers they run,
With eager haste to find
The promis'd Christ, the God unknown,
The Saviour of mankind.

2. Ready our record to receive,
From every side they press,
Made willing to repent, believe,
And live thy witnesses:
O thou who hast their hearts prepar'd,
Display thy pardning love,
And qualify for their reward,
And lodge them safe above.

"He that reapeth receiveth wages, and gathereth fruit unto life eternal: that both he that soweth, and he that reapeth, may rejoice together."—John 4, v. 36.

1. The reaper of thy fields receives
In part his wages here,
Thrice happy in thy service lives,
Thy Spirit's minister:
His heart thy peace and blessing glads,
With joy he labours on,
And every added convert adds
A jewel to his crown.

2. He gathers fruit who sinners wins,
And fruit that shall remain,
While souls redeem'd from all their sins
With him the prize obtain;
Who many turns to righteousness,
To him the grace is given,
To honour God by his success,
To gain, and people heaven.

3. The earnest of his glorious hire,
He humbly holds it fast,
Till blest with all his heart's desire,
With joys that ever last,
When all who sow'd the gospel-word
With all the reapers meet,
And in the presence of their Lord
Behold their bliss compleat.

"Herein is that saying true, One soweth, and another reapeth. I sent you to reap that &c."—John 4, v. 37, 38.

1. The prophets spake of Jesus' grace,
The seed immortal sow'd,
Th' Apostles reap'd the ransom'd race,
And brought a world to God:
The Prophets and Apostles too
For us the way prepar'd,

And if their footsteps we pursue,
We share their full reward.

2. Entred into their labours we,
And prosper'd in our deed,
Avail us of their ministry,
And thro' their toil succeed;
We preach the Lord our righteousness,
The world thro' Christ forgiven,
And God, to seal his word of grace,
Reveals his Son from heaven.

"Many of the Samaritans believed on him, for the saying of the woman."—John 4, v. 39.

1. Jesus a sinful soul converts
And sends her to convert the men,
Master of all his creature's hearts;
His power is thus in weakness seen,
And thus, his counsel to fulfil,
Th' Almighty sends by whom he will.

2. Shall men, the great, and learn'd, and wise
His feeble instrument disdain,
(Whoe'er of Jesus testifies,)
Or wisdom from a woman gain,
And gladly at her bidding go
Their Saviour from himself to know?

"So when the Samaritans were come unto him, they besought him that he would tarry with them: and he abode there two days."—John 4, v. 40.

Convinc'd to Thee, O Lord, we come,
And instant in thy Spirit pray,
Enter, and make our hearts thy home,
With poor converted heathens stay,
Thro' life's short day our Teacher be,
Our God thro' all eternity.

"Now we believe, not because of thy saying: for we have heard him ourselves, and know that this is indeed the Christ, the Saviour of the world."—John 4, v. 42.

1. This is the faith we humbly seek,
The faith which with Thyself we find:
Speak to our souls, in mercy speak,
Thou Friend and Saviour of mankind,
Messiah, sent us from above,
To teach the world, that God is Love.

2. Call'd by thy gospel-messenger
We gladly his report believe,
But when of thine own mouth we hear,

The truth we savingly receive,
And partners of thy Spirit know
That God is manifest below.

3. By that inspoken word of thine
Thou dost thy Deity reveal,
The Saviour of the world is mine,
Sav'd from my sins, I surely feel,
The real Christ of God Thou art,
Thy unction speaks it in my heart.

"He went unto him, and besought him that he would come down, and heal his son."—John 4, v. 47.

The father's fondness for his son,
His forwardness to ask a sign,
False notions of the God unknown
Which would th' Omnipotent confine,
Jesus with kind compassion sees,
His weaknesses with meekness bears,
Relieves a sinner in distress,
And grants his most imperfect prayers.

"Except ye see signs and wonders, ye will not believe."—John 4, v. 48.

Oft have I heard, O Lord, and read
Thy wondrous works perform'd of old,
Yet unconvinc'd by word or deed,
My free and full assent withhold:
Such is my stubborness of will,
Help'd by preventing grace in vain,
Unless I see thy power and feel,
I still an infidel remain.

"Come down, ere my child die."—John 4, v. 49.

Tis not confin'd to time or place
The virtue of thy saving grace,
Whene'er our wants to Thee we tell,
Thy power is present, Lord, to heal:
Ev'n now thou seest with pitying eye
A sinner sick, and doom'd to die:
But if thou speak the word, my soul
Is at the point of death made whole.

"Jesus saith, Go thy way; thy Son liveth. And the man believed the word that Jesus had spoken unto him."—John 4, v. 50.

1. He spake, and Jesus' word alone
Effects the double miracle,
The distant body of the son,
The father's heart a word can heal:
Credence to God the father gives,
Heal'd of his incredulity
His son restor'd to health believes,
Believes the cure he doth not see.

2. This is the miracle I need,
Saviour of souls, for this I pray,
Let virtue out of Thee proceed,
And take the plague of sin away:
The fever of fierce passion chide,
Command it, Jesus, to depart,
The fever of desire and pride,
And cure my unbelieving heart.

"The father knew that it was at the same hour, in the which Jesus said unto him, Thy son liveth."—John 4, v. 53.

His word, the sign of Jesus' will,
Performs the thing it signifies,
The power omnipotent to heal
His efficacious word applies:
Say to me, Lord, Thy soul is heal'd,
And heal'd it shall this moment be,
And with thy sinless Spirit fill'd,
I live a sacrifice to Thee.

"Himself believed, and his whole house."—John 4, v. 53.

1. 'Tis not enough for me to know
The things which God for me hath done,
His works I should to others show,
And make his mighty wonders known:
I cannot hide them in my heart,
I must proclaim his power abroad,
His miracles of grace assert,
And give the glory all to God.

2. The faith which in my heart I feel,
I humbly with my mouth confess,
That others too his praise may tell,
My Saviour's witnesses increase,
That all his family beneath
May magnify, with those above,
The God who saves our souls from death,
The quickning power of Dying Love.

"This is again the second miracle that Jesus did, when he was come out of Judea into Galilee."—John 4, v. 54.

The first effect of grace Divine
Is at the soul's espousals shew'd,
It changes water into wine,
And gives our faith a taste of God:
The second sign to life restores
The soul that Jesus word receives,
And man th' eternal God adores,
And God in man eternal lives!

JOHN CHAPTER FIVE

"There is at Jerusalem a pool, which is called Bethesda, having five porches."—John 5, v. 2.

O Jesus, I see
My Bethesda in Thee;
Thou art full of compassion and mercy for me:
Thy blood is the pool

Both for body and soul,
And whoever steps in, is made perfectly whole.

"In these lay a great multitude of impotent folk, of blind, halt, withered, waiting for the moving of the water."—John 5, v. 3.

Jesus, Thou art the house of grace,
Where all our sin-distemper'd race
A cure for every ill may find,
Those that in mercy's porch attend
Till thy balsamic power descend
To heal the sick, and halt, and blind;
A time to Thee who dare not set,
But thy appointed season wait,
And long, and pray to be made whole,
Till thy good Spirit from the sky
Come down, th' atoning blood t' apply,
And plunge us in the crimson pool.

"An angel went down at a certain season into the pool, and troubled the water: whosoever then first &c."—John 5, v. 4.

Angel, and Porch, and Pool Thou art,
And when thou dost thy zeal exert,
And stir thine own compassions up,
The lazar-soul that comes to Thee,
Is heal'd of his infirmity,
Is made partaker of his hope:
Soon as thy yearning bowels move,
Approaching in the time of love,
Whoe'er believes, and enters in,
Though wither'd, impotent, and blind,
Is by the Healer of mankind
Sav'd, in a moment sav'd, from sin.

"A certain man was there, which had an infirmity thirty and eight years."—John 5, v. 5.

For half a mournful century
I have afflicted been,
And groan'd beneath the tyranny
Of my own bosom-sin:
Th' inveterate obstinate disease
I struggled with in vain;
And hardly now at last confess,
There is no help in man.

"When Jesus saw him lie, and knew that he had been now a long time in that case, he saith unto him, Wilt thou be made whole?"—John 5, v. 6.

1. Thou dost my helpless case behold
With pity's melting eye:
A soul unsav'd, a sinner old
Attach'd to earth I lie:
Weigh'd down with guilt, o'rewhelm'd, opprest,

I feebly mean to pray,
And ere I utter my request,
Thou knowst what I would say.

2. The ulcers which I hide from man,
I cannot hide from Thee,
Who knowst my sinfulness and pain,
My life of misery:
Born, altogether born in sin,
In sin I still abide,
And heal'd I never yet have been,
Or felt thy blood applied.

3. Such is the desperate wickedness
Of this deceitful heart,
In love alas! with my disease,
From sin I will not part;
My nature doth to sin alone
Continually incline:
Let thy effectual will be shown,
And that shall conquer mine.

"The impotent man answered him, Sir I have no man, when the water is troubled, to put me into the pool."—John 5, v. 7.

1. An impotent desire I feel
At times to be made whole,
But who shall undertake to heal
My long-distemper'd soul?
Not one of all our sinful race,
When Christ his grace would give,
Can help me to accept his grace,
Can help me to believe.

2. While tortur'd here with lingring pains
I languish for my cure,
Another and another gains,
And feels his pardon sure:
Pardon may all the world receive
Of their transgressions past,
But let me, Lord, at last believe,
Let me be sav'd at last.

"Jesus saith unto him, Rise, take up thy bed, and walk."—John 5, v. 8.

Thy word enables me to rise,
Sin, and th' occasions to forsake,
Thy word my pardon'd soul supplies
With strength thy work to undertake;
And lo, I walk, to health restor'd,
In all the footsteps of my Lord.

"And immediately the man was made whole, and took up his bed, and walked."—John 5, v. 9.

Why hast thou, Saviour, by thy grace
The miracle of healing shown,
But that I may thy goodness praise,
The way of thy commandments run,
With steady zeal my Guide pursue,
And bear thine utmost will, and do?

"And on the same day was the sabbath."—John 5, v. 9.

Whene'er Thou dost a sinner heal
Languid, and weary, and opprest,
His pardon he exults to feel,
Enters into that sacred rest,
And antedates the joy above,
The sabbath of eternal Love.

"He that made me whole, the same said unto me, Take up thy bed, and walk."—John 5, v. 11.

1. Saviour, who by thy balmy blood
Hast all my sins and sorrows heal'd,
My soul thou hast with strength endued,
Thy mercy and thine arm reveal'd,
And blest me with sufficient grace
To walk in all thy righteous ways.

2. If man forbid and Thou injoin,
Thy word shall my direction be,
I own th' authority Divine,
Take up my cross and follow Thee,
Till fashion'd like my Head, I rise,
And find my mansion in the skies.

"What man is he that which said unto thee, Take up thy bed and walk?"—John 5, v. 12.

The Man whose word is life and power,
Whose word and will and act are one,
Who only could to health restore,
And fill my soul with strength unknown,
The man who hath my sins forgiven
He bids me walk with him to heaven.

"He that was healed wist not who it was."—John 5, v. 13.

But I my good Physician know,
Whose blood was shed to buy my cure,
Whose grace the pardon did bestow,
And seal'd it on my conscience sure;
My soul to save, from heaven he came,
And heal'd by telling me his name.

"Jesus had conveyed himself away, a multitude being in that place."—John 5, v. 13.

Jesus conveys himself away,
That ministers applause may shun,
If Christ by them his power display,
Or make his great salvation

known,
The instruments themselves should hide,
And God alone be glorified.

"Afterward Jesus findeth him in the temple, and said unto him, Behold, thou art made whole: sin no more, lest a worse thing come unto thee."—John 5, v. 14.

1. The Saviour still delights to find
His patients in the house of prayer,
Shews himself good, and doubly kind
To all that humbly seek him there,
Their souls with grace confirming meets,
Their cure continues and compleats.

2. For Thee I in thy temple stay,
For Thee before thine altar lie:
Thou Lamb who bear'st my guilt away,
Wilt thou not farther sanctify,
Give always what Thou once didst give,
And in mine inmost essence live?

3. Tell me again, that Thou hast heal'd
The worst of all the sinsick race,
Assure me of my pardon seal'd,
Repeat the word of saving grace,
And bid me in thy Spirit's power
Go conquering on, and sin no more.

4. Continual need of Thee I have
My faith to give, confirm, increase;
I sink, if Thou forbear to save,
Relapse into my old disease,
Lose all my power, and life, and zeal,
And justly claim the fiercest hell.

5. But O I never, never need
Thy grace abuse and sin again,
I may from strength to strength proceed;
I shall thy promis'd help obtain,
Retrieve the perfect health of love,
And take my place prepar'd above.

"Therefore did the Jews persecute Jesus, and sought to slay him."—John 5, v. 16.

And shall we think it strange, or new,
That wicked men revile the good,
With cruel enmity pursue,
And thirst to drink the martyrs blood?
Who most possess of Jesus mind,
And truth, and meek benev'lent love,
Shall most of Jesus treatment find,
And gain the brightest crown above.

"My Father worketh hitherto, and I work."—John 5, v. 17.

1. God over all forever blest,
Jehovah, and Jehovah's Son,
From doing good Thou canst not rest,
With thine eternal Father one:
His works of grace shall never cease,
The property of Love Divine
Is to communicate and bless,
And all his attributes are thine.

2. Thy Providence preserves, maintains,
And rules the universe it made,
Thy Spirit moves, and acts, and reigns
In all that hang upon thine aid:
Thy Father is in Thee employ'd;
Thou dost his works and Thou alone;
The power, and majesty of God,
Essence, and will is all thy own.

"Therefore the Jews sought the more to kill him &c."—John 5, v. 18.

1. Because Thou sav'st us from our fall,
Thy foes against thy life conspire,
Because Thou dost thy Father call
Thy proper, own, eternal Sire:
Thou dost thy Godhead testify,
Thy power divine on sinners prove,
An Equal of the Lord most-high,
A Martyr both of truth and love.

2. Tis thus the world thy love repays,
Which makes to dying sinners known
The truth that saves our ruin'd race,
Uplifting rebels to a throne:
And all who dare the truth defend
The treatment of their Lord receive,
And all who on their God depend
Are deem'd by man not fit to live.

"The Son can do nothing of himself, but what he seeth the Father do: for what things soever he doeth, these also doeth the Son likewise."—John 5, v. 19.

1. O glorious inability
Which shews the perfect power supreme!
He cannot work, distinct from Thee,
Thou canst not work, distinct from Him:
In virtue, mind, and nature One,
Beyond the reach of human thought,
Whate'er is by thy Father done,
By Thee is in that instant wrought.

2. He shews and does the work Divine,
At once Thou seest and dost the same;

Thy act is his, and his is thine:
He is, Thou art, the Great I AM!
Incomprehensible we own
Th' adorable necessity:
Nor He nor Thou canst act alone,
No more than God can cease to be.

"For the Father loveth the Son &c."—John 5, v. 20, 21.

1. Sole Object of thy Father's love,
A draught of all his great designs
From Him Thou hast receiv'd above,
And dost whate'er his will enjoins:
Equal to his, Thou shew'st thy power
Omnipotent the dead to raise,
Bodies Thou canst, and souls restore
To all the vigorous life of grace.

2. Thou dost on whom Thou wilt bestow
The various life deriv'd from Thee:
Thee thy believing people know
Fountain of immortality,
Thy sovereign Godhead we confess,
By whom the Holy Ghost is given,
And then the plenitude of grace,
And then th' eternal life of heaven.

"The Father hath committed all judgment unto the Son."—John 5, v. 22.

Eternal Judge of quick and dead
Thee, Jesus, I my Lord adore,
From whom my sentence must proceed,
And tremble at thy boundless power!
Judge me not in thy wrath severe,
But in the mildness of thy grace;
Afflict, rebuke, and chasten here,
But never drive me from thy face.

"That all men should honour the Son, even as they honour the Father."—John 5, v. 23.

Thee, Jesus, God supreme, the Son,
Ev'n as the Father we adore,
Equal to the Most-high we own,
The same in majesty and power;
In Thee his character express,
The brightness of his glory see:
And will no other Lord confess,
No other God adore, but Thee.

"He that heareth my word, and believeth on Him that sent me, hath everlasting life, and shall not come into condemnation, but is passed from death unto life."—John 5, v. 24.

1. If blest with faith that works by love,
Blest with eternal life Thou art,
Thou hast the life of those above,

The seed of glory in thy heart:
For God in Christ is Love to man,
And when to the believer given,
The soul doth in itself contain
The pure essential bliss of heaven.

2. Wou'dst thou increase of faith receive?
The Saviour's word persist to hear,
Injoy thy priviledge, and live
From every charge of conscience clear;
Believing Him who sent his Son,
And pass'd from death to life divine,
Thou knowst the quickning Three in One
Father, and Son, and Spirit thine.

"The hour is coming, and now is, when the dead shall hear the voice of the Son of God: and they that hear shall live."—John 5, v. 25.

1. When Jesus first pronounc'd the word,
They found the Resurrection come,
Dead bodies heard their quickning Lord,
And Lazarus forsook the tomb:
Dead souls He every day doth raise:
They hear his voice, and faith receive,
And live the sinless life of grace,
And soon the life of heaven shall live.

2. Jesus, the only God and true,
The Father's co-eternal Son,
Life mortal, and immortal too
Thy gift unspeakable we own:
The Word of life, the Life reveal'd
And manifest to man Thou art;
And conscious of my pardon seal'd,
I find Thee in my faithful heart.

"For as the Father hath life in himself &c."—John 5, v. 26, 27.

Pure, independent life divine
Thy Sire doth in himself possess:
Pure, independent life is thine,
Who judgest all in righteousness:
Thou dost or life, or death ordain,
Such is thy Father's high decree,
And (for Thou art the Son of man)
Mankind receive their doom from Thee.

"Marvel not at this: for the hour is coming, in the which all that are in the graves shall hear his voice; And shall come forth, they that have done good &c."—John 5, v. 28, 29.

1. I cannot doubt the power Divine,
Dead souls, or bodies dead to save:
Death oft hath heard that voice of thine,
Heard from the bed, the bier, the

grave:
That voice our mouldring dust again
Shall from earth's lowest centre hear,
And ocean pay its debt of man,
And all before thy throne appear.

2. Whose works, and lives, and hearts were good
They shall with joy and triumph rise,
Obtain the crown by grace bestow'd,
The life with Christ above the skies:
But who on earth have evil done
The day shall all their deeds reveal,
Their righteous doom they cannot shun,
But rise, to be thrust down to hell.

"My judgment is just; because I seek not mine own will, but the will of my Father."—John 5, v. 30.

O may I never seek my own,
But thy most acceptable will,
So shalt thou make thy counsel known,
Thy mind concerning me reveal,
My heart to all thy ways incline,
And make thy righteous judgment mine.

"If I bear witness of myself, my witness is not true."—John 5, v. 31.

1. And shall meer man of men demand
His saying simply to receive,
Before the proofs we understand,
Before we see the witness live,
And evidence his sins forgiven
By walking like an heir of heaven?

2. We ought not to his word alone
Or confident assertions trust;
The life must join to make it known,
The works to shew the doer just,
And all the Spirit's fruits, to prove
A Christian perfected in love.

"These things I say, that ye might be saved."—John 5, v. 34.

He spake that they might hear,
And faith by hearing come,
He spake with kind intent sincere
To save, and not to doom;
With real, serious will
He wish'd them justified,
Who in their sins continued still
Till in their sins they died.

"He was a burning and a shining light: and ye were willing for a season to rejoice in his light."—John 5, v. 35.

1. A minister should burn and shine,
Inflam'd with pure celestial love,
Glad to impart the light divine,
Himself inlighten'd from above:
His life should our instruction be,
One exercise of fervent zeal,
That all the light of truth may see,
That all the fire of love may feel.

2. Joyful to see the light appear,
If Christ his minister ordain,
The world admire, the adders hear,
And dart into the dark again:
They soon against conviction fight,
The unaccepted truth repel,
And quench the burning shining light
Who shews their works, the works of hell.

"I have greater witness than that of John: the works that I do, bear witness of me."—John 5, v. 36.

The judgment blind of erring man,
The verbal testimony's vain,
Unless our actions testify
And more substantial proof supply:
But when our faith by works is show'd,
When all our works are wrought in God,
His record then the world receive;
They must behold how Christians live.

"Ye have not his word abiding in you: for whom he hath sent, him ye believe not."—John 5, v. 38.

Who in the Saviour sent confides,
In him th' ingrafted word abides,
He hath the great Jehovah seen,
And heard the voice of God to man;
By faith th' Unsearchable he knows,
And daily in the knowledge grows,
Till pure from sin his soul ascends,
And faith fill'd up in vision ends.

"Search the Scriptures, for in them ye think ye have eternal life, and they are they which testify of me."—John 5, v. 39.

1. Christ himself the precept gives,
(Let who will the word despise)
Bids me in the sacred leaves
Trace the way to paradise,
All his oracles explore,
Read, and pray them o're and o're.

2. Who with true humility
Seek Him in the written word,
Christ in every page they see,
See, and apprehend their Lord:
Every scripture makes him known,
Testifies of Christ alone.

3. Here I cannot seek in vain:
Digging deep into the mine,
Hidden treasure I obtain,
Pure, eternal Life Divine,
Find Him in his Spirit given,
Christ the Way, the Truth of heaven.

"Ye will not come to me, that ye might have life."—John 5, v. 40.

1. Will they not? alas for them,
Dead in sin who Christ refuse!
He did all the world redeem,
All unto salvation chuse:
Sinners, come, with me receive
All the grace he waits to give.

2. In ourselves the hindrance lies,
Stopt by our own stubborn will:
He his love to none denies,
He with love pursues us still:
Sinners, come, and find with me
Only heaven in his decree.

"If another shall come in his own name, him ye will receive."—John 5, v. 43.

Coming in thy great Father's name
Who first rejected Thee,
Allow'd each bold impostor's claim
With blind credulity:
And still we see the world that can
God and his truth deny,
They greedily assent to man,
They all believe a lie.

"How can ye believe, which receive honour one of another, and seek not the honour that cometh from God only?"— John 5, v. 44.

1. Ye patient of applause and fame,
Bold to usurp the Christian name,
No more your souls deceive;
Who seek the praise that comes from men,
Ye boast your hearsay faith in vain;
Ye cannot yet believe.

2. By fellow-worms carest, belov'd,
Ye cannot be by God approv'd,
Vile favourites of his foe,
Who incense from the world receive,
In fair repute, and honours live,
And have your lot below.

3. Awake out of your pleasing dream,
Renounce yourselves, the world's esteem
The world's reproach despise,
As sojourners on earth unknown,
Wish to be prais'd by God alone,

Your Father in the skies.

4. Your pride and want of faith lament,
And then believe whom God hath sent
To speak your sins forgiven,
Your sinful nature to remove,
And perfected in humble love
To give you thrones in heaven.

JOHN CHAPTER SIX

"A great multitude followed him, because they saw the miracles which he did on them that were diseased."—John 6, v. 2.

I the miracles have seen
Wrought in these thy Spirit's days
On the sinsick souls of men,
Miracles of healing grace:
Wherefore with the multitude
Saviour, Lord, I follow Thee,
Let thine ancient works be shew'd,
O repeat them all on me.

"Jesus went up into a mountain, and there he sat with his disciples."—John 6, v. 3.

Jesus here his wisdom shows
Mixt with tenderness of love,
Not to urge his envious foes
Doth out of their sight remove;
Silent, he declines applause,
Pious to the mount retreats,
Humbly from the world withdraws,
Meekly with his followers sits.

"He saith unto Philip, Whence shall we buy bread, that these may eat?"—John 6, v. 5.

Faithless and ungrateful men,
Why should ye distrust your God?
Can He not his own sustain,
He who fills the world with food?
Souls, and bodies too to feed
Still his love is always near:
And if miracles ye need,
Miracles again appear.

"This he said to prove him."—John 6, v. 6.

Satan tempts, our faith t' o'rethrow,
Christ, to strengthen and improve,
That we may our weakness know,
With the virtue of his love:
Gracious souls by want he tries,
Takes upon himself their cares;
Then abundantly supplies,
Tells them, all he has is theirs.

"There is a lad here, which hath five barlyloaves, and two small fishes: but what are they among so many?"—John 6, v. 9.

1. Less will in his hands suffice,

Who the corn doth yearly bless,
Grains to harvests multiplies,
Gives the hundred-fold increase:
Careful for all living things,
God, whose Providential call
From earth's fruitful bosom brings
Food and nourishment for all.

2. God omnipotently near
Leaves us first our wants to feel,
Then he doth for us appear,
Then he doth his arm reveal:
Succour'd in our greatest need,
Learn we thus his grace to prize,
At his hands receive the bread
Sent as manna from the skies.

"Now there was much grass in the place: so the men sat down, in number about five thousand."—John 6, v. 10.

1. God commands the grass to grow,
Fodder to the cattle gives,
Yet his noblest work below
Man his goodness disbelieves,
Anxious for thy family,
Doubtful of thy Saviour's power,
Thousands fed by Jesus see,
Fed that thou mayst doubt no more.

2. Countless miracles unseen
Daily are by Jesus done,
That the careful sons of men
May confide in Him alone,
May their gracious Owner know,
God who answers the request,
Feeds his family below,
Leads them to an endless feast.

"He distributed to the disciples, and the disciples to them that were set down, as much as they would."—John 6, v. 11.

Hungring after heavenly food
If we for the blessing stay,
He that fed the famish'd croud
Sends us not unblest away:
Waiting on our bounteous Lord
Who our faith's obedience prove,
Jesus feasts us by his word,
Fills our hearts with joy and love.

"Gather up the fragments."—John 6, v. 12.

Gather we still the fragments up
Which from our Master's table fall,
Whate'er may feed our faith and hope,
The sacred crumbs, preserve them all;
Let not one gracious thought be lost,
The faintest, least desire of good
More than a thousand worlds it cost,
It cost the Lamb his richest blood.

"They filled twelve baskets with the fragments."—John 6, v. 13.

Poor, fainting souls our God relieves,
And thus our unbelief confounds,

Above what we can hope he gives,
His grace miraculous abounds,
His blessing all our wants exceeds;
And he who ministers the word
Himself inriches, while he feeds
The hungry followers of his Lord.

"When they had seen the miracle that Jesus did, they said, This is of a truth that Prophet that should come into the world."—John 6, v. 14.

How long hast Thou vouchsaf'd to feed
Thy follower in the wilderness!
And yet I know thee not indeed,
Nor truly by my life confess:
Prophet Divine, rais'd up for me,
Thine utmost power of love exert,
Then shall I all thy wonders see,
And hear my Teacher in my heart.

"When Jesus perceived that they would come and take him by force, to make him a king, he departed again into a mountain himself alone."—John 6, v. 15.

I.

How few by his example led
Jesus' obscurity desire,
Its proffer'd pomp and grandeur dread,
And gladly from the world retire!
Join'd to the poor inglorious few
Fain would I, Lord, the people shun,
Thee to the sacred mount pursue,
And live conceal'd with Thee alone.

"When Jesus perceived that they would come and take him by force, to make him a king, he departed again into a mountain himself alone."—John 6, v. 15.

II.

1. Who dost all worldly state decline,
Thee I by holy violence take,
Present my heart thy humble shrine,
And Thee my King by faith I make:
Thou promisest my King to be,
Thou cam'st from heaven to dwell with man,
And wilt not hide thyself from me,
But in my ravish'd bosom reign.

2. Accomplish then thy love's design,
Set up thy gracious kingdom here,
And stamp'd with holiness divine,
I bear thy royal character,
I sink baptiz'd into thy name,
All earthly dignities despise,
And singly seek with stedfast

aim
A crown of glory in the skies.

"It was &c. The sea arose, by reason of a great wind that blew."—John 6, v. 17, 18.

1. Horribly the waves and wind
Of fierce temptation roar,
When our Lord we cannot find
In present peace and power;
When we mourn his help delay'd,
The darkness of his absence feel,
Wrapt in sin's profoundest shade
As in the gloom of hell.

2. Oft alas the penal night
Doth from his wrath proceed;
Oft his grace withdraws the light,
And fills our hearts with dread;
Storms without, and fears within
He lets arise, our faith to prove,
Leaves us in th' abyss of sin
The objects of his love.

"It is I, be not afraid."—John 6, v. 20.

He who rules the lower air
Stirs up the troubled sea,
Tempts, and urges to despair,
But cannot conquer me,
Cannot; for my present Lord
(When passion and the world runs high,)
Speaks the comfortable word
And tells my heart, Tis I!

"Then they willingly received him into the ship: and immediately the ship was at the land whither they went."—John 6, v. 21.

1. Hurricanes the ship defies,
If Thou art in the ship,
Swiftly toward the haven flies,
And bounds along the deep!
Saviour, in thy church appear,
Give all our hearts thy voice to know,
Then redeem'd from sin and fear
We to perfection go.

2. Borne upon the wings of love,
We in thy Spirit's might,
Swiftly to our Center move
And urge our rapid flight:
Life is in a moment o're,
While all thy saints of Thee possest
Reach with shouts the happy shore,
And on thy bosom rest.

"When the people saw that Jesus was not there, they came to Capernaum, seeking for Jesus."—John 6, v. 24.

1. Come let us anew
Our Saviour pursue,
Though now out of sight,
We shall find him again, if we seek him aright.
Us who often hath fed
With spiritual bread,
Will his comforts restore
And his kingdom bring in to the

diligent poor.

2. Invisibly near,
He will quickly appear,
No more to depart,
In his Spirit He comes to abide in our heart:
Then united in love
His fulness we prove,
In his presence remain,
And never lose sight of our Saviour again.

"Ye seek me, not because ye saw the miracles, but because ye did eat of the loaves, and were filled."—John 6, v. 26.

Nature thy gifts requires
With fond voluptuous aim,
To satisfy its own desires,
Not to exalt thy name:
Drawn by the sweets of grace,
Saviour we follow on;
But few are found who seek thy face,
For thy own sake alone.

"Labour not for the meat which perisheth, but for that meat which endureth unto life everlasting, which the Son of man shall give unto you."—John 6, v. 27.

1. The world with useless care
Throughout their life's short day,
That perishable meat prepare,
That wealth which cannot stay;
But few their pains bestow,
As creatures born to die,

And feed by faith on Christ below,
Till to his throne they fly.

2. Thou art the Bread of life
That meat which shall remain:
Be it our only care and strife
Thy blessed Self to gain;
Give, Lord, and always give
Th' immortalizing Food,
And strengthen us by grace to live
The sinless life of God.

"What shall we do, that we might work the works of God?"—John 6, v. 28.

Hast thou indeed done well?
The action is not thine;
The Spirit is its Principle,
Its rule the will Divine;
To Him from whom it flow'd
It doth directly tend,
And wrought in the pure love of God
His glory is its End.

"This is the work of God, that ye believe on Him whom He hath sent."—John 6, v. 29.

1. The first great work of God
Is in my heart begun,
Who now believe, Thou hast bestow'd
On me thy darling Son;
Hast sent Him from the sky,
That sinners may receive
The Man who liv'd for all to die,
Who died in all to live.

2. Father of all, in me
The heavenly gift increase,
The faith that works by charity,
And teems with holiness,
That having done thy will
I the reward may gain,
And meet my Saviour on the hill,
And in his presence reign.

"What sign shewest thou, that we may see, and believe thee?"—John 6, v. 30.

Wonders we daily see
Of power and grace Divine,
Yet blind thro' infidelity
We still demand a sign:
Thou giv'st the sign requir'd,
Thou dost the veil remove,
And with thy Spirit's life inspir'd
We see, believe, and love.

"Moses gave you not that bread from heaven; but my Father giveth you the true Bread from heaven."—John 6, v. 32.

Moses could not give the Bread,
Nor yet the Sign bestow,
Jesus doth from God proceed,
His Gift to all below:
Who that precious Gift receives,
Sent from the Father's throne above,
Eats the Manna true, and lives
The life of sinless love.

"The bread of God is he which cometh down from heaven, and giveth life unto the world."—John 6, v. 33.

Bread of God, for Thee I lift
My hungry longing heart,
The true Bread, the Father's Gift
To all the world Thou art;
Thou bestow'd on all mankind
Dost sinners dead to life restore:
Thee reveal'd by faith we find,
And live for evermore.

"Then said they unto him, Lord, evermore give us this bread."—John 6, v. 34.

Lord, they ask'd a good unknown
Which Thou would'st not deny:
Thee that living Bread we own
That Manna from the sky
Thee we every moment need
T' increase the life inspir'd by Thee,
Feed our spirit still and feed
Thro' all eternity.

"I am the bread of life."—John 6, v. 35.

Thee the Principle and Food
Of life divine we bless:
Raise in us the life of God
Of faith and righteousness,
Mixt, incorporated with man,
Our grace continually improve,
Still with fresh supplies sustain,
And raise to perfect love.

"He that cometh to me shall never hunger; and he that believeth on me shall never thirst."—John 6, v. 35.

End of our inlarg'd desires,
Eternal Verity,
Nothing more the soul requires
Which knows and feeds on Thee,
Blest, beyond conception blest,
Partaker with the saints above,
Here inthron'd in heavenly rest,
And satisfied with Love.

"Ye also have seen me, and believe not."—John 6, v. 36.

1. God made man on earth appear'd,
And mighty wonders wrought;
Sinners saw their Lord and heard,
And yet believed him not:
Still thy Spirit, Lord, is near,
Yet still unknown to me Thou art,
Till Thou giv'st the hearing ear
And preachest to my heart.

2. Now thy miracles of grace
Repeat, O God in me,
Now reveal thy lovely face
And give me eyes to see;
Present with thy servant dwell,
Into mine inmost spirit given,
Give me in Thyself to feel
The hidden life of heaven.

"All that the Father giveth me shall come to me; and him that cometh to me I will in no wise cast out."—John 6, v. 37.

1. Thy Father gave Thee all mankind:
But drawn by unresisted grace
Who follow on their Lord to find
Their Lord they surely shall embrace,
To those dear wounds for refuge flee,
And full salvation gain in Thee.

2. The soul that would on Thee rely,
Jesus, Thou never wilt disdain,
Or leave him in his sins to die,
But purg'd from every guilty stain
With open arms of love receive,
Forever in thy joy to live.

3. Saviour, for thy own promise sake
Vouchsafe the blessing I implore,
Me, me into thy favour take,
To perfect holiness restore,
And to thy Father's house admit,
And give me on thy throne to sit.

"I came down from heaven, to do the will of Him that sent me."—John 6, v. 38.

Descending from thy Father's throne,
Thou cam'st to execute his will,
The souls peculiarly thine own
To bless, and sanctify, and seal,

And raise whoe'er his voice obey,
Thy saints triumphant—in that day.

"And this is the Father's will, which hath sent me &c."—John 6, v. 39.

Wast Thou not sent, my Lord, for me?
And did not the Paternal Grace
Give this poor helpless soul to Thee?
Receive me then to thine embrace,
And place me by thy side above,
To glorify thy faithful love.

"This is the will of him that sent me, that every one which seeth the Son, and believeth on him, may have everlasting life: and I will raise him up in the last day."—John 6, v. 40.

1. Who can resist th' Almighty will,
Or frustrate what our God ordains?
The practical believer still
Eternal life in Christ obtains,
And, faithful unto death shall rise,
To share his kingdom in the skies.

2. Salvation is of faith alone,
And who by faith my Saviour see,
I have the Life, I have the Son,
The glorious Hope reveal'd in me:
And when my Friend the Judge comes down,
I mount, and claim the promis'd crown.

"No man can come to me except the Father which hath sent me, draw him: and I will raise him up at the last day."—John 6, v. 44.

1. Father, Thou hast our hearts inclin'd,
Or we had never sought thy Son,
We still thy powerful drawings find,
And cannot rest in grace begun;
Till Thou thine own desires fulfil,
And Jesus in our hearts reveal.

2. To this, O God, Thou hast us wrought
That now we might thy Son confess,
Led by preventing grace and taught
Add us to Jesus witnesses,
Command the light of faith to shine,
And fear gives place to love divine.

3. His Spirit send, to seal us his,
As members of his body here,
Joint heirs of everlasting bliss,
That when he doth with clouds appear,
We all may to his joy succeed,
And reign triumphant with our

Head.

"Every man that hath heard, and hath learned of my Father, cometh unto me."—John 6, v. 45.

Taught of himself my God to fear,
Jesus, thy Father's voice I hear,
The softly-whispering grace,
Which bids me come, as lost, to Thee,
For wisdom, peace, and liberty,
For life, and righteousness.

"Not that any man hath seen the Father, save he which is of God, he hath seen the Father."—John 6, v. 46.

1. From his, into thy school receive,
And help me, Saviour, to believe,
In God with Thee the same:
Thou only dost the Father know,
Thou only canst to sinners show
His nature and his name.

2. Witness of truth, and Channel too,
Th' Invisible appears in view,
If Thou thyself reveal;
I then injoy the blisful sight,
I see him by thy Spirit's light,
And all his goodness feel.

"He that believeth on me hath everlasting life."—John 6, v. 47.

1. Author of faith implant in me
That root of immortality,
That never-failing root,
Whence every grace and virtue grow;
And then th' eternal life bestow,
The ripe celestial fruit.

2. But if in me reveal'd Thou art,
I have the Earnest in my heart,
The Witness and the Seal:
Come then mine unbelief remove,
And by the Spirit of life and love
In me forever dwell.

"I am that Bread of life."—John 6, v. 48.

1. Jesus, that Bread of life we own
(Essential Life which ne'er begun
And cannot cease to be)
The Word of life, display'd above,
Begotten by his Father's love
From all eternity.

2. Jesus we own the Angel's Bread
Before these heavens and earth were made,
And since our world began
Reveal'd in mortal flesh below,
We all by faith may Jesus know
The Bread of life to man.

3. Author of faith and Finisher,
We taste his gracious sweetness here,
The manna of his love
Sure antepast of heavenly bread
Which shall our ravish'd Spirits feed
With endless Life above.

"Your fathers did eat manna in the wilderness, and are dead. This is the bread that cometh down from heaven, that a man may eat thereof and not die &c."—John 6, v. 49, 50, 51.

1. Form'd in the region of the air,
The figure might their strength repair,
A while from death reprieve,
But the true Bread from heaven sent down
Who taste in God's eternal Son
We evermore shall live.

2. While in this wilderness we dwell,
Our living, quickning Principle,
Thou, Saviour, from above
Dost with Thyself vouchsafe to feed,
And daily thro' thy members spread
The life of faith and love.

3. Long as eternal ages last,
Our food shall neither cloy nor waste,
Our souls with love supplied
Shall on Jehovah's fulness feast,
In Thee alone forever blest,
Forever satisfied.

"How can this man give us his flesh to eat?"—John 6, v. 52.

1. Th' Unfathomable mystery!
Let others ask, how can it be:
Th' imperishable meat
Which Thou to all wou'dst freely give,
With prostrate reverence we receive,
Thy sacred flesh we eat.

2. The Fountain of my life, and Head,
The Victim dying in my stead,
That I thy life may know,
Thyself, in various ways design'd
To quicken me and all mankind,
Thou dost on all bestow.

"Except ye eat the flesh of the Son of God, and drink his blood, ye have no life in you."—John 6, v. 53.

1. How blind the misconceiving croud,
Who in the literal grossness dream
They eat thy flesh, and drink thy blood!
Alas, there is no life in them:
And who partake th' external sign,
Without the hidden mystery
They eat the bread, and drink the wine,
But never feed, O Lord, on Thee.

2. What is it then thy flesh to eat?
O give mine inmost soul to know
The nature of that heavenly meat
Ordain'd to quicken all below:
What is it, Lord, to drink thy blood?
Explain it to this heart of mine,
And fill me with the life of God
The love, the holiness Divine.

"Whoso eateth my flesh, and drinketh my blood, hath eternal life; and I will raise him up at the last day."—John 6, v. 54.

Who now his flesh and blood partake,
Partakers of the life Divine,
We soon shall see our Lord come back
His members all in one to join;
And feeding on this living Bread,
This earnest of my endless bliss,
I too shall rise to meet my Head
I too shall see him as He is.

"My flesh is meat indeed, and my blood is drink indeed. He that eateth my flesh, and drinketh my blood, dwelleth in me, and I in him."—John 6, v. 55, 56.

Saviour, thy flesh is meat indeed!
Thy nature to thy church made known
Doth every saint with manna feed,
Till every saint with Thee is one,
Till blended with its heavenly Food
The soul thy gracious fulness feels
And all transform'd we dwell in God,
And God in us forever dwells.

"As the living Father hath sent me, and I live by the Father; so he that eateth me, even he shall live by me."—John 6, v. 57.

Stupendous miracle of love!
Archangels cannot tell me how
I live by Thee, my Life above,
As by the living Father Thou!
But sure as Thee thro' faith I eat,
Thy Spirit's substance I receive,
And one with my mysterious Meat
Thro' all eternity shall live.

"This is that bread which came down from heaven: not as your fathers did eat manna, and are dead: he that eateth of this bread shall live forever."—John 6, v. 58.

Give me on Thee, the living Bread,
To live, till here my journey end,
Thou Bread of heaven, a pilgrim lead
To realms from which Thou didst descend:
Eternal Bread, the true desire
Of everlasting joys impart,
And my translated soul inspire
With all Thou hast and all Thou art.

"This is an hard saying, Who can bear it?"—John 6, v. 60.

Hard to conceive without thy love,
Impossible without thy light,
Jesus, mine unbelief remove,
That I may know the truth aright:
That Thou should'st give thy flesh to man,
Our reasoning pride can never bear:
Make thy mysterious saying plain,
And teach my heart by dwelling there.

"When Jesus knew in himself, that his disciples murmured at it, he said unto them, Doth this offend you?"—John 6, v. 61.

Doubts may in true disciples rise:
They cannot, Lord, offended be,
Or like the murmuring world, despise
The truths not yet reveal'd by Thee:
By faith their scruples they suppress,
With meek humility submit,
And waiting for the light of grace,
Bewail their blindness at thy feet.

"What and if ye shall see the Son of man ascend up where he was before?"—John 6, v. 62.

When Jesus in the clouds ye see
Ascending to his pompous throne
Inrob'd in all his majesty
The Father's co-eternal Son,
Surrounded with his dazling quire,
Blessing the church he leaves below;
No marvel if ye then inquire
How can this God his flesh bestow?

"It is the Spirit that quickneth, the flesh profiteth nothing."—John 6, v. 63.

1. Thy word in the bare literal sense,
Though heard ten thousand times, and read,
Can never of itself dispense
The saving power which wakes the dead:
The meaning spiritual and true
The learn'd expositor may give,
But cannot give the virtue too,
Or bid his own dead spirit live.

2. But breathing in the sacred leaves
If on the soul thy Spirit move,
The re-begotten soul receives
The quickning power of faith and love;
Transmitted thro' the gospel-word
Whene'er the Holy Ghost is given,
The sinner hears, and feels restor'd
The life of holiness and heaven.

"The words that I speak unto you, they are spirit, and they are life."—John 6, v. 63.

1. Jesus descended from the sky,
The Power of God in man Thou art;
Thyself, to whom I now apply,
Speak thy own words into my heart:
Thy words are more than empty sound,
Inseparably one with Thee,
Spirit in them and life is found,
And all the depths of Deity.

2. While feebly gasping at thy feet
A sinner in my sins I bow,
O might I now my Saviour meet,
And hear, and feel thy sayings now!
Speak, and thy word the dead shall raise,
Shall me with spirit and life inspire;
Speak on, and fill my soul with grace,
And call me to that deathless quire.

"No man can come unto me, except it were given unto him of my Father."—John 6, v. 65.

1. Faith is not on all bestow'd:
Thou who hast the grace receiv'd,
Fear to lose the gift of God;
Thou who never hast believ'd,
Hope that precious faith t' obtain
Bought by Jesus on the tree
Bought for every child of man
Freely offer'd now to Thee.

2. Drawn by efficacious grace
Toward thine unknown Saviour move,
Taught of God to seek his face,
Wait for his redeeming love:
When Thou dost the Son receive
Made by his great Father known,
Sav'd by sovereign mercy, give
All the praise to God alone.

"From that time many of his disciples went back, and walked no more with him."—John 6, v. 66.

Souls are by temptation shewn
Jesus who a while pursue;
Trials make them fully known,
Separate 'twixt the false and true:
Thro' thy quick and powerful word,
Lord, Thou soundest every heart:
Then they feel the two-edg'd sword,
Then the hypocrites depart.

"Will ye also go away?"—John 6, v. 67.

Yes; unless Thou hold me fast,
After all thy love to me,
I shall faithless prove at last
Treacherously depart from Thee:
That from Thee I may not go,
Leave me not to my own will;
My Companion here below,
Guide me to thy heavenly hill.

"Lord, to whom shall we go? thou hast the words of eternal life &c."—John 6, v. 68, 69.

1. Master, what a school is thine!
Truth and life thy words impart:
Thou Thyself the Truth Divine
Thou the Life eternal art;
Both we by thy teaching know,
Truly here we learn to live:
Here Thyself Thou dost bestow,
Light and love forever give.

2. Whither shall we go from Thee:
Lord to whom for life repair?
All besides is misery,
Death, delusion, and despair:
Wherefore to Thyself we cleave;
Thee the living God we own,
Only by thy Spirit live,
Find our heaven in Thee alone.

"We believe, and are sure, that Thou art the Christ, the Son of the living God."—John 6, v. 69.

Jesus, Thee I surely know
Son of God, and God most-high:
Thou wast manifest below
Whom the angels glorify;
Partner of my flesh and blood,
God's eternal Son Thou art,
Christ, thyself th' eternal God
Living, reigning in my heart.

"Have not I chosen you twelve? and one of you is a devil."—John 6, v. 70.

1. He leaves them all in humble fear,
While Judas he forbears to name,
That every faithful soul sincere
May ask, "if I the traitor am,"
That each his helplessness may own,
Suspicious of himself alone.

2. O may I, Lord, with jealous care
Watch over my own feeble heart,
Mistrust myself, of sin beware,
And least I should from Thee depart,
My soul into thy keeping give,
And pray, and tremble, and believe!

JOHN CHAPTER SEVEN

"Jesus would not walk in Jewry, because the Jews sought to kill him."—John 7, v. 1.

1. To 'scape thy persecuting foes
Thy power Thou dost not interpose,
Or call for heaven's vindictive fire,
But yield, and quietly retire:
The death Thou dost at present shun,
Not fearfully from danger run
But seek thy Father's will to do,
And in his time to suffer too.

2. By Thee instructed, we suppress
Our rash impatient eagerness,
Nor court the persecutor's sword,
But wait the season of our Lord,

Wisely from our destroyers flee,
Till stopt by the divine decree,
We suffer in the will of God,
And write our vict'ry in our blood.

"Now the Jews feast of tabernacles was at hand."—John 7, v. 2.

1. The feast of tabernacles
With joyful exultation,
Thine Israel, we Observe to Thee
The God of our salvation;
From sin's Egyptian bondage
Who didst thine own deliver,
Jesus, we praise Thy pardoning grace,
And love that lives forever.

2. We travel thro' this desart
Of trouble and vexation,
In booths remain Till we obtain
A lasting habitation;
The true celestial Canaan
To us by promise given,
The better feast Th' eternal rest,
Th' inheritance of heaven.

"If thou do these things, shew thyself to the world."—John 7, v. 4.

1. Who works the works of God
Must oft expect to hear
The dire advice of flesh and blood,
"Before the world appear,
"Go, shew thyself to man,
"A champion in the cause,
"For all thy piety is vain
"Without the world's applause."

2. But deaf to nature's voice,
Jesus we follow Thee,
And hidden from mankind, rejoice
In thy obscurity,
Happy, if Thou approve
Our works in secret done,
If by our humble faith and love
We please our God alone.

"For neither did his brethren believe in him."—John 7, v. 5.

Who love the praise of man
Their unbelief confess,
Though walking in a shadow vain
Of formal godliness;
They slight the Saviour's word
Who seek their own renown,
Refuse their self-denying Lord,
His sufferings and his crown.

"Jesus said unto them, My time is not yet come: but your time is always ready."—John 7, v. 6.

1. Who their own desires pursue
Their want of faith declare,
Their own violent will to do
They always ready are,
God's appointed time out-run
And full of selfish forwardness
Boldly snatch the gift unknown
Th' anticipated grace.

2. Now, just now, is nature's word
Impatient of delay!

Guided by thy will, O Lord,
I for thy leizure stay,
Dare not set a time to Thee,
Or dictate, When thyself to show:
Give whate'er Thou wilt to me,
And as Thou wilt bestow.

"The world cannot hate you."—John 7, v. 7.

1. The world will always love their own,
Who countenance their sin,
Or let them quietly sleep on,
Till Tophet takes them in:
But O! their choicest favourites are
The minister and priest,
The guides who prudently forbear
To interrupt their rest.

2. Who in the worldly spirit live,
And with the many go,
Favour and praise from man receive,
The good they seek below;
Not hated for religion's sake,
In Satan's arms secure
They slumber on; and thus they make
Their own damnation sure.

"But me it hateth, because I testify of it, that the works thereof are evil."—John 7, v. 7.

1. The world with persecuting spight
The sons of God blaspheme,
And hate and shun th' officious light
Which doth their deeds condemn;
The witnesses of Jesus grace
The saints they cannot bear
Who against all their evil ways
By word and life declare.

2. Confessing whom our hearts adore,
We feel their enmity:
O might we, Lord, deserve it more
By more resembling Thee!
O might we all thy Spirit breathe,
The wicked to reprove,
And testify in life and death
Thy purity of love!

"Go ye up unto this feast."—John 7, v. 8.

To that sacramental feast
Numbers without Jesus go,
In the outward form they rest,
Care not Him their Lord to know;
Christians leaving Christ behind,
To his house in vain repair,
Never at his table find,
Never wish to find him there.

"I go not up yet unto this feast, for my time is not yet full come. When he had said these words unto them, he abode still in Galilee."—John 7, v. 8, 9.

Jesus, I thy wisdom need,
With exact fidelity
Well to time my every deed
When and as ordain'd by Thee:
Till thy counsel is reveal'd,

Let me in my calling rest,
Feel at last thy time fulfil'd,
Then on thy perfection feast.

"The Jews sought him at the feast, and said, Where is he?"—John 7, v. 11.

Thyself Thou dost from them conceal
That seek thee not aright,
But sinners who their blindness feel
Thou wilt restore to sight;
Thou wilt the seeking mourner chear,
And give the weary rest:
And when Thou dost my Lord appear,
Thy presence makes the feast.

"Some said he is a good man: others said, Nay; but he deceiveth the people. Howbeit no man spake openly of him, for fear of the Jews."—John 7, v. 12, 13.

1. The judgment of the world how blind
Who treat the members like their Head!
As base deceivers of mankind
Whoe'er in Jesus footsteps tread,
Their Lord to Calvary attend,
And bear his burthen to the end.

2. None dares in their behalf to speak,
Abandon'd and decried by all,
No favour but from God they seek,
On Him they for protection call,
On Him their Advocate rely,
Till meekly on his cross they die.

"Now about the middle of the feast, Jesus went up into the temple, and taught."—John 7, v. 14.

1. At length the time is quite fulfil'd,
The moment come, when God had will'd
To manifest his Son,
Jehovah, in the temple seen,
Begins t' instruct the sons of men,
And make the Godhead known.

2. The Christ foretold by ancient seers,
The Lord in his own house appears,
To teach, and not declaim,
To answer all his love's design,
And with authority Divine
Declare his Father's name.

3. By thy example, Lord, repress
Our ministerial forwardness,
And teach us when, and where,
And how our office to fulfil,
And the whole counsel of thy will
Before the world declare.

"How knoweth this man letters, having never learned?"—John 7, v. 15.

1. Jesus, thy ministers receive
A light which study cannot give;
Divinely taught they are,
To propagate thy truths below
And teach the doctrines which they know
By diligence in prayer.

2. Thy law is in their inward parts,
Thy Spirit inspires their faithful hearts
With wisdom from above,
He gives the meaning of thy word,
And much they know of their dear Lord,
For much they pray and love.

3. The scorn of men, the worldling's fool
Commences in thy Spirit's school
Unto salvation wise,
The heavenly path to sinners shows,
And mighty in the scripture goes
Their Leader to the skies.

"Jesus answered them, and said, My doctrine is not mine, but his that sent me."—John 7, v. 16.

1. An herald of the grace divine
Can say "My doctrine is not mine,
"But his who sent me forth,
"Freely what I receive to give,
"And tell the world, They all may live
"Thro' Jesus' dying worth."

2. The truths he speaks are not his own,
God teaches him, and God alone,
The mystery to explain,
Opens his mouth to preach the word,
And tells our hearts, It is the Lord,
Who gives such power to man.

"If any man will do his will, he shall know of the doctrine, whether it be of God, or whether I speak of myself."—John 7, v. 17.

1. Lord, that I may the doctrine know,
A will to do thy will bestow,
An humble ready mind
To follow truth, where'er it leads:
And then the light from Thee proceeds,
And then my God I find.

2. My simple, childlike heart inspire
With fervour of intense desire
Thee, only Thee to please;
And make thy great salvation known,
And bring thy docile follower on
To perfect holiness.

3. Thou canst not speak distinct

from Him
Who sent thee, Saviour, to redeem
This longing soul of mine:
Come then, dear Lord, thy counsel show,
And give me in thy love to know
The plenitude Divine.

"He that seeketh his glory that sent him, the same is true, and no unrighteousness is in him."—John 7, v. 18.

1. A teacher sent from God, designs
Jehovah's glory, and declines
Whate'er might raise his own;
T' exalt his heavenly Lord he seeks,
In honour of his Master speaks,
And lives for God alone.

2. O that I thus with upright aim
May magnify my Saviour's name,
And only seek his praise,
My truth and faithfulness approve,
Sav'd by the power of perfect love
From all unrighteousness!

"Did not Moses give you the law? and yet none of you keepeth the law."—John 7, v. 19.

The law thy servant Moses gave,
But not the power our souls to save,
But not th' obedient heart:
Jesus, we more and more rebel,
Till Thou the gospel-grace reveal,
And tell us who Thou art.

"Why go ye about to kill me?"—John 7, v. 19.

1. Why? Thou thyself hast told us why:
Because we thy commands defy,
Only inclin'd to ill,
With cruel enmity pursue,
And persecute our Lord anew,
And in thy members kill.

2. Because we could not keep thy laws,
Thy murtherers nail'd thee to the cross;
And there Thou bearst away
The sins of reprobate mankind,
And buy'st the power which all may find
Thy perfect will t' obey.

"Jesus answered and said unto them, I have done one work &c."—John 7, v. 21.

1. When virtue's advocate replies
As far from passion as from fear,
The answer soft and meekly wise
Becomes his Saviour's minister,
Who calmly sensible complains,
And truth and Jesus cause maintains.

2. For wisdom, Lord, on Thee I wait:

Instruct me when to hold my peace,
And when in words to vindicate
The works of genuine righteousness,
And stop the bold impiety
Which blames the good that flow'd from Thee.

"Judge not according to appearance, but judge righteous judgment."—John 7, v. 24.

1. 'Tis not, O Lord, th' external part
Which pleases or displeases Thee,
The principle, the end, the heart
Thou dost in every action see,
Thou only know'st the doer's aim,
The will, the temper, and the frame.

2. But partial, ignorant, and blind
We rashly judge as things appear,
Censorious, hasty, and unkind
Judge by the hearing of the ear,
And oft as sway'd by hate or love,
The good condemn, the ill approve.

3. Jesus, send forth thy truth and light,
That with thy love of equity
Inspir'd, we may pronounce aright
The sentence which proceeds from Thee,
As partners in thy judgment join,
And reign in righteousness Divine.

"Is not this he, whom they seek to kill? But lo, he speaketh boldly, and they say nothing unto him."—John 7, v. 25, 26.

1. The tongues, the hands, the hearts of men
Are subject to Divine controul,
God over all doth still restrain
Their rage against the faithful soul,
The faithful soul hath nought to fear,
Though Satan and his host are near.

2. Thoughtless of what the world intends,
A Christian speaks and labours on:
Jesus his instrument defends,
Immortal till his work is done;
Jesus the conquering faith supplies,
And then bestows the heavenly prize.

"Then they sought to take him: but no man laid hands on him, because his hour was not yet come."—John 7, v. 30.

1. Father, in thy hands we are
The members of thy Son,
Trust thy Providential care,
And hang on Thee alone,
Till thy sovereign goodness

please,
And Thou the sacred fence remove,
Neither fiends nor men can seize
The objects of thy love.

2. When thy wise permissive will
Shall leave us to their power,
Let the world our bodies kill,
In thine appointed hour:
Safe till then for God we live;
And when our souls from earth are driven,
Trust thee, Father, to receive,
And give us thrones in heaven.

"Many of the people believed on him."—John 7, v. 31.

God hath chose the simple poor,
As followers of his Son,
Rich in faith, of glory sure,
To win the heavenly crown:
Him the vulgar still embrace
By the great and learned denied,
Scorn'd by all the foes of grace,
And daily crucified.

"They said, When Christ cometh, will he do more miracles than these which this man hath done?"—John 7, v. 31.

All the world's disputers vain
Refuse the truth to know,
Slight the argument so plain
Of God reveal'd below:
Who his gracious wonders see,
The humble, unopposing croud
Hence conclude that this is HE,
The Christ, th' eternal God!

"The Pharisees and the chief priests sent officers to take him."—John 7, v. 32.

See the heavenly Man of God,
How patiently He stands!
Lets the men athirst for blood
Extend their ruffian hands;
Checks the fury of his foes,
But not by judgments from above,
Only signs of meekness shows,
And miracles of love!

"Then said Jesus, Yet a little while am I with you."—John 7, v. 33.

Those who will not, while they may,
Their Lord and God receive,
Soon outlive their gracious day,
And never can believe:
While I yet can make it sure,
Let me the proffer'd Blessing seize,
Seize a moment, to secure
Mine everlasting peace.

"And then I go unto Him that sent me."—John 7, v. 33.

Suffering saints, with comfort mourn,
For your discharge is near,
Soon ye shall to God return,
And at his throne appear:
There the wicked vex no more,
There your weary spirits rest,

Far beyond the tempter's power,
Reclin'd on Jesus breast.

"Ye shall seek me and shall not find me: and where I am, thither ye cannot come."—John 7, v. 34.

1. Those who will not seek him now,
While life and strength remain,
When their dying heads they bow,
Would seek the Lord in vain:
Casting now his words behind,
Seiz'd by the hellish messenger,
Nothing they in death shall find
But darkness and despair.

2. Jesus, Lord, to Thee I give
The glory, power, and praise;
Thou hast help'd me to believe,
And half unveil'd thy face:
O stir up my faithful heart
To seek, and still pursue the prize,
Till arriving where Thou art
I grasp thee in the skies.

"Will he go to the dispersed among the Gentiles, and teach the Gentiles?"—John 7, v. 35.

Yes: He hath the Gentiles sought,
Dispers'd and wandring wide,
Outcasts by his Spirit taught,
And truly justified:
Sinners still He doth receive,
While Pharisees reject his grace,
Teaches us to love, and live
The life of righteousness.

"Jesus stood and cried, saying, If any man thirst, let him come unto me, and drink."—John 7, v. 37 &c.

1. Ye thirsty for God To Jesus give ear,
And take thro' his blood The power to draw near,
His kind invitation, Ye sinners, embrace,
The sense of salvation Accepting thro' grace.

2. Sent down from above Who governs the skies,
In vehement love To sinners he cries,
"Drink into my Spirit, Who happy would be,
"And all things inherit, By coming to Me."

3. O Saviour of all, Thy word we believe,
And come at thy call, Thy grace to receive:
The blessing is given, Wherever Thou art;
The earnest of heaven Is love in the heart.

4. To us at thy feet The Comforter give,
Who gasp to admit Thy Spirit, and live:
The weakest believers Acknowledge for thine,
And fill us with rivers Of water Divine.

"He that believeth on me, as the scripture hath said, out of his belly shall flow rivers of living water."—John 7, v. 38.

1. The sinner that hath, O Jesus, from Thee
That scriptural faith, Thy vessel shall be,
Peace, mercy, and blessing To others impart,
And joy never ceasing, Which springs from his heart.

2. Pour'd out from above Thy Spirit in him,
In rivers of love To sinners shall stream:
With spiritual graces, Which ever o'reflow,
The world he refreshes, The desart below.

"This spake he of the Spirit, which they that believe on him should receive: for the Holy Ghost was not yet given, because that Jesus was not yet glorified."—John 7, v. 39.

1. No; the Spirit's dispensation
Was not then on earth begun,
Jesus in his bloody passion
Had not laid the ransom down,
Had not by his dying merit
Bought the universal grace,
Thro' his prayer obtain'd the Spirit,
Pour'd him out on all our race.

2. But we now by faith adore thee,
Jesus, high above all height,
Re-instated in thy glory,
Re-possest of all thy right;
Thou hast with thy Father pleaded
Thine oblation on the tree;
Thou hast in thy suit succeeded,
Gain'd the Holy Ghost for me.

3. Now He is sent down from heaven,
Witness of thy power above,
Is to true believers given,
Source of all our joy and love:
Yes; we now thy bliss inherit,
Now our Pentecost is come:
Thou hast seal'd us by thy Spirit,
Mark'd for thine eternal home.

"When they had heard this saying, they said, Of a truth this is the prophet. Others said, This is the Christ."—John 7, v. 40, 41.

The promise made, but not fulfil'd
Thy hearers, Lord, with joy receiv'd,
Before the precious truth was seal'd,
The Prophet Thee, the Christ believ'd:
And shall not we thy Godhead own,
And testify thy Spirit given,
Thro' seventeen hundred ages known,
And daily still sent down from heaven.

"Shall Christ come out of Galilee? Hath not the scripture said &c."—John 7, v. 41, 42.

1. I want the faith which reasons not,
Though rational, implicit too,
That simply by thy Spirit taught,
Persuaded all thy words are true,
No seeming contrariety
May make me stumble, Lord, at Thee.

2. Useless disputes, reflections vain,
Questions obscure be cast aside;
The doubts I cannot yet explain
I leave to my unerring Guide:
And He my heavenly path shall show,
And all the truth I need to know.

"So there was a division among the people because of him."—John 7, v. 43.

1. The world offended at our Lord,
Is still in every age the same:
To bring a sharp divisive sword,
Not a deceitful peace He came,
His followers from his foes to part,
And shew the ground of every heart.

2. The truth his confessors defend
His faithless enemies deny;
Those in their Saviour's cause contend
These still persist and crucify,
Till Jesus his great power assumes,
And the millennial kingdom comes.

"And some of them would have taken him; but no man laid hands on him."—John 7, v. 44.

The world their hands can never lay
On one secur'd in thine,
Till Thou permit them, Lord, t' obey
And answer thy design:
They then with malice blind fulfil
Thine unperceiv'd decree,
The body of thy witness kill,
And send his soul to Thee.

"The officers answered, Never man spake like this man."—John 7, v. 46.

1. When our God the gospel gives
Cloth'd with his own Spirit's might,
Then the open'd heart believes,
Then our soul's restor'd to sight.
We its hidden beauty see,
Taste the sweetness of the word,
Feel its powerful energy,
Wondring own our heavenly Lord.

2. He disarms the hostile mind,
He doth all its hate remove;
By his word transform'd we find

Holy peace and humble love:
Never mortal spake like Him!
More than man He needs must be:
Is He not the God supreme?
Answer, Lord, thyself in me!

"Then answered them the Pharisees, Are ye also deceived?"—John 7, v. 47.

1. When Jesus we presume to praise,
Struck with his wonder-working word,
The world their ancient clamour raise,
Against th' admirers of our Lord,
As weak, deluded fools despise,
When Christ begins to make us wise.

2. Deceiv'd by Truth we cannot be:
But you your wretched selves deceive,
Blind Pharisees, who say ye see,
In a vain formal shadow live,
And mock the power ye will not feel,
Till Satan cheats you into hell.

"Have any of the rulers, or of the Pharisees believed on him?"—John 7, v. 48.

1. We still the old objection hear,
Have any of the great, or wise,
The men of name and character
Believ'd on Him the vulgar prize?
Our Saviour to the rich unknown,
Is worshipp'd by the poor alone.

2 The poor, we joyfully confess,
His followers and disciples still,
His friends and chosen witnesses,
Who know his name, and do his will,
Who suffer for our Master's cause,
And only glory in his cross.

"This people who knoweth not the law are cursed."—John 7, v. 49.

1. Boasters of a religious show,
Who the unlearned poor disdain,
Howe'er the literal law ye know,
Its curse doth still on you remain,
Who have not the whole law fulfill'd,
It speaks your condemnation seal'd.

2. The poor, the death-devoted croud
Their Lord with humble faith receive,
They gladly know their pardning God,
Freed from the legal curse they live,
The Spirit of pure obedience prove,
And all the law fulfill'd in love.

"Nicodemus saith unto them (he that came to Jesus by night, being one of them)."—John 7, v. 50.

Who first convers'd with Christ by night,
Defends him now in open day,
Arm'd by the word of Jesus might
The malice of his foes to stay,
He quells them with resistless zeal,
And baffles all the rage of hell.

"Doth our law judge any man, before it hear him, and know what he doeth?"—John 7, v. 51.

1. Who suffer in their Saviour's cause,
Must never marvel, or complain
Of violent wrongs, and broken laws;
By merciless oppressive man
Condemn'd unheard they always were,
And still their Master's portion share.

2. Witnesses of th' atoning blood,
Have ye been once arraign'd and tried?
As outlaws by your foes pursued,
Persist, and patiently abide,
Assur'd your cause shall soon be known,
And the great Judge pronounce, Well-done.

"Art thou also of Galilee?"—John 7, v. 52.

1. Dar'st thou oppose the pop'ular cry,
For blacken'd innocency plead?
Expect the ready world's reply,
No stronger argument they need,
But answer by reproaching thee,
"And art thou too of Galilee?"

2. Determin'd then thy lot expect,
Who canst the Christian sect defend,
Thou must be of the Christian sect,
Revil'd, and patient to the end,
With God's afflicted people rise,
To claim thy kingdom in the skies.

"And every man went unto his own house."—John 7, v. 53.

One question puts them all to flight,
From the bold champion of his Lord:
And when with the same beasts we fight,
And speak in faith the given word,
They cannot stand before our face;
One Christian shall a thousand chase.

JOHN CHAPTER EIGHT

"Jesus went unto the mount of Olives: And early in the morning he came again into the temple."—John 8, v. 1, 2.

Let us to the mount retreat,
And rest with Christ awhile,
Rest from persecution's heat,
And evangelick toil,
Patient grace by prayer obtain
For labouring on with strength renew'd,
Then go forth to fight again,
And work the works of God.

"All the people came unto him; and he sat down, and taught them."—John 8, v. 2.

Answering to their pastor's zeal,
The sheep betimes appear,
Eager and impatient still,
They flock the word to hear,
Listen, while the rich despise,
The great neglect, the learn'd dispute,
Priests against the truth arise,
And zealots persecute.

"The scribes and Pharisees brought unto him a woman taken in adultery."—John 8, v. 3.

1. Rejoicing in iniquity
The messengers of Satan see,
The servants of his will
Who watches us by day and night,
And seeks with unrelenting spite
To tempt, surprize, and kill.

2. But Jesus came the world to save,
Poor guilty souls who nothing have
In their defence to plead,
Who wait the sentence to receive,
Outcasts of men; that these may live,
He suffer'd in their stead.

"They set her in the midst."—John 8, v. 3.

They drag her out to public view,
Zealots who mercy never knew,
Who all remorse disown,
Drag her to death with hands unclean,
And fierce against another's sin,
Insult before they stone!

"Now Moses in the law commanded us, that such should be stoned: but what sayst thou?"—John 8, v. 5.

1. In vain would Christ's insidious foes
The servant to the Lord oppose:
The law to satisfy,
Not to destroy, from heaven He came,
That I, believing on his Name,
Might live, and never die.

2. Moses may frown, if Jesus smiles;
Justice and grace He reconciles;

His yearning bowels move
To sinners who their sins confess,
He cloathes them with his righteousness,
He saves them by his love.

"But what sayest thou?"—John 8, v. 5.

Thou sayst, the law is good and just:
Yet if I in thy mercy trust,
The law condemns in vain:
Thou sayst, I to thy wounds may flee,
And find my life restor'd in Thee,
And never sin again.

"This they said, tempting him, that they might have to accuse him."—John 8, v. 6.

1. He must unjust or cruel seem,
The sinner, or the law condemn,
Mercy or truth offend,
His zeal, or his compassion show;
Absolve her? he is virtue's foe,
And sin's acknowledg'd Friend.

2. The Serpent speaks in guileful men,
He tempts us first to sin, and then11
Accuses those that yield:
But Jesus he in vain assay'd,
That Bruiser of the serpent's head
His blunted tools repel'd.

"But Jesus stooped down, and with his finger wrote on the ground as though he heard them not."—John 8, v. 6.

Hark, how the hellish bloodhounds cry!
As Love himself would doom to die
A speechless criminal!
Their clamours fierce he will not hear,
Who still inclines his open ear
To misery's softest call.

"He that is without sin among you, let him first cast a stone at her."—John 8, v. 7.

1. What wisdom in our heavenly Lord!
His power accompanies his word,
And keen conviction darts,
Righteous, and merciful, and meek,
He sends the hypocrites to seek
An answer in their hearts.

2. He teaches us to cast aside
The cruel zeal of virtuous pride,
And first inquire within,
(Before we dare an harlot stone,)
Impeccable am I alone,
And never born in sin?

"And again he stooped down, and wrote on the ground."—John 8, v. 8.

Content to blast their wicked aim

He stoops again, and spares their shame,
The secret in their breast
Discover'd by his piercing word,
He leaves: the troubled sect is stir'd;
Let conscience do the rest!

"And they which heard it, went out."—John 8, v. 9.

1. Conscience, thou voice of God in man,
Accus'd by thee, we strive in vain
Thy clamours to suppres:
A thousand witnesses thou art;
And God is greater than our heart,
And all its evils sees.

2. Thy voice outspeaks, and strikes us dumb,
When greater sinners we presume
With rigour to condemn,
It makes us hide our guilty head,
Who vilest profligates upbraid,
And judge ourselves in them.

"And Jesus was left alone, and the woman."—John 8, v. 9.

1. The gospel stands in Moses place:
The foes of Jesus and his grace
Are scatter'd by a word,
Th' accusers all are fled and gone,
Misery with Mercy left alone,
The sinner with her Lord.

2. If left alone with Thee I am,
Though cover'd o're with guilt and shame,
I nothing have to fear;
My Saviour in my Judge I meet,
And wait, a sinner at thy feet,
Thy pardning voice to hear.

"When Jesus had lift up himself, and saw none but the woman, he said unto her, Woman, where are those thine accusers? hath no man condemned thee?"—John 8, v. 10.

1. He rises in the power of love,
Lifts himself up, his grace to prove,
And silent victory!
Be comforted, thou trembling soul,
Thy fears and sorrows to controul,
He turns his eyes on Thee.

2. "Where are the men that call'd so loud
"For justice, and the sinner's blood,
"Thy chast accusers where?"
(Jesus triumphantly demands,
And neither earth nor hell withstands
When Mercy means to spare.)

3. "Not one among them all, not one,
"To cast the first vindictive stone!
"On thine iniquity

"Can none inflict the judgment due?
"Are Pharisees adulterers too,
"And scribes as weak as thee?"

"She said, No man, Lord."—John 8, v. 11.

And what tho' every man condemn,
And every fiend conspire with them
Hellish with human pride
To doom a sinner in distress,
The Judge (if thou thy guilt confess)
The Judge is on thy side.

"And Jesus said unto her, Neither do I condemn thee: go, and sin no more."—John 8, v. 11.

1. Thine Advocate in Jesus see!
Tis He that speaks the word, tis He
That takes the prisoner's part:
Not to condemn the world he came:
Believing now in Jesus name
Ev'n now absolv'd thou art.

2. Who shall accuse th' elect of God,
Protected by th' atoning blood?
Tis God that justifies,
That bids thee go, and sin no more,
Go in thy Saviour's peace and power,
And trace him to the skies.

"He that followeth Me, shall not walk in darkness."—John 8, v. 12.

Jesus, I believe in Thee,
Yet my way I cannot see,
Yet I cannot see thy face,
Dark, and dead, and comfortless,
But if blind I follow on
Feeling for the God unknown,
I cannot long in darkness stay;
It must at last be chas'd away,
And turn'd into the perfect day.

"He that followeth me, shall have the light of life."—John 8, v. 12.

1. O for that chearing Light,
That Light of life within,
Which scatters all the shades of night,
The hellish gloom of sin!
Jesus thyself impart,
Light of the world remove
This unbelief, and fill my heart
With all the life of love.

2. Resolv'd, I follow Thee,
Till Thou thy love reveal,
In feeble faith's obscurity
My deadly darkness feel;
Believing against hope
The promise I embrace:
And I shall soon be lifted up,
And I shall see thy face.

"Though I bear record of myself, yet my record is true: for I know whence I came and whither I go; but ye cannot tell whence I come, and whither I go."—John 8, v. 14.

1. Eternal thanks to Thee,
Thou self-discover'd Light,
Thro' whom we thy credentials see,
And learn to judge aright:
Thee, Jesus, we receive
Our Saviour from above,
The wonders of thy life believe,
The wonders of thy love.

2. Thou cam'st from God, we know,
And dost with sinners stay,
That we may in thy footsteps go,
Nor miss the heavenly way:
Thou dost thy church attend,
Our Comforter and Guide,
To keep us, and when time shall end,
To carry home thy bride.

"And yet if I judge, my judgment is true: for I am not alone, but I and the Father that sent me."—John 8, v. 16.

Thou canst not, Lord, subsist alone,
As different, or distinct from Him,
With God inseparably one,
The same eternal God supreme:
Thy judgments are thy Father's too,
His judgments and decrees are thine,
And therefore all thy works are true,
And works of Righteousness Divine.

"I am one that bear witness of myself, and the Father that sent me, beareth witness of me."—John 8, v. 18.

1. Jesus by his meer word, alone
True witness of himself could bear:
Yet God did first attest his Son,
And by a voice from heaven declare;
The Father sent his Wel-belov'd,
By mighty signs his mission seal'd,
And Jesus' heavenly tempers prov'd
His soul with all the Godhead fill'd.

2. Tis thus a Follower of the Lamb
Doth real testimony give,
By works, not words, his grace proclaim
And shew the world how Christians live;
Tis thus the sons of God evince
Their birth illustrious from above,
From outward and from inward sins
Redeem'd by meek and lowly love.

"Ye neither know me nor my Father: if ye had known me, ye should have known my Father also."—John 8, v. 19.

1. They who never knew the Son
Thro' his own Spirit's light,
Never have the Father known,
Or worship'd God aright;
Only Jesus can declare
The great eternal Deity:
Atheists, Lord, they surely are,
That disbelieve in Thee.

2. But thy true disciples pray,
To us the Father show,
Thou his majesty display
Which none besides can know:
Thou his glorious Image art,
Himself descended from above:
Finding Thee within our heart
We know that God is Love.

"No man laid hands on him, for his hour was not yet come."—John 8, v. 20.

Who his mind on God hath stay'd,
Is kept in perfect peace,
Neither troubled nor afraid
He lives his Lord to please,
Careless of approaching ill,
Himself to Jesus work he gives,
Lives to answer all his Will,
In snares and deaths he lives!

"I go my way, and ye shall seek me, and shall die in your sins: whither I go, ye cannot come."—John 8, v. 21.

1. Wo to the men whom Jesus leaves,
Who force their Saviour to depart!
Up to their own desires He gives,
Their own obduracy of heart:
They seek him then, but seek too late,
Who long refus'd his love to feel,
They sink beneath his judgments weight,
They sink with all their sins to hell.

2. Thou didst foretell the fearful doom
Of that self-reprobated race,
That we in this our day may come,
And humbly seek, and find thy grace:
Entring into thy love's design,
We give thee, Lord, our broken heart:
Us to Thyself so closely join
That neither life nor death may part.

"Ye are from beneath, I am from above: ye are of this world, I am not of this world."—John 8, v. 23.

As members of that heavenly Man
Christians indeed are from

above,
Not of this world of shadows vain,
We our celestial country love:
Let worldlings love the things below,
A nobler good to us is given,
That all our spotless lives may show
The spirit and the taste of heaven.

"If ye believe not that I am He, ye shall die in your sins."—John 8, v. 24.

1. I would believe that Thou art He
Who came from heaven to die for me:
Saviour of men, the power supply,
Nor leave me in my sins to die:
A sinner on thy mercy cast,
I mourn for my offences past;
O for thy own dear sake forgive,
And sav'd by faith my soul shall live.

2. If now thy previous grace I feel,
Which melts my stubbornness of will,
If crush'd by unbelief I groan,
And languish for a God unknown,
One ray of life and comfort dart,
One spark of faith into my heart,
And let me feel thy sprinkled blood,
And see thee now my Lord, my God!

"They said unto him, Who art thou? And Jesus saith unto them, Even the same that I said unto you, from the beginning."—John 8, v. 25.

1. Thee, Jesus, thee th' eternal Lord,
Jehovah's uncreated Son,
Jehovah's unbeginning Word,
The first great Cause of all we own,
Thee by thy works and doctrines find
The Light and Life of all mankind.

2. In words, in deeds Thou dost declare
Thy own divine almighty power,
Yet harden'd infidels forbear
Thy sovereign Deity t' adore,
They will not know thee who Thou art,
Or feel thee living in their heart.

3. A life Thou hast which ne'er begun,
Which no decay or end shall know;
A life Thou didst assume, lay down,
To save this wretched world below:
And thro' thy loss the sons of men
May all thy life eternal gain.

"I have many things to say, and to judge of you: but he that sent me is true; and I speak to the world those things which I have heard of him."—John 8, v. 26.

I.

1. Jesus, who dost alone contain
The blessings of eternity,
Thou know'st the ill that is in man,
Thine only eye his heart can see,
Yet wilt Thou not the whole declare,
Or shew us more than we can bear.

2. Instructed by thy tenderest love
O that thy ministers may know,
The covering when they must remove,
And when thy moderation show,
Suppress what should not be reveal'd,
And leave the heart with Thee conceal'd.

"I have many things to say, and to judge of you: but he that sent me is true; and I speak to the world those things which I have heard of him."—John 8, v. 26.

II.

1. Fountain of truth, forever full,
Hail Thou great Father of our Lord!
Thy bosom was his heavenly school:
He heard, not yet th' incarnate Word;
From all eternity He knew,
That Thou art wise, and good, and true.

2. With Thee substantially the same,
With Thee inexplicably one,
He only doth declare thy name,
He makes to man thy nature known,
And taught by Him, we sweetly prove
Thy truth, thy wisdom, and thy love.

"When ye have lift up the Son of man, then shall ye know that I am, and that I do nothing of myself; but as my Father hath taught me, I speak these things."—John 8, v. 28.

1. What multitudes who never know,
Till they have crucified, their God!
He then doth his compassion show,
And draw and wash them in his blood,
Into his cross's school receive,
And teach them fully to believe.

2. Thy murderers, now we learn of Thee
That Thou art the supream I AM,

Equal to God in majesty,
With God eternally the same
Thy passions and thy actions shine
With worth and dignity Divine.

3. Essential Truth, thy words are His,
And following them we cannot stray,
They point us to celestial bliss,
Fresh life into our souls convey;
Till sav'd and sanctified in one,
They speak us up into thy throne.

"And he that sent me is with me: the Father hath not left me alone: for I always do those things which please him."—John 8, v. 29.

1. The Sender (for it cannot be)
Is never separate from the Sent,
Who join'd to his Divinity
Our flesh, his sacred instrument,
The Father leaves him not alone,
But lives eternal in his Son.

2. Obedient to his Father's will,
The Son for us obtain'd the grace
All his commandments to fulfil,
T' abide in all his righteous ways,
To walk in all well-pleasing here,
And pure before his face t' appear.

"If ye continue in my word, then are ye my disciples indeed."—John 8, v. 31.

Continuing in the outward word,
I read, and hear, believe, and do:
But give me thy good Spirit, Lord,
T' approve me thy disciple true:
Thou art the Truth that makes us free,
Abide, eternal Word in me.

"And ye shall know the truth, and the truth shall make you free."—John 8, v. 32.

Then shall I in the Word abide,
Establish'd and confirm'd in grace,
Thy promise to the utmost tried
With firm fidelity embrace,
And know the Truth, as I am known,
With God most intimately one.

"We were never in bondage to any man? How sayest thou, Ye shall be made free?"—John 8, v. 33.

1. O the vanity of man!
Fast bound in misery,
Gaul'd with Satan's iron chain,
He boasts that he is free;
Still inthrall'd in heart and mind,
"He needs not be by Christ restor'd,"
Bold, and ignorant, and blind
Rejects his pardning Lord.

2. Jesus, full of truth and grace,
To me my bondage show,
That I gladly may embrace
The gift Thou would'st bestow,
Find redemption in thy blood,
The joy of thy disciples prove,
Live with all the sons of God
The life of perfect love.

"Whosoever committeth sin, is the servant of sin."—John 8, v. 34.

1. Slaves we all by nature are,
To every vice inclin'd,
Foil'd, and prisoners took in war,
Our conqueror's yoke we find:
We to sin ourselves have sold,
And basely bow'd to passion's sway;
By a thousand lusts controul'd,
We dar'd not disobey.

2. By the guilt and tyranny
Of cruel sin opprest,
Lord, we will not come to Thee
For freedom and for rest:
Break this adamantine chain,
Who only canst the soul release,
Change the stubborn will of man,
And bid us go in peace.

"The servant abideth not in the house forever: but the son abideth ever."—John 8, v. 35.

Soon out of the house of God
The slave of sin is cast,
Cast into a fiery flood,
And pains that alway last:
But the child of faith and love
His full recompence shall gain
In his Father's house above
Eternally remain.

"If the Son shall make you free, ye shall be free indeed."—John 8, v. 36.

1. Thee, Redeemer of mankind,
Jehovah's favourite Son,
Let a wretched captive find,
Who for deliverance groan:
Real liberty from sin,
The true substantial freedom give,
Give thy Spirit, and within
My heart forever live.

2. Then, my God, and not till then
I shall indeed be free,
Free from the desires of men,
From all iniquity,
Free from every thought of ill,
Free to rejoice and always love,
Free to do thy perfect will
As angels do above.

"I speak that which I have seen with my Father: and ye do that which ye have seen with your father."—John 8, v. 38.

God and his hellish enemy
Divide the human throng:
Sinner, thy true condition see,
Thou must to one belong:
God, if his pleasure thou fulfil,
Thee for his child shall own,
But if thou dost the devil's will,
Thou art the devil's son.

"If ye were Abraham's children, ye would do the works of Abraham."—John 8, v. 39.

1. Not by the Christian name alone
The Christian man is shew'd,
Words cannot evidence a son
Of Abraham and of God;
No confident assertions vain
No single act can prove
That I am truly born again,
And God sincerely love.

2. I must in Abraham's footsteps stay,
Pursue him to the skies,
My houshold teach the heavenly way,
My Isaac sacrifice;
My life must speak the faith within,
In even tenor flow,
Demonstrate I am sav'd from sin,
And God my Father know.

"Ye seek to kill me, a man that hath told you the truth, which I have heard of God: this did not Abraham."—John 8, v. 40.

Who in the faith of Abraham tread,
Obediently receive
The truth that doth from God proceed,
And lovingly believe:
But his pretended children still
Reject the truth abhor'd,
Malign the witnesses, and kill,
And drive them to their Lord.

"We have one Father, even God."—John 8, v. 41.

1. The children of that wicked one
Conceal their sin and shame,
With daring pride the God unknown
They for their Father claim,
Their guilt disdaining to confess
They make their misery sure,
And while they cherish their disease
Can never find a cure.

2. Sinner, the painful truth admit
By hell no more beguil'd,
And prostrate own at Jesus feet
Thou art the devil's child;
Devilish thy works, and life, and heart;
But ransom'd by his blood,
Believe that thou his purchase art,
And thou art born of God.

"If God were your Father, ye would love me, for I proceeded forth, and came from God; neither came I of myself, but he sent me."—John 8, v. 42.

1. Children of God by faith, we owe
Our hearts and lips, O Christ, to thee:
Thou didst proceed from God we know,
His Son from all eternity,

Thou cam'st his heavenly Messenger,
And didst in mortal flesh appear.

2. Wherefore we thankfully believe,
Enter into thy strange design,
To Thee thy praise and glory give,
Thou great Philanthropist Divine,
With warmest gratitude approve,
And our Almighty Lover love.

"Why do ye not understand my speech? Even because ye cannot hear my word."—John 8, v. 43.

1. Strangers to your redeeming Lord,
Self-hardned from his righteous fear,
Ye cannot understand his word,
For dead in sin ye will not hear:
His knowledge he withholds from none;
The bar is all in you alone.

2. By blinding passions prepossest,
Thro' grace consent to let them go;
And ye may be in Jesus blest,
And ye his saving truths shall know,
Taste the good word to sinners given,
And praise your Teacher sent from heaven.

"Ye are of your father the devil, and the lusts of your father, ye will do: he was a murtherer from the beginning &c."—John 8, v. 44.

A child of hell with Satan joins,
His ready instrument of ill,
Enters into the fiend's designs,
(Who comes to steal, deceive, and kill;)
Envious against the truth he fights
Which would his direful deeds bewray,
And like, his murthering sire, delights
The souls of innocents to slay.

"He is a liar, and the father of it."—John 8, v. 44.

Th' original of evil see,
Of all deceit and wickedness!
Satan, the homicide is he,
Deceiver of our helpless race:
To plunge us in eternal woe
He preaches still his ancient lie,
"Sin on; and if to hell ye go,
"Ye shall not there forever die."

"Because I tell you the truth, ye believe me not."—John 8, v. 45.

Corrupt alike in heart and mind,
Till re-begotten from above,
To falsehood as to sin inclin'd,
We neither truth nor virtue love;
Wisdom himself averse we hear,
Abhorring good to evil cleave,
To truth divine a lie prefer,

And Satan before Christ believe.

"Which of you convinceth me of sin?"—John 8, v. 46.

"Convinc'd of sin I cannot be,"
Thou sayst it, Lord, and Thou alone:
Born, wholly born in sin, to Thee
My heart's iniquity I own:
But if Thou bless me with thy mind
And safe conceal my life above,
The world no sin in me shall find
Kept by the power of perfect love.

"If I say the truth, why do ye not believe me?"—John 8, v. 46.

The truth Thou sayst, the Truth Thou art:
Why do I not believe in Thee?
Do I not, Lord, desire to part
With all my sin and misery?
Some secret ill, some bar unknown,
Some idol must obstruct my will:
O speak, and take away the stone,
And pardon on my conscience seal.

"He that is of God heareth God's words: ye therefore hear them not, because ye are not of God."—John 8, v. 47.

The sons of God with faith sincere,
Attend and know their Father's word,
The sheep their heavenly Shepherd hear,
And glad confess, It is the Lord!
But ah, the unbelieving croud
His word, his truth, his doctrine slight,
And deaf to all the calls of God,
Rush blindfold to eternal night.

"Say we not well that thou art a Samaritan and hast a devil?"—John 8, v. 48.

They brand Him whom they will not know
(God in his miracles confest)
"Their church's and their nation's foe,
"By a proud lying spirit possest!"
Blasphemers of the Lord Most high
They no remorse or scruple feel,
But uttering the infernal lie
Applaud themselves for speaking well.

"Jesus answered, I have not a devil; but I honour my Father, and ye do dishonour me."—John 8, v. 49.

1. With meekness and majestic grace
Jesus their hellish charge denies:
His word to the blaspheming race
Becomes the Lord of earth and skies!
Silent so oft He answers here,
His Father's greatness to

maintain,
Stampt with Jehovah's character,
And God's Ambassador to man!

2. His minister the World should bear,
Their general calumnies despise:
But when to fix the charge they dare,
Tax'd with the thing his soul defies
The man whom Christ did truly send
Must then throw off the crime abhor'd,
And while he doth himself defend
He guards the honour of his Lord.

"I seek not mine own glory: there is one that seeketh and judgeth."—John 8, v. 50.

A messenger requir'd to speak,
The bounds of his defence will know,
Nor ever his own glory seek,
Or fiercely judge his bitterest foe,
Content the slander to repel
He speaks, of Jesus mind possest,
With wisdom mild, and temper'd zeal,
And leaves his life to do the rest.

"Verily, verily I say unto you, If any man keep my saying, he shall never see death."—John 8, v. 51.

Justly doth our humble Lord
His doctrine magnify:
"He that keeps the Saviour's word
Shall not forever die:"
Life he sets before us here
The true eternal life above;
Thus thro' faith we persevere
In pure obedient love.

"Then said the Jews, Abraham is dead and the prophets."—John 8, v. 52.

No: with God they greatly live
A life on earth unknown,
Now the glorious end receive
Of faith in Abraham's Son;
Prophets, patriarchs fulfil'd
Th' anticipated word of grace,
Saw their Lord in part reveal'd,
And now they see his face.

"Jesus answered, If I honour myself, my honour is nothing &c."—John 8, v. 54.

If the Son of God forbear,
The Lord and God most-high,
Which of us shall ever dare
Himself to glorify?
Prostrate at thy throne of grace,
Thy creatures, Lord, we humbly own,
Sinful worms of earth to raise
Belongs to Thee alone.

"Yet ye have not known him; but I know him: and if I should say, I know him not, I shall be a liar like unto you: but I know him, and keep his saying."—John 8, v. 55.

Every real worshipper
Who serves the God he loves,
Thus attests his grace sincere,
And by his actions proves:
Faith by works itself will show:
But liars are they all who say
God they for their Father know,
The God they disobey.

"Your father Abraham rejoiced to see my day."—John 8, v. 56.

1. In figures, types, and promises
Our father Abraham saw his day,
His Seed which should the nations bless,
Bear all our curse of sin away
An universal Saviour rise,
And bring us back our paradise.

2. O that the joy which then o'reflow'd
The patriarch's heart were fixt in mine,
While gazing on th' incarnate God,
O'repower'd with extasies divine,
With all his weight of blessings blest,
I sink on my Redeemer's breast!

3. Thy day is come, but never past:
Jesus, I long thy day to see:
Vouchsafe my favour'd soul a taste
Of that supreme felicity,
That rapture which thy presence gives,
And every saint thro' faith receives.

4. Before mine eyes of faith appear,
In all thy charms of heavenly grace;
Or rather let me view thee here
A Lamb expiring in my place,
Pour out my soul in tears of love,
And die, to share thy joy above.

"Thou art not yet fifty years old."—John 8, v. 57.

Broken the Man of griefs appears,
The Man of griefs He stands confest,
Not by the weight of numerous years,
But by our numerous sins opprest,
Faded in youth, grown old so soon,
He shews his sun must set at noon.

"Before Abraham was, I am."—John 8, v. 58.

1. "When Abraham was not born, I AM,
"I AM from all eternity!"
Jehovah sounds in Jesus Name,

God over all we worship Thee;
Sole self-existing God Thou art,
Ador'd in every faithful heart.

2. Not a new-made dependant God,
But Sovereign, Absolute, Most-high,
Thou cam'st to save us by thy blood,
Thou cam'st for sinful man to die,
That all mankind might live forgiven
Thro' Thee, the only God in heaven.

"Then took they up stones to cast at him."—John 8, v. 59.

1. Jesus, the Man Divine Thou art!
Before created things begun,
Thou dost thy Deity assert
Jehovah's Fellow and his Son,
Th' incomprehensible I AM,
With God eternally the same.

2. Equal to the great God supreme,
Thyself Thou dost with justice make:
They sacrilegiously blaspheme
Thro' stubborn, hellish pride mistake
Who thy Divinity disown,
And wish to drag thee from thy throne.

"But Jesus hid himself, and went out of the temple &c."—John 8, v. 59.

1. Thou dost thy Godhead testify,
Thine own eternal power maintain,
Nor for the truth refuse to die,
But sav'st thyself for sharper pain,
Waiting to suffer in our stead,
And in thy Father's time to bleed.

2. Thou dost out of the temple go,
Not to a single sect confin'd;
Thy blood in freer streams must flow
A sacrifice for all mankind,
That all mankind by faith may see
The one eternal God in Thee.

JOHN CHAPTER NINE

"And as Jesus passed by, he saw a man which was blind from his birth."—John 9, v. 1.

1. How sad our state by nature is,
How dark, disconsolate, forlorn!
We have not known the way of peace,
In unbelief and misery born,
Depriv'd of that celestial Light,
With stumbling steps we wander on,
And nothing find but grossest night,
And sin, and death, and hell

begun.

2. That heavenly Light appear'd below,
Pass'd thro' this mortal life for me,
When doubly blind, I could not know
My God, or my Redeemer see:
On me He cast a pitying look
Which chas'd the shades of death away,
And all my chains of darkness broke,
And made my soul a child of day.

"Who did sin, this man or his parents, that he was born blind?"—John 9, v. 2.

Let every child of Adam own
The cause of all his sufferings here:
The cause is sin, and sin alone,
And death and hell are in the rear!
My parents' sin ingender'd pain,
Intail'd eternal death on me;
Who still in misery bound remain,
Till Christ appears, to set me free.

"Neither hath this man sinned, nor his parents: but that the works of God should be made manifest in him."—John 9, v. 3.

God cannot take delight to grieve
The wretched helpless sons of men,
But may awhile in weakness leave,
That all his power may soon be seen:
His work is to restore the blind;
And when he doth the scales remove,
Our Lord by his own light we find
And praise the pardning God of love.

"I must work the works of him that sent me."—John 9, v. 4.

Long as my day of life remains,
My business is to work for God,
T' employ my utmost strength and pains
For Him who bought me with his blood:
No respite from the toils of love
I ask, till life's short season end:
Suffice for me, to rest above,
To rest with my eternal Friend.

"The night cometh, when no man can work."—John 9, v. 4.

I.

The Light for a few moments shines,
That every soul his course may run,
And joining in the Lord's designs,
Labour till all his work is done:
But when the Sun of righteousness
Withdraws from man his Spirit's

light,
And leaves us wholly void of grace;
His absence is eternal night.

"The night cometh, when no man can work."—John 9, v. 4.

II.

Most sensibly, O Lord, I know,
My night of death approaches fast;
My time for work, my course below
Is in another moment past:
O then cut short thy work of grace,
This moment finish it in me,
And let the next conclude my race,
And bring me to my goal and Thee.

"As long as I am in the world, I am the Light of the world."—John 9, v. 5.

1. The world's bright Day did then appear,
When present in his body here
Our Lord vouchsaf'd to shine:
His heavenly life and doctrine shew'd
The Majesty of real God,
Th' eternal Light Divine.

2. But present in thy Spirit still,
Jesus, Thou dost Thyself reveal,
In this thy church below;
And every soul, though wrapt in night,
May see thine all-inlivening light,
And Thee his Saviour know.

3. Light of the world, appear to all,
To raise the nations from their fall,
Thy beams of glory dart,
Our sin and ignorance disperse,
And chear our gladden'd universe,
And shine in every heart.

4. Come, O Thou Day-spring from on high,
Forth from thy chamber in the sky
To poor benighted man,
That visited and led by Thee
We all our way to heaven may see,
And life eternal gain.

"He anointed the eyes of the blind man with the clay."—John 9, v. 6.

1. Man made of earth by earth He heals!
The creature is whate'er He wills
Who gave it first to be:
Clay in th' Almighty's hands restores
Our bodily, or mental powers,
And gives the blind to see.

2. The weakest instrument Divine,
Water, or earth, or bread and

wine
Can work upon the soul:
Thou giv'st the means their saving use,
And then thy virtue they transfuse,
And make the sinner whole.

3. Thy touch medicinal we prove,
Our blindness it doth still remove,
The unction of thy grace
Opens our faith's inlighten'd eyes,
And lo! with rapturous surprize
We see thy lovely face!

"Go wash in the pool of Siloam .... He went his way, and washed, and came seeing."—John 9, v. 7.

1. When Jesus bad me first believe,
My spirit did its sight receive,
Though long by nature blind;
To Christ at his command I went,
And found him by his Father Sent,
The Saviour of mankind.

2. His Spirit drew me to the Pool
Which makes a world of sinners whole,
The purple Fountain shew'd,
The balm infallible applied,
And pointed out the Crucified,
And plung'd me in his blood.

3. T'was there I wash'd my sins away,
I triumph'd in the gospel-day,
To paradise restor'd:
And clearly still I all things see;
But nothing half so fair as Thee,
So heavenly as my Lord.

"The neighbours said, Is not this he that sat and begged?"—John 9, v. 8.

The sinner blind is always poor,
And begging waits at Mercy's door:
He waits when now restor'd to sight,
A suppliant still for farther light,
Humbly resolv'd thro' life to sit
A beggar at his Saviour's feet.

"Some said, This is he: others said, He is like him: but he said, I am he."—John 9, v. 9.

1. Inlighten'd by his God alone
A sinner sav'd is hardly known,
No more the slave of hell and sin,
But humble, meek, and pure within,
In love renew'd, and born again,
The Christian is another man!

2. Yet well he knows himself the same,
And owns "The beggar blind I am:"
With open'd eyes he always sees
His pardon'd sin, and past disease,
Different thro' grace in heart and will,
But of himself a sinner still.

"Therefore said they unto him, How were thine eyes opened."—John 9, v. 10.

We ask a soul no longer blind,
Who chas'd the darkness of thy mind,
Open'd thine inward eyes to see
That all on earth is vanity,
To see the true celestial road,
And fix thy faithful heart on God?

"He answered and said, A man that is called Jesus, made clay &c."—John 9, v. 11.

1. Thro' vanity I will not tell,
Nor yet thro' fear the truth conceal,
But own in love's simplicity
The things my God hath done for me:
He of his own accord past by
And saw the blind with pitying eye.

2. The Man, the God they Jesus call,
My Saviour, and the Friend of all
Anointed with his grace my soul,
And said Go, wash in Siloam's pool;
Obedient to his Spirit's word,
I went; I wash'd; and saw my Lord.

"Then said they unto him, Where is he?"—John 9, v. 12.

Jesus! where is He to be found,
Whose mercy doth to all abound?
O that the blind would all inquire,
Impatient, for the world's Desire,
Till Christ his healing light imparts,
And shews his presence to their hearts!

"He said, I know not."—John 9, v. 12.

A sinner once to sight restor'd
Need never miss his pardning Lord:
Nor shall he of his loss complain,
Who strives the Saviour to retain,
And only seeks the things above
With humble fear, and grateful love.

"It was the sabbath-day when Jesus made the clay, and opened his eyes."—John 9, v. 14.

Jesus the sabbath's Lord we praise,
Who carrying on his great designs,
His miracles of power and grace,
Redemption to creation joins,
He bids the soul with pardon blest
From its own works forever cease,
Receives into his people's rest,
And keeps with him in perfect peace.

"The Pharisees asked him how he had received his sight. He said unto them, He put clay upon mine eyes, and I washed, and do see."—John 9, v. 15.

1. Pharisees inquire in vain
How we receiv'd our sight,
Will not bow to God made man,
Believing in the Light:
God in human clay reveal'd,
Who heal'd us by his blood applied,
Rests with all his works conceal'd
From all the sons of pride.

2. Jesus hides himself from those,
Who with an evil heart
Seek the truth, the truth t' oppose,
And spitefully pervert:
When their Saviour they repel,
The Light their pride disdains t' adore
Leaves them inexcusable,
And blinder than before.

"Some said, This man is not of God, because he keepeth not the sabbath-day. Others said, How can a man that is a sinner, do such miracles?"—John 9, v. 16.

From the man, outrageous spite
To judgment false proceeds,
Equity pronounces right
Of persons from their deeds:
They appearances look thro'
Who darkness hate and light approve,
They believe the Saviour true
Who truth and goodness love.

"And there was a division among them."—John 9, v. 16.

Jesus, thy disciples here
The judging world divide,
Prais'd by some as men sincere,
By others vilified:
Various as their passions, Lord,
The thoughts of men will ever be;
Thus they verify thy word,
And treat thy church like Thee.

"They say unto the blind man, What sayest thou of him, that he hath opened thine eyes?"—John 9, v. 17.

Strange malignity of men!
Who credulous of ill
All the proofs of good disdain
Which court their stubborn will!
Light from heaven if we receive,
They only question, to disprove,
Good they never can believe
Of those they will not love.

"He said, He is a prophet."—John 9, v. 17.

Jesus' upright confessor
Discharging what he owes
Speaks without reserve or fear
The truth before its foes,
Vindicates the instrument
Who open'd a blind sinner's

eyes,
Witnesses the Prophet, sent
His Saviour, from the skies.

"The Jews did not believe that he had been blind, and received his sight, until they called the parents, and asked them &c."—John 9, v. 18, 19.

Who the work of God oppose
Thro' obstinate despight,
Every avenue they close
Against the hateful light;
Pharisees the truth to shun,
Unwearied pains and trouble take;
Doubting if the thing were done
They it undoubted make.

"He is of age, ask him."—John 9, v. 21.

Few will risk the consequence,
And dare the truth confess,
Standing bold in the defence
Of Jesus witnesses:
Prudently, themselves to clear,
The burthen they on others lay:
But they must to God appear,
And answer in that day!

"The Jews had agreed already, that if any man did confess that he was Christ, he should be put out of the synagogue."—John 9, v. 22.

1. And have they not agreed it now,
While us who dare acknowledge Him,
To the one God in Jesus bow,
God self-existent and supreme,
Out of the church they still reject,
And force into a separate sect!

2. But O, most gracious God and true,
Defeat their dire malicious aim,
Who hate the Lord they never knew,
Abhor the followers of the Lamb,
And would as schismaticks oppress,
And slay thy patient witnesses.

3. Sole, independant God most-high,
Exalted on thy throne above,
The flock who on thy blood rely
For peace and purity of love,
Kept in the British fold defend,
Kept in the fold till time shall end.

"Give God the praise: we know that this man is a sinner."—John 9, v. 24.

1. Hear what the wise and learned say!
"This man, pretending to do good,
"To shew the blind their heavenly way,
"And teach th' illiterate multitude,
"The sabbath he profanely breaks,
"And contrary to order speaks."

2. We hear, but cannot think with them,
Or to their bold assertions trust,
Or from appearances condemn,
Blindly, implicitly unjust,
But Jesus' ministers receive:
And thus the praise to God we give.

"That he is a sinner I know not: one thing I know, that I was blind, and now see."—John 9, v. 25.

1. We still among the poor may find
A soul to sudden sight restor'd,
A sinner now no longer blind
A generous witness for his Lord,
Who speaks, and simply perseveres,
And neither man nor devil fears.

2. Born blind I was, and bred in sin,
Bound, like the fiends, in chains of night:
But Thou hast shone my heart within,
Surrounded with stupendous light;
And clearly, Lord, my Way I see,
My End, my present Heaven in Thee.

"Then said they to him again, What did he to thee? how opened he thine eyes?"—John 9, v. 26.

1. Envious and proud, in every age
The world against our Lord conspire,
With restless, unrelenting rage
Into his gracious work inquire
With stubborn infidelity
They ask, they urge, how can it be?

2. The wonders wrought in this our day,
Which thy experienced people know,
Saviour, they study, to gainsay,
Our faith by cavilling t' o'rethrow,
The Spirit mock, the inward Light,
And rob Thee of thy gracious right.

3. Yet will we still the truth maintain,
Born and inlighten'd from above,
And tell the faithless world again
Thy miracles of power and love:
We know what Thou to us hast done,
But how—appears to Thee alone.

"Wherefore would ye hear it again? will ye also be his disciples?"—John 9, v. 27.

1. An answer plain and full we give,
When friends, or candid foes demand,
Willing our witness to receive,
The truth to know and understand:

The truth we then with joy impart,
And speak to thy disciples heart.

2. Weary of publishing thy grace
To listening souls, we cannot be:
But if they proud objections raise,
Resist the light, and will not see,
And judges of thy work appear,
They are not worthy, Lord, to hear.

"Then they reviled him, and said, Thou art his disciple."—John 9, v. 28.

And let the railing world exclaim:
I wish them all to follow Thee:
I glory in the sacred shame
Pour'd by their blindfold rage on me:
Thy poor revil'd disciple I
As such rejoice to live and die.

"We know that God spake unto Moses: but as for this fellow, we know not whence he is."—John 9, v. 29.

1. Ye know not, for ye will not know,
Jesus descended from the sky,
The Substance whom your shadows show,
The Prophet great, the Lord Most-high,
The Light, the Life, the Truth, the Way
Which leads to everlasting day.

2. Strangers to his converting grace,
Opposers of his Spirit's power
Ye scorn our Saviour to confess,
The Opener of our eyes t' adore,
Who Christ undauntedly proclaim
Our God eternally the same.

"The man answered, Why herein is a marvellous thing &c."—John 9, v. 30.

1. The poor, wayfaring man,
Inlighten'd from above,
Doth valiantly the truth maintain,
And more than conqueror prove;
The Man who nothing knows
But Jesus on his side
Withstands an host of learned foes,
And baffles all their pride.

2. Learning and power contend
Against the truth in vain,
Whoe'er the cause of Christ defend
The vict'ry must obtain:
For still the truth of God
Doth in its witness fight,
Confounds the unbelieving croud,
And puts the world to flight.

"Ye know not whence he is, and yet he hath opened mine eyes."—John 9, v. 30.

His understanding's eyes,
His mouth is open'd too,
The blind is brought divinely

wise
A way he never knew;
With reasons strong and clear
With wisdom not his own
He proves—the hand of God is here
And God the work hath done.

"We know that God heareth not sinners; but if any man &c."—John 9, v. 31.

Even we, the vulgar, know,
Who God disdains to fear,
And on in sin presumes to go,
His prayer He will not hear:
But if with contrite sighs
The wretch for mercy groan,
A sinner vile in his own eyes
In God's account is none.

"But if any man be a worshipper of God, and doth his will, him he heareth."—John 9, v. 31.

Who God in truth adore
And walk in all his ways
He makes the channels of his power,
The vessels of his grace,
Sends to declare his will,
And sinful souls convert:
And daily thro' his word they heal
The blindness of the heart.

"Since the world began was it not heard that any man opened the eyes of one that was born blind."—John 9, v. 32.

Conviction is from God:
Since first the world began
Was never man who knew or shew'd
The sinfulness of man:
The Spirit of truth alone
Of unbelief reproves,
He makes the human darkness known,
And by his light removes.

"If this man were not of God, he could do nothing."—John 9, v. 33.

Ye Scribes with learning fraught,
Ye doctors of the law,
By an illiterate beggar taught,
The just conclusion draw:
A man can nothing do
Of God uncall'd unsent,
But saving souls in him we view
Our Saviour's instrument.

"Thou wast altogether born in sins, and dost thou teach us? and they cast him out."—John 9, v. 34.

1. The marks of wicked pastors see!
Fierce war against the sheep they wage,
Treat them with scornful cruelty,
And minded of their duty, rage:
Pleaders for rules—and union

too,
The sheep out of the fold they drive,
And then as schismaticks pursue,
And count them then not fit to live.

2. Yet will we not their sentence fear;
Th' unjust themselves, not us, condemn:
Cast out we find our Saviour near,
Cut off, not from our Head, but them:
Without the pale we cannot be,
Whose life is hid with Christ above,
Who cleave, dear Lord, to thine and Thee
With stedfast faith and humble love.

"Jesus heard that they had cast him out; and when he had found him, he said unto him, Dost thou believe on the Son of God?"—John 9, v. 35.

1. The furious world rejecting those
Who seek in holiness t' excel,
Foes to themselves, eternal foes,
Themselves they from the church expel,
They separate from the saints indeed,
(The saints by formalists abhor'd)
And make the members like their Head
And drive them closer to their Lord.

2. Our loving Lord the outcasts seeks
Whom Satan's synagogue expels,
He finds, and words of comfort speaks,
And to our hearts himself reveals:
He gives us faith, and faith's increase,
And while on us his Spirit rests,
Our souls o'reflow with joyous peace,
And heaven is open'd in our breasts.

"He answered and said, Who is he, Lord, that I might believe on him?"—John 9, v. 36.

1. Happy the self-mistrusting man
Who for thyself of thee inquires,
Thou wilt not let him ask in vain,
But grant in his thine own desires:
For faith divine the sinner's heart
Is open'd by docility,
But Thou of both the Giver art,
And all our good proceeds from Thee.

2. The man whom God to this hath wrought
Instruction readily receives,
And found by Him who came unsought,
He first inquires, and then believes;

Inlighten'd by his Saviour's grace,
Convinc'd of his converting power,
His soul shall soon with joy embrace
And Christ in spirit and truth adore.

"Jesus said unto him, Thou hast both seen him, and it is he that talketh with thee."—John 9, v. 37.

What comfortable words are thine,
Physician of the helpless poor!
They speak our Comforter Divine,
They speak our heart-felt pardon sure:
Thy words are words of truth and grace,
Spirit, and light, and life they give;
We hear; we see the Speaker's face,
We see the face of God, and live.

"And he said, Lord, I believe: and he worshipped him."—John 9, v. 38.

The sudden faith Thou hast bestow'd,
Saviour, I must in words express,
Adore the true eternal God,
And thee my God, my Lord confess:
For this alone I Thee intreat,
This only good on earth desire,
To live, adoring at thy feet,
And meekly at thy feet expire.

"For judgment I am come into the world: that they &c."—John 9, v. 39.

1. Righteous, Lord, thy judgments are!
When men their misery own,
Thou thy mercy dost declare,
And make thy Godhead known:
Foolish, ignorant, and blind,
We first our unbelief confess,
Then the Light from heaven we find,
The Lord our Righteousness.

2. But the wise, and learn'd, and proud,
Refuse themselves t' abase,
Scorn t' admit their fall from God,
And total want of grace,
Justly are they left by Thee,
Who still against thy Spirit fight,
Left in their obscurity,
Or blinded by the Light.

"Some of the Pharisees said, Are we blind also?"—John 9, v. 40.

Of their ignorance they show
The most undoubted sign,
Dark as hell who will not know
Their need of light divine
Pharisees untaught by grace,
Yet learned in their own esteem:
None of all our blindfold race
Is half so blind as them.

> "If ye were blind, ye should have no sin: but now ye say We sin; therefore your sin remaineth."—John 9, v. 41.

1. Ignorance in which ye dwell
Excusable had been,
Were it quite invincible
It is not wilful sin:
But your knowledge ye assert,
And cast your helps and means aside;
Hence the veil is on your heart,
And all your faith is pride.

2. Would you own with humble grief
Your want of light and love,
Christ would help your unbelief,
And all your guilt remove:
But with arrogant disdain
Your blindness if ye still deny,
Infidels ye must remain,
Till in your sins ye die.

JOHN CHAPTER TEN

> "Verily verily I say unto you, He that entreth not by the door into the sheepfold, but climbeth up some other way, the same is a thief and a robber."—John 10, v. 1.

1. Ye reverend thieves and robbers hear,
Who steal into the church's fold,
Usurp the sacred character
Thro' love of ease, or lust of gold,
Or hire yourselves, the flock to feed,
And basely minister for bread!

2. Not by the Door ye enter in,
Who seek your family to raise,
Or introduc'd by Simon's sin
Hard labour—for the highest place:
Ambition climbs that other way,
And all the slaves who serve for pay.

> "He that entreth in by the door, is the shepherd of the sheep."—John 10, v. 2.

1. A pastor good in God's esteem
Who enters in by Christ the Door,
Inwardly call'd and mov'd by Him,
Obeys the Spirit's secret power,
And for his awful charge design'd
By Heaven, he casts the world behind.

2. He only at God's glory aims,
And lives to serve the Saviour's will:
The love of souls his heart inflames;
He tends the sheep with fervent zeal,
Himself to this one thing applies,
And gives his life in sacrifice.

> "To him the porter openeth."—John 10, v. 3.

1. To him the Doorkeeper above

The Father manifests his Son,
Opens the treasures of his love,
Makes his mysterious wisdom known,
The pastor into Christ receives,
And the true Door of utterance gives.

2. God only can his Son reveal,
And Jesus' ministers ordain,
Jehovah must their mission seal;
Or man lays on his hands in vain:
Thou, Father, Thou that Porter art;
Display my Saviour in my heart.

"And the sheep hear his voice."—John 10, v. 3.

His voice the sheep rejoice to hear,
Nor fear, in following that, to stray,
They know their Saviour's minister,
And man for Jesus sake obey,
His word as God's, not his, receive,
The gospel hear, the gospel live.

"And he calleth his own sheep by name, and leadeth them out."—John 10, v. 3.

1. Inspir'd with goodness from above
His sheep he doth for Jesus claim,
He visits all with tenderest love,
He knows, and calls them all by name,
Each precious soul he counts his own,
His friend, his brother, and his son.

2. His own, and not another's sheep,
Watchful by day and night he tends,
Intrusted by his Lord to keep
From ravening wolves, and roaring fiends,
He knows their wants, their burthens bears
And all their feeble sorrows shares.

3. Out of an evil world of wo,
Out of its pomps and pleasures vain,
Out of their fond pursuits below,
Out of the base desires of men,
Out of themselves to Christ he leads,
And Christ supplies his people's needs.

"When he putteth forth his own sheep, he goeth before them and the sheep follow him: for they know his voice."—John 10, v. 4.

1. In all the paths of righteousness,
Of silent peace, and joy unknown,
The first to practise what he says,
A faithful guide he leads them on,
A shining light before them goes,

In every point their duty shews.

2. The wisdom and the power of God
In hearing him, they hear, and feel,
Admire the grace on man bestow'd,
(A man who speaks and lives so well,)
And while his life confirms his word,
Pursue the follower of their Lord.

"A stranger will they not follow, but will flee from him: for they know not the voice of strangers."—John 10, v. 5.

A stranger to the truth of grace
They from their genuine shepherd know,
Abhor his doctrines and his ways,
After his life refuse to go,
And trembling at delusion nigh
As from a thief and robber fly.

"This parable spake Jesus unto them: but they understood not what things they were which he spake unto them."—John 10, v. 6.

1. Strangers both to themselves and Thee,
The robbers of thy church remain,
They will not understand and see
The difference so severely plain,
Themselves the thieves they will not own,
Or at thy feet for mercy groan.

2. Open, O Lord, their blinded eyes,
Blinded by the infernal god;
Or in thy people's cause arise,
Whom thou hast purchas'd with thy blood,
Redeem the sheep to hirelings sold,
And chase the thief out of thy fold.

"Verily, verily I say unto you, I am the Door of the sheep."—John 10, v. 7.

1. Thee, Jesus, Thee I fall before
Who only art the church's Door,
With importunity
I knock, and never will depart;
Open, dear Lord, thy loving heart,
And take me into Thee.

2. If Thou the grace of faith bestow,
Thyself I by thy Spirit know
My true eternal Rest,
Entrance into thy church I find,
Thro' Thee to all thy people join'd,
And shelter'd in thy breast.

"All that ever came before me, are thieves and robbers: but the sheep did not hear them."—John 10, v. 8.

1. Invaders of the ministry,

Who ran before, unsent by Thee,
The God they never knew,
Who profits and preferments gain;
They spoil the helpless souls of men,
They rob and murther too.

2. But them the flock will never hear,
Will never follow or revere
The covetous and proud
As pastors after thine own heart,
Who take the dire destroyer's part,
And slay the saints of God.

"I am the door: by me if any man enter in he shall be saved, and shall go in and out and shall find pasture."—John 10, v. 9.

1. Lord, I believe, and enter in,
Sav'd, in a moment sav'd from sin
Its guilt and tyranny;
Beyond the murdering shepherd's power,
Where neither men nor fiends devour,
I dwell secure in Thee.

2. Thro' Thee, and thine atoning blood
I come with free access to God,
His dear adopted son:
Thy blood shall all my wants supply,
And bear me up beyond the sky
To that eternal throne.

3. Pasture I find in every place,
I feed upon the word of grace
To all believers given;
And fill'd with love, shall soon confess
Thou art the Gate of holiness,
Thou art the Gate of heaven.

"The thief cometh not, but to steal and to kill, and to destroy."—John 10, v. 10.

1. Lo, the ruthless felon comes,
Hallow'd by unhallow'd hands,
Honour to himself assumes,
Bold the church's goods demands,
From the poor their right he takes,
Havock of the needy makes!

2. The old thief and murderer
Comes unseen to seize his prey,
In his trusty agent here
Comes, immortal souls to slay,
By their wicked pastor's zeal
Drags the wandring sheep to hell.

"I am come that they might have life, and that they might have it more abundantly."—John 10, v. 10.

1. That the doubly dead might live,
Lord, Thou wast on earth reveal'd,
That we might thy mind retrieve,
By thy promis'd Spirit seal'd,
Pardon'd, perfectly renew'd,
Sav'd with all the life of God.

2. Answer then thy blest design,
Bring to me the life of grace,
Bring me larger life divine,
Fill my soul with holiness,
Fit me for the life above,
All that life of heavenly love.

"I am the good Shepherd: the good Shepherd giveth his life for the sheep."—John 10, v. 11.

The Shepherd good indeed Thou art,
I feel thy goodness at my heart:
No goodness out of Christ I see:
Goodness himself has died for me,
For me, and all the stragling kind
Thou didst the costly ransom find,
Thy life was the stupendous price,
And bought my peace, my paradise.

"But he that is an hireling and not the shepherd, whose own the sheep are not, seeth the wolf coming, and leaveth the sheep, and fleeth."—John 10, v. 12.

1. The workman's worthy of his food;
But if with eagerness pursued
He loves his wages here,
Labouring for filthy lucre's sake,
He justly to himself must take
The hireling's character.

2. The man whom covetous desire
Impels to minister for hire,
We mercenary call:
But O, what title shall we give
A wretch who dares the hire receive,
And never works at all?

3. If want, or pestilence be near,
If danger and the wolf appear,
Or persecution rise,
Aghast the lowring storm he sees,
And proving that they are not his,
Deserts the sheep, and flies.

"The hireling fleeth, because he is an hireling, and careth not for the sheep."—John 10, v. 13.

The hire more than the sheep he loves,
And basely from his post removes,
While their own shepherd stays,
He hides himself, requir'd t' appear
Their advocate, and dumb thro' fear
The little flock betrays.

"I am the good Shepherd, and know my sheep, and am known of mine (as the Father knoweth me, and I know the Father) and I lay down my life for the sheep."—John 10, v. 14, 15.

1. The Shepherd good, Thou dost approve
With kind regard, and cordial

love
The sheep redeem'd below,
The sheep with firm fidelity
Cleave to their Shepherd good, and Thee
With pure affection know.

2. Jehovah, with Jehovah one,
Thou knowst him, Lord, as Thou art known,
And (O! how can it be?)
That union inexpressible
Thou dost with thy great Father feel
Thy members feel with Thee.

3. For this Thou dost thy life lay down,
That gather'd by thy death alone
The sheep no more may rove,
But all thy heavenly nature find,
To Thee inexplicably join'd,
And simplified by love.

"And other sheep I have which are not of this, fold: them also I must bring; and they shall hear my voice; and there shall be one flock, and one Shepherd."—John 10, v. 16.

1. Millions of sheep so dearly bought,
Immortal souls redeem'd of old,
Jesus, Thou hast already brought,
And added to the Christian fold:
Whole nations have thy call obey'd,
Gentiles and Jews thy gospel known,
And join'd to Thee their common Head
Thy church throughout the earth is One.

2. One God the children all confess,
One Head the members all adore,
One Spirit of faith and holiness,
Who fills them with his love and power;
One flock, one body, and one bride,
So closely join'd in mind and heart,
That neither earth nor hell divide,
That neither life nor death can part.

3. Yet millions still uncall'd remain
Wide wandring in the wilderness:
Thee, Saviour, let thy love constrain
To bring in every sheep that strays:
O let them hear and flock to Thee
From north, and south, and east, and west,
Together all thy glory see,
And in their Shepherd's bosom rest.

4. The secret whisper of thy love,
The small still voice shall bring them home,
Though far as hell from heaven they rove
From God, they to thy church shall come,
For thy own gracious promise sake

Thou wilt incline their hearts t' obey,
One undivided people make,
And give us all one perfect way.

5. Then jarring sentiments shall cease,
And discord's voice be heard no more,
While in the truth of holiness
Thy church with one consent adore,
Flesh of thy flesh, bone of thy bone,
The members each to each shall join,
Cemented by thy blood alone,
And one with unity Divine.

"Therefore doth my Father love me, because I lay down my life, that I may take it again. No man taketh it from me &c."—John 10, v. 17, 18.

1. Submissive to thy Father's will,
Jesus, Thou didst thy life lay down,
Didst of thine own accord fulfil
The strange design of love unknown
Obedient to his love's decree,
Thou didst the general ransom pay:
Thy deed was absolute, and free,
And yet Thou couldst not disobey.

2. Love only did my Lord constrain
Thy life so freely to resign,
A sacrifice for guilty man;
A grateful sacrifice divine:
Love would, not let my Saviour rest,
Sole cause of the stupendous deed,
It drew thee from thy Father's breast,
It made the Man of sorrows bleed.

3. Deserving in thy proper right
Thou hence obtain'st thy Father's love,
And rais'd by thy own Spirit's might,
Appear'st our Advocate above;
Great Patron of the ransom'd race,
Well-pleas'd He always is with Thee:
And Thou hast merited his grace,
And Thou hast bought his love for me.

"Many of them said, He hath a devil, and is mad; why hear ye him?"—John 10, v. 20.

The Wisdom of our God made man
Jesus was vilified, blasphem'd,
Heard with aversion, and disdain,
A madman, and demoniac deem'd!
Thou zealous follower of thy Lord,
The crown of all thy labours see,
Expect from man the same reward,

And bow thy head on Calvary.

"How long dost thou keep us in suspense? If thou be the Christ, tell us plainly."—John 10, v. 24.

1. Nature impatient of delay
Would force the Lord to shew his power:
"Now, now, we cry, thyself display,
"Now, now—for we can wait no more,
"Thy mysteries all at once explain,
"For God is bound to wait on man!"

2. But a believing child of grace
Tarrys the leizure of his Lord,
Waits upon Him, who hides his face,
Continues patient in the word,
Manner and time to Jesus leaves,
And what his Saviour wills, receives.

"The works that I do in my Father's name, they bear witness of me."—John 10, v. 25.

Who in the steps of Jesus treads,
The surest testimony gives,
He speaks less by his words than deeds,
The truth's authentic witness lives;
And lo! throughout his life is show'd
The wisdom and the power of God!

"Ye believe not; because ye are not of my sheep."—John 10, v. 26.

1. The sheep with meek docility
Expect, the Shepherd's voice to hear,
Jesus, by faith they cleave to Thee;
Obedience is their character,
Obedience doth their faith approve,
And tender fear, and humble love.

2. Saviour, on me the faith bestow
Which joins a sinner to the sheep:
And when thy pardning voice I know,
To Thee and thine united keep,
Till in that awful day I stand
Among the sheep at thy right-hand.

"My sheep hear my voice, and I know them, and they follow me."—John 10, v. 27.

1. The sheep with true simplicity
Attend, and taste, and keep thy word,
They lead the life approv'd by Thee,
Follow their active, suffering Lord,
Copy thy life of love and pain,

And labour all thy mind to gain.

2. They prove thine acceptable will,
Thine image more and more put on,
Their vileness more and more they feel,
Their race assign'd with patience run,
Thy followers to the end endure,
And make their own election sure.

"I give unto them eternal life, and they shall never perish, neither shall any pluck them out of my hand."—John 10, v. 28.

1. The faith Thou dost ev'n now bestow,
Ev'n now the life eternal give,
And Thee their Lord who truly know
The hidden life of glory live;
Their souls are in those hands of thine,
Kept by the power of love divine.

2. Obsequious to thy dear commands
Alone with Thee who safely dwell,
Sin shall not pluck out of thy hands,
Nor all the force of earth or hell;
And if the Truth can never lie,
Believing souls can never die.

"My Father who gave them me, is greater than all: and none is able to pluck them out of my Father's hand. I, and my Father are one."—John 10, v. 29, 30.

1. God over all in power supream,
Thy Father doth thy sheep defend,
They never can be forc'd from Him
Who loves thy members to the end,
Who keeps the souls on Thee bestow'd
Th' irrevocable gift of God.

2. Saviour, I in thy word confide,
Nothing throughout eternity
The Head and body shall divide,
Or tear my faithful soul from Thee,
Whom, by thy Spirit taught, I own
Forever with thy Father One.

3. One God in essence and in power
Mine utmost Saviour I proclaim,
The Father and the Son adore
From all eternity the same,
That I may one in spirit be
With God to all eternity.

"Jesus answered them, Many good works have I shewed you &c."—John 10, v. 32.

Jesus answer'd them to shew

We should at times reply,
To the persecuting foe
Our actions justify,
Bold before the world confess
The crime of publishing the word,
Advocates for truth, express
The temper of our Lord.

"For a good work we stone thee not, but for blasphemy."—John 10, v. 33.

Will the foes of Jesus own
They hate us for his sake?
Us they as blasphemers stone,
And righteous vengeance take;
"Wretches who the Spirit feel,
"Pretend to know their sins forgiven,
"Say, that now in God they dwell
"And live the life of heaven!"

"Say ye of him, whom the Father hath sanctified, Thou blasphemest; because I said, I am the Son of God?"—John 10, v. 36.

1. Christ, the Character express
Of God's substantial power,
Image of his holiness
Jehovah we adore!
Him his Father sanctified
Before the worlds or time begun,
Plac'd forever at his side
His co-eternal Son.

2. Fulness of his sanctity,
The only God supreme,
Being's Source, I AM is He,
Who did our world redeem;
When in Christ the Father came
To consecrate his human shrine,
Dwelt in that corporeal frame
The Plenitude Divine.

3. "One I and my Father are!"
One God in persons three
By the Spirit we declare
The tri-une Deity:
Blasphemy denies in vain
The glories of Jehovah's Son:
One with God, Thou must remain
Thro' endless ages One.

"If I do not the works of my Father, believe me not."—John 10, v. 37.

Christ himself, unless he wrought
His Father's works, alone,
Willing was not to be thought
The great Jehovah's Son:
And would we be own'd untried?
Believ'd, before the proofs are shew'd?
No; let works the doubt decide,
And speak us born of God.

"But if I do; though ye believe not me, believe the works."—John 10, v. 38.

Re-begotten from above,
In Christ, and creatures new,
Sinners, by our works we prove
That our report is true,
Witness what we surely know,
That man may still the Spirit receive:
Let our words for nothing go;

Ye must our lives believe.

"That ye may know and believe, that the Father is in me, and I in him."—John 10, v. 38.

Jesus' real witnesses
We live for this alone
That ye may with us confess
The Father in the Son,
That ye may believe aright,
And fill'd with God, rejoice to prove
All the length, and breadth, and height,
And depth of Jesus love.

"Therefore they sought again to take him; but he escaped out of their hands, And went away again beyond Jordan."—John 10, v. 39, 40.

When the wicked seek to slay
Who Jesus testify,
Following Him, we 'scape away,
And from their violence fly,
Faithfully the truth commend,
And people to his guardian care,
Calmly on our Lord attend
In solitude and prayer.

"John did no miracle: But all things that John spake of this man were true."—John 10, v. 41, 42.

1. Voice of all the prophets old,
Their End the Baptist shew'd,
Pointing out whom they foretold
The heavenly Lamb of God:
Jesus his forerunner's word
By words, by wonders, verified,
Liv'd our gracious faithful Lord,
Confirm'd the truth, and died.

2. Searching, Lord, if Thou art He
Who should our souls restore,
Clearly we thy Godhead see,
And thine eternal power;
Ancient prophecies compare
With those stupendous works of thine,
Thus convinc'd to all declare
Thou art that Man Divine!

"And many believed on him there."—John 10, v. 42.

Still in spite of earth and hell,
Sinners their Lord embrace,
In their inmost souls they feel
The miracle of grace:
End of every outward sign,
Jesus, Thou dost the faith impart;
Then I know that Thou art mine,
Jehovah in my heart!

JOHN CHAPTER ELEVEN

"Lord, behold, he whom thou lovest is sick."—John 11, v. 3.

1. The prayer which God delights to hear,
With stedfast faith and humble fear
The sinner's wants before him lays,
And meekly for an answer stays,

Nothing prescribes to the Most-
high
Whose pity hears the softest sigh,
But waits the blessing from above,
And minds the Saviour of his love.

2. Saviour, with kind compassion see
Thy ransom'd creature's misery,
The sinner whom Thou lov'st am I,
But sick, and at the point to die;
Tempted, and weak, in sin and pain,
Here at thy feet I still remain:
Thou know'st my case, Thou hearst me groan,
In death—Thine only will be done!

"This sickness is not unto death, but for the glory of God, that the Son of God might be glorified thereby."—John 11, v. 4.

I.

His own great glory He intends,
When God the pain, or trouble sends:
Out of the earth it doth not rise,
But comes in mercy from the skies;
It comes, our groveling souls to raise,
And quicken'd with the life of grace,
We seek the solid joys above,
And bless our Saviour's chastning love.

"This sickness is not unto death, but for the glory of God, that the Son of God might be glorified thereby."—John 11, v. 4.

II.

Jesus, my soul's infirmity
Is known, is suffer'd still by Thee,
Yet wilt Thou not thy help deny,
Or leave me in my sins to die:
Surely Thou shalt my sickness heal,
Thy love in season due reveal,
That sav'd I may proclaim thy grace,
And live to thine eternal praise.

"Now Jesus loved Martha, and her sister, and Lazarus."—John 11, v. 5.

I.

And me—may every soul subjoin!
The Friend of Lazarus is mine:
My Friend from all eternity,
He lov'd, he died himself for me!

"Now Jesus loved Martha, and her sister, and Lazarus."—John 11, v. 5.

II.

The suffering I this moment prove
Is a fresh token of his love:
I hear the rod, by Jesus sent,
Which cries "Be zealous, and repent!"
Because Thou lov'st, Thou dost chastise:
And quicken'd by the scourge I rise,
And yield, when all th' affliction's past,
That fruit which shall forever last.

"When he had heard therefore that he was sick, he abode two days still in the same place where he was."—John 11, v. 6.

1. He waits; to manifest his grace,
To help his dying friend, delays,
The sickness lingers to remove,
But not thro' want of power or love.
Thus our Physician from the sky
Lets a beloved patient die,
And then exerts his power to save,
And lifts the sinner from the grave.

2. Jesus, if such thy love's design
Toward this weak, sinsick soul of mine,
If still thou dost thine aid forbear
To sink me down in just despair;
I'l suffer all the mortal pain,
And dead to God, in death remain,
Till my almighty Saviour come,
And call my soul out of its tomb.

"Let us also go into Judea again."—John 11, v. 7.

He shuns his murtherers no more,
But goes at God's appointed hour
To lay the ransom down,
He goes to suffer in our stead,
And, life restoring to the dead,
Surrenders up his own.

"Master, the Jews sought of late to stone thee; and goest thou thither again?"—John 11, v. 8.

For this into their hands He goes,
Gives himself up, to save his foes,
By dying in their place:
The voluntary Victim dies,
And thro' one bloody sacrifice
Atones for all our race.

"Are there not twelve hours in the day? If any man walk in the day, he stumbleth not &c."—John 11, v. 9, 10.

1. The faithful, in their Saviour's sight,
Walk on as children of the light,
In calm security;

Nor earth nor hell their steps o'rethrow,
Who in the ways of duty go,
And Christ their Pattern see.

2. Light of the world they Him confess;
The glorious Sun of righteousness
On all their paths He shines;
And labouring with intrepid zeal
They their appointed work fulfil,
And answer his designs.

3. On Christ while humbly they rely,
His only will and glory eye,
They cannot fall, or sin:
Himself into their hearts he gives,
Irradiates all their powers, and leaves
No stumbling-block within.

4. But strangers to his saving grace,
Sinners pursue their dreary ways,
Without his Spirit's light
Blindfold, in sin they stumble on,
And sink at last despairing down
Into eternal night.

"Our friend Lazarus sleepeth."—John 11, v. 11.

1. Period of my griefs and woes,
Welcome death's desir'd repose!
Death my day of labour ends;
Death is sleep to Jesus' friends:

2. Weary, weary, and opprest,
Faint and languishing for rest,
Fain I would forget to weep,
Close my eyes in lasting sleep;

3. Free from pain recline my head,
Mouldring in its earthen bed,
Till the sinner's constant Friend,
Judge of quick and dead descend.

4. Then my dust his voice shall hear,
Springing from the sepulchre,
Join its mate, and soar away,
Mingle in the blaze of day!

"And I am glad for your sakes that I was not there, to the intent ye may believe."—John 11, v. 15.

1. Thy mercy grants the sinner's prayer;
Thy greater love doth oft defer
The promis'd good to give,
That help'd in the most desperate case
We thy transcendant power may praise,
And perfectly believe.

2. Thy presence bids our troubles cease;
Thy absence makes our faith increase,
While patient and resign'd
We humbly for thy coming stay,
Till fitted thro' our Lord's delay
Thine utmost love we find.

"Then said Thomas unto his fellow-disciples, Let us also go, that we may die with him."—John 11, v. 16.

1. Not thro' a sad desponding fear,
When danger, pain, and death are near,
We would with Christ abide;
But with divine conformity
Partake his passion on the tree,
And languish by his side.

2. Made willing in the strength of grace,
Saviour thy portion we embrace:
Thou know'st thy people's heart,
Who come to suffer for thy name,
Resolv'd that neither grief nor shame,
Nor pain, nor death shall part.

"When Jesus came, he found that he had lien in the grave four days already."—John 11, v. 17.

Parted from God, the soul is dead,
Buried alive the graceless soul,
His conscience as with worms o'respread,
No sepulchre is half so foul!
The poor, habitual sinner lies
Long dead in trespasses and sins,
And cannot wake, and cannot rise
Till call'd by life's immortal Prince.

"Many came to Martha and Mary, to comfort them concerning their brother."—John 11, v. 19.

We kindly share a mourner's woe
Stript of the friend a while bestow'd;
No pity for a soul we show
Who long by sin has lost its God:
No comfort can that soul receive
But with the hope of Jesus' grace,
Who helps poor sinners to believe,
And still delights the dead to raise.

"Then Martha, as soon as she heard that Jesus was coming, went and met him; but Mary sat still in the house."—John 11, v. 20.

Forth by our good desires we go
Our dear, approaching, Lord, to meet
Or wait, his secret will to know,
And in the house expecting sit;
With forward zeal, like Martha, run,
To Jesus of our loss complain;
Or calmly sad, like Mary, moan,
Till He returns, and ends our pain.

"But I know, that even now, whatsoever thou wilt ask of God, God will give it thee."—John 11, v. 22.

Hadst Thou, O Lord, been always here,
My soul thro' sin had never died:
But now in my behalf appear,
My Spokesman at thy Father's side:
He cannot turn away from Thee,
Thou must prevail, I surely know;
Whate'er thou dost request for me
He will for thy dear sake bestow.

"Jesus saith unto her, Thy brother shall rise again."—John 11, v. 23.

The good we eagerly require
Thou still with-holdest from thine own,
To cool th' impatience of desire,
And make us ask in faith alone;
To stop our unbelieving haste,
Dispose and teach us to receive;
And then Thou shewst thy power at last,
And then Thou dost thy Spirit give.

"I am the Resurrection and the Life: he that believeth on me, though he were dead, yet shall he live: And whosoever liveth, and believeth on me, shall never die. Believest thou this?"—John 11, v. 25, 26.

1. With faith thy saying we receive,
Thee, Lord, the Resurrection own,
Th' essential Life of all that live
Surrounding, or beneath, thy throne:
Life of the world to come Thou art,
Life of the saints in flesh confin'd,
And wouldst thy quickning Spirit impart
To raise the souls of all mankind.

2. The faith Thou dost on us bestow
Restores our souls to life again,
Th' eternal Life in Thee we know,
The gracious glorious life obtain,
The antepast, in perfect peace
In thy unsinning mind we prove,
And feel that real holiness
That life infus'd of heavenly love.

3. Our souls rais'd up to die no more,
Jesus, Thou dost persist to save;
And Thou, whom all thy saints adore,
Shalt call our bodies from the

grave;
We all who live by faith in Thee,
Who on thine only love rely,
Possest of immortality
The second death shall never die.

"Yea, Lord: I believe that thou art the Christ, the Son of God, which should come into the world."—John 11, v. 27.

1. Yes, Lord: I stedfastly believe
Thou the desir'd Messias art,
Thee, Prophet, Priest, and King receive
With joy into my loving heart;
Son of the living God most-high,
His fulness all resides in Thee,
Yet didst Thou live on earth, and die
To live eternally in me.

2. The Saviour-God so long foretold,
The Ransomer of Jacob's race,
Of all mankind to Satan sold,
My God, my Saviour I confess:
Come in the flesh Thou art I know;
Thou wilt fulfil thine own design,
Destroy the devil's works below,
And fill our souls with life divine.

"The Master is come, and calleth for thee."—John 11, v. 28.

Happy is the family
Strong in faith, and much in prayer!
Jesus, they belong to Thee,
Thou art Lord and Master there,
Thou art worshipp'd, and rever'd,
Thou art glorified alone;
Nothing but thy word is heard,
Nothing but thy will is done.

"As soon as she heard that, she arose quickly, and came unto him."—John 11, v. 29.

Man in ministring relief,
Miserable comforter,
Aggravates the mourner's grief,
Burthens whom he means to chear:
Mary turns from such away,
Her immortal Friend to meet,
Goes to Christ without delay,
Seeks her comfort at his feet.

"When Mary saw him, she fell down at his feet, saying unto him, Lord, if thou hadst been here, my brother had not died." —John 11, v. 32.

Jesus' feet her refuge are:
There accustom'd to complain,
Mary breathes her mournful prayer,
Washes them with tears again,
Cries, in humble faith sincere,
"Death could not with Life abide:
"Life Itself, hadst Thou been here,
"Lord, my brother had not died."

"When Jesus therefore saw them weeping, he groaned in the spirit."—John 11, v. 33.

1. Jesus in the spirit groans
Human wretchedness to see,
Sin's severe effects bemoans,
Sorrow and mortality;
Takes upon himself our pains,
Groans, and weeps, and prays, and cries,
All our weaknesses sustains,
All our sufferings sanctifies.

2. When his troubled members feel
All the bitterness of sin,
Still with groans unspeakable
Groans the Comforter within!
By a load of woes opprest,
Woes too great for life to bear,
Still the sinner smites his breast,
Smites his breast—and God is there!

"Jesus troubled himself (Greek)."—John 11, v. 33.

Passion's turbulent excess,
Pure from sin, he could not feel;
Rational was the distress,
Wholly subject to his will:
He who did our nature take,
Would its sinless frailties know,
Freely suffer'd for our sake,
Made himself the Man of woe.

"He said, Where have ye laid him? they say, unto him, Lord, come, and see."—John 11, v. 34.

Where have ye the sinner laid?
In his Maker's hands no more,
Till the Quickner of the dead
Doth to second life restore:
In corruption's pit he lies:
Jesus, come, with pity see,
Speak, and bid the soul arise,
Call him forth to live for Thee.

"Jesus wept."—John 11, v. 35.

I.

Jesus weeps, our tears to see,
Feels the soft infirmity,
Feels, whene'er a friend we mourn
From our bleeding bosom torn!
Let him still in spirit groan,
Make our every grief his own,
Till we all triumphant rise,
Fly to meet him in the skies.

"Jesus wept."—John 11, v. 35.

II.

1. Jesus weeps for sinners blind,
Mourns the death of all mankind;
Blesses us with sacred showers,
Sheds his tears to hallow ours;
Weeps, to make our case his own,
For our guilty joys t' atone,
Wipes at last the mourner's eyes,
Sorrow's source forever dries!

2. Till that happy day I see,
Lord, I would lament with Thee,
Griev'd along the valley go,
Griev'd, but not for things below;
This my only burthen prove,
I have lost the life of love,
Never can myself forgive,
Till with Thee in heaven I live.

"Then said the Jews, Behold how he loved him."—John 11, v. 36.

When with eyes of faith we see
Jesus fasten'd to the tree,
Very man, and very God
Pouring, not his tears, but blood,
Grateful on the sight we gaze,
Cry in passionate amaze,
See, his tender mercy prov'd!
See, how well the world He lov'd!

"Could not this man, which opened the eyes of the blind, have caused that even this man should not have died?"—John 11, v. 37.

Presumptuous men, thro' malice blind,
Would fain the times and seasons know,
Fault with eternal Wisdom find,
And teach him when his power to show,
Insult him for his kind delay,
And when he works, the Saviour stay.

"Jesus therefore again groaning in himself, cometh to the grave."—John 11, v. 38.

1. Their sin extorts th' indignant groan,
Their proud obduracy of heart,
Which scorns his benefits to own,
Which will his saving grace pervert,
Though God himself, in person come
To call their souls from nature's tomb.

2. He curbs the strugling grief within,
That thus we may our zeal suppress,
Urg'd to resent our neighbour's sin,
Shock'd by a world of wickedness,
And silently the anguish bear,
Or vent our burthen'd souls in prayer.

"It was a cave, and a stone lay upon it."—John 11, v. 38.

1. Who lies in unbelief confin'd,
His heart is as a loathsom grave,
Loathsom, and dark, corrupt, and blind,
While grace in vain attends to save,
Harden'd by habitudes of sin,
It will not let salvation in.

2. Habitual sin shuts up the tomb,

And stops the avenues of grace,
Till shining in the dungeon's gloom,
Glory supreme himself displays,
And Holiness corruption seeks,
And Light Divine to darkness speaks.

3. Jesus, Thou hast the hindrance shewn,
The sin that doth my soul beset,
I feel the hard and pondrous stone,
I pant beneath th' enormous weight,
Till pity brings Redemption near,
And Love unbars the sepulchre.

"Jesus said, Take ye away the stone."—John 11, v. 39.

1. Thou bidst us take away the stone,
Thou bidst us put our sins away:
But, Lord, the power is thine alone
Thro' which we can thy word obey,
From every act of sinning cease,
And gain the gift of righteousness.

2. The power which thy command conveys,
The previous, penitential power,
Workers together with thy grace
We all may use, and wait for more,
May outward obstacles remove,
And gasp for the pure life of love.

"Lord, by this time he stinketh: for he hath been dead four days."—John 11, v. 39.

I.

Reason and faith together strive,
Just as the mighty work is wrought:
How can a putrid carcass live,
Or how, out of corruption brought,
My soul in holiness arise,
And live the life of paradise!

"Lord, by this time he stinketh: for he hath been dead four days."—John 11, v. 39.

II.

The slave of fashionable sin,
Who spends his life in pleasures vain,
Specious without, but foul within,
Offensive both to God and man,
The pestilent example gives,
Is dead, and stinks, while yet he lives.

"Jesus saith unto her, Said I not unto thee, If thou wouldest believe, thou shouldest see the glory of God?"—John 11, v. 40.

1. Lord, thy saying I receive,
As spoken now to me,
If the promise I believe
I shall thy glory see,
Shall from mine offences freed

Both see and feel thy saving power,
Rise triumphant from the dead,
And die, and sin no more.

2. Gladly I believe the word,
And wait the truth to prove,
To thine image here restor'd,
The life of spotless love:
Walking in my Saviour's sight
I here shall find thine utmost grace,
Then with all the sons of light
Behold thy open face.

"Jesus lift up his eyes, and said, Father, I thank thee, that thou hast heard me &c."—John 11, v. 41, 42.

1. Ready to conclude thy race
With this great miracle,
Lord, Thou dost thy Father praise,
Thou dost Thyself reveal:
Heard in this, in every hour,
Thou all thy wondrous works hast done,
By thine own essential power,
With God forever One.

2. Sovereign Lord of life and death
Thy right Divine receive,
All who by thy mercy breathe
Should to thy glory live;
God supream in majesty
Thee, Jesus, I with joy confess
Sent from God to quicken me,
And all our ransom'd race.

"He cried with a loud voice."—John 11, v. 43.

1. When th' Almighty Jesus cries,
Hears the soul in paradise,
Hasts the summons to obey,
Re-assumes his mortal clay,
To our dying life restor'd,
Lives again to serve his Lord.

2. All that voice of God shall hear,
All forsake the sepulchre,
Put again their bodies on,
Stand arraign'd before the throne;
Then the awful Judge we see:
Now, my God, He pleads for me!

"Lazarus, come forth."—John 11, v. 43.

1. Jesus, quickning Spirit, come,
Call my soul out of its tomb,
Dead in sins and trespasses,
Thou art able to release,
Canst the life of grace restore,
Raise me up to sin no more.

2. That almighty word of thine
Fills the dead with life divine:
Speak again, and bid me go,
Perfect liberty bestow,
O repeat my sins forgiven,
Loose, and lift me up to heaven.

"He that was dead came forth."—John 11, v. 44.

Jesus, we testify thy power
From all degrees of death to

save:
Thee, Lord of life, our souls adore,
Rais'd from the bed; the bier; the grave!

"He that was dead came forth, bound hand and foot with grave-clothes &c."—John 11, v. 44.

1. Senseless no more in sin I dwell,
But leave my guilty nature's tomb,
Thy Spirit's quickning virtue feel,
And forth at thy command I come;
Yet bound I in thy sight appear,
Of death the fatal tokens have,
And recent from the sepulchre,
Expect thy farther power to save.

2. I wait, till Thou my Lord repeat
And seal the word of pardning love,
Loose by thy word my hands and feet,
The bandage from my sight remove:
My God I then shall clearly see,
Perform the works of righteousness,
And walk in glorious liberty,
And run with joy the heavenly race.

3. If ministers thy grace ordain
And use their instrumental power,
Yet Thee, great Ransomer of men,
Thee only shall my soul adore
Thy truth that makes me free indeed,
Thy word it is that sanctifies,
And faithful in thy steps I tread
To find my Life beyond the skies.

"Then many of the Jews which came to Mary, and had seen the things which Jesus did, believed on him."—John 11, v. 45.

How good to visit Jesus' friends,
How happily the visit ends!
A mourner sad they come to chear,
And find the heavenly Comforter,
His gracious miracles they see
Proofs of th' incarnate Deity,
The precious gift of faith receive,
And rais'd themselves to God they live.

"Then gathered the chief priests and the Pharisees a council, and said, What do we? for this man doth many miracles."—John 11, v. 47.

What should ye do, who see
The wonders of his grace?
Believe in his Divinity
And Christ your Lord embrace,
The signs and tokens know,
While God his arm reveals,

And proves his work reviv'd below
By twice ten thousand seals.

"If we let him thus alone, all men will believe on him; and the Romans shall come and take away both our place and nation."—John 11, v. 48.

1. Self-righteous Pharisees
The sinners' Friend oppose,
And priests in every age increase
The number of his foes;
While yet they might receive
Th' eternal Son of God,
They neither will themselves believe,
Nor suffer us that wou'd.

2. Ye venerable men,
Who 'gainst your Saviour fight,
Imaginary ills ye feign,
And real dangers slight:
Least Rome your church o'rethrow,
Affectedly ye fear,
And thoughtless of your hellish foe,
Ye dread his successor.

3. Strangers to Jesus blood
Ye no conviction have,
Rejecting Him by God bestow'd
Your sinful souls to save:
But tremble at the day
Which shall his wrath reveal,
When Satan takes your souls away,
And shuts them up in hell.

"It is expedient for us, that one man should die for the people, and that the whole nation perish not."—John 11, v. 50.

1. As patriots wise and good
Fir'd for the nation's weal,
Th' ambitious, covetous, and proud
Their base designs conceal:
Their credit, wealth, and power
T' insure is all their aim,
And when the wolves thy flock devour,
They use religion's name.

2. Religion is their care,
Yet still themselves they seek,
The temple of the Lord they are,
Yet thus their actions speak
"Let truth and justice die
"With every righteous one,
"So we may live, install'd on high,
"And rule the church alone."

"This spake he not of himself: but being high priest that year, he prophesied that Jesus should die for that nation &c."—John 11, v. 51, 52.

1. Wisdom and power to God belong!
Thou dost o'rerule the pontiff's tongue
Beyond himself, to prophesy:
The year of thy redeem'd is come
Thy outcasts must be gather'd home,
And one for all the people die:

Such thy unchangeable decree;
Thy Son the Sacrifice shall be,
And bleed in a whole nation's place:
He dies; but not for Jews alone,
His blood shall ransom and atone
For every child of Adam's race.

2. He hath for all been offer'd up,
The world's Desire, the nation's Hope
Partition's wall hath broken down:
His death's effects we all partake,
Gentiles and Jews his body make,
Gather'd, and sanctified in one:
Thou dost to every longing heart
The Spirit of thy Son impart,
Thro' which we Abba Father cry,
While in the power of simple love
The fellowship of saints we prove,
And join thy church beyond the sky.

"Jesus therefore walked no more openly among the Jews, but went thence into a country near to the wilderness, and there continued with his disciples."—John 11, v. 54.

I.

By the ordinance divine,
And not thro' servile fear,
Persecution we decline,
Till call'd of God t' appear:
Issuing then from our retreat,
We openly maintain thy cause,
Dauntless, Lord, thy murtherers meet,
And suffer on thy cross.

"... But went thence into a country &c."—John 11, v. 54.

II.

Happy place that could afford
A safe retreat to Thee,
Screen my persecuted Lord
From hellish cruelty!
Hunted still by zealots blind,
Abhor'd by fiends and men Thou art:
Shelter here vouchsafe to find,
Within my happy heart.

JOHN CHAPTER TWELVE

"Then Jesus came to Bethany, where Lazarus was, which had been dead."—John 12, v. 1 &c.

1. Life to a soul if Jesus give,
He will not then neglect and leave
His Lazarus restor'd,
But visits and confirms the grace,
The tender life of righteousness,
And feeds him with the word.

2. The sinner sav'd is Jesus guest,
(Whose presence makes th' angelic feast,
Whose glory fills the skies:)
He banquets on redeeming love,
Nor envies those he left above,

The saints in paradise.

"Then they made him a supper, and Martha served &c."—John 12, v. 2, 3.

1. The church which keeps its Lord's commands,
The house of true obedience stands,
And Jesus entertains:
Tis there He kindly condescends
To sup with his believing friends,
And in their hearts remains.

2. Martha renews her pious care,
Attends him in his members there
And furnishes the treat,
Sinners to gracious life restor'd
Enjoy the presence of their Lord,
And at his table sit.

3. Mary, devoted Mary, lies
Low at his feet with flowing eyes,
And loose, dishevel'd hair,
On Him whom more than life she loves
Pours out the faith which God approves,
And all her soul in prayer.

"She wiped his feet with her hair: and the house was filled with the odour of the oinment."—John 12, v. 3.

1. His love the pardon'd sinner shows,
And freely on the poor bestows
What freely he receives;
He clasps them with a kind embrace,
Wipes off the sorrow from their face,
And all their wants relieves.

2. Riches, as fast as they increase,
Not as an ornamental dress,
But a superfluous load
He uses for the noblest ends,
On Jesus in his saints expends,
And serves the church of God.

3. The ointment's on the members spill'd,
The house is with its odour fill'd,
And prayers and praises rise,
Grateful to his dear Lord above;
And God in Christ with smiles of love
Accepts the sacrifice.

"He was a thief, and had the bag."—John 12, v. 6.

Money with God of no esteem
He doth to thieves and traitors trust,
But precious souls are kept by Him,
Are safe with Jesus Christ the just:
Judas the church's goods may steal,
He cannot make our souls his prey,
Though help'd by him who comes from hell
The sheep to spoil, and kill, and

slay.

"Then said Jesus, Let her alone (Gr., forgive her)."—John 12, v. 7.

The world who only seek their own
Compassion for the poor pretend,
But judge who live for God alone,
And all on their Redeemer spend:
They may external works approve
Whene'er the needy we relieve,
But our excess of zealous love
To Christ, they never can forgive.

"Against the day of my burying hath she kept this."—John 12, v. 7.

The things we most affect and prize
We offer Christ in sacrifice,
His costliest gifts to Him restore,
And wish our utmost all were more;
Our Lord as for his tomb prepare,
Languish to rest with Jesus there,
And weeping, till his face appears,
We still embalm him with our tears.

"The poor always ye have with you."—John 12, v. 8.

We bless thee, Saviour, for the grace
Which left thy deputies behind:
The poor on earth supply thy place,
That man may still to God be kind:
Our alms expecting to receive
The Head we in the members see;
And what to them we do, or give
We give, or do it, Lord, to Thee.

"They came, not for Jesus sake only, but that they might see Lazarus also, whom he had raised from the dead."—John 12, v. 9.

1. Ye who curiously desire
The works of Christ to see,
Come; but farther grace require,
And his disciples be:
Him who rais'd us from the dead,
Expect your sinful souls to raise;
Feel the Spirit of our Head,
And live to Jesus praise.

2. Burst the barriers of the tomb
Thro' his almighty word:
All mankind to Him may come,
And glorify the Lord:
Ye who sleep in death awake,
While Christ his quickning power exerts,
Seek him for his own dear sake,
And find him in your hearts.

"The chief priests consulted, that they might put Lazarus also to death: Because that by reason of him many of the Jews went away, and believed on Jesus."—John 12, v. 10, 11.

1. Impious priests in every age
Thy servants death contrive,
Persecute with cruel rage
Whom Thou hast made alive,
Hate thy faithful witnesses;
While crouds our resurrection see,
Wonder at our life of grace,
And turn themselves to Thee.

2. O that more might see us live,
As risen from the grave,
Gladly our report receive,
And prove thy power to save!
Let them, Lord, the world desert,
Thyself that quickning Spirit own,
Give thee all their loving heart,
And live for Thee alone!

"Much people took branches of palm trees, and went forth to meet him, and cried, Hosanna, blessed is the King of Israel, that cometh in the name of the Lord."—John 12, v. 12, 13.

1. The people still go forth to meet,
And Jesus with hosannas greet,
The King of saints, the God supreme,
His Sender comes reveal'd in Him.

2. Receive him in Jehovah's name,
Jehovah is with Christ the same,
Receive him in his Spirit bestow'd,
The fulness of the tri-une God!

3. He comes, He comes, on earth to reign,
He brings us back our power again,
The sovereignty which Adam lost,
With Father, Son, and Holy Ghost.

4. In us who Christ our God adore,
He doth his kingdom here restore,
And in our faithful hearts we prove
The reigning power of Jesus love.

5. The Author of our joy we bless,
The King of peace and righteousness,
Triumphant in the earnest given;
For present love is present heaven.

6. We soon shall meet him in the sky,
And ceaseless hallelujah cry,
Palms in our hands, as conquerors, bear,
And glory on our foreheads wear!

"Fear not, daughter of Sion; behold thy King cometh, sitting on an asses colt."—John 12, v. 15.

1. Pomp and magnificence He leaves
To kings who need their weakness hide,
No dignity from man receives
Who comes but to encounter pride,
To make the world, and sin submit,
And trample death beneath his feet.

2. Meekness and love compose his train:
Sion, rejoice thy King to see!
He comes o're willing hearts to reign
By patience and humility:
Ye need not fear the sinner's Friend
Who comes your sins and fears to end.

3. Sinners by gentleness He wins,
And sweetly bends them to his sway;
Receive your mild, pacific Prince,
Injoy the happiness t' obey,
Delight his easy yoke to prove,
And bless his law of life and love.

"These things understood not his disciples at the first: but when Jesus was glorified, then remembred they that these things were written of him, and that they had done these things unto him."—John 12, v. 16.

1. Ah, Lord, my ignorance I own,
Thy mind I cannot yet conceive,
But wait, till Thou, to make it known,
Thy own revealing Spirit give,
Thy lively oracles t' explain,
And plant thy reigning power in man.

2. I read, but cannot comprehend
The depth of thy mysterious word;
But when Thou dost thy Spirit send,
I there shall find my pardning Lord,
By thy own light discover Thee,
And born of God, thy kingdom see.

3. Inthron'd again above the skies,
Thou hast obtain'd the Comforter,
Who opens our inlighten'd eyes,
By humble faith, and childlike fear,
Brings to our mind thy words of grace,
And all thy depths of love displays.

4. The veil remov'd we then

perceive,
Th' inexplicable book unseal'd,
Thy sovereign Deity believe
In whom the scriptures are fulfil'd,
Who dost thy gracious sway maintain,
And in our hearts triumphant reign.

"The people that was with him when he called Lazarus out of his grave, and raised him from the dead, bare record."—John 12, v. 17, 18.

1. We, Jesus, have heard Thy wonderful fame,
The power of thy word To sinners proclaim,
With hearty thanksgiving Acknowledge thy grace,
The living, the living Should publish thy praise.

2. Our spirits were dead, And buried in sin;
But waken'd and freed From death we have been,
The true Resurrection We found in our graves:
And Jesus' affection Whole multitudes saves.

3. Come then at his call Our Jesus to meet!
His wonders on all He waits to repeat:
The proofs of his favour Ye all shall receive,
And friends of your Saviour And witnesses live.

"The Pharisees therefore said among themselves, Perceive ye how ye prevail nothing? behold, the world is gone after him."—John 12, v. 19.

1. Who with hate implacable
The Lord of life oppose,
Pharisees against their will
Their own foul hearts disclose:
Men who would the world engage
Their own blind followers to be,
Lo, the world, with envious rage,
Gone after Christ they see!

2. Who with envy now behold
His messengers success,
(Like your predecessors old)
Your baffled pride confess:
Ye that love the praise of men,
Must surely forfeit their esteem,
If the love of Jesus reign,
And all go after Him.

"We would see Jesus."—John 12, v. 21.

Fain would I my Redeemer see,
As when extended on the tree
He groan'd beneath my sinful load,
He pour'd out all his guiltless blood;
Above, I want this only sight,
To view the Lamb in his own light,
T' adore the lustre of those scars
Which brightens all the morning-

stars!

"Philip cometh and telleth Andrew; and again, Andrew and Philip told Jesus."—John 12, v. 22.

How pleasing is the harmony,
When Jesus' ministers agree,
In bringing souls to Him conspire,
And point them to the world's Desire;
His followers true, no envious zeal
No vain self-preference they feel,
His glory seek, and not their own,
And live t' exalt their Lord alone.

"The hour is come, that the Son of man should be glorified."—John 12, v. 23.

Son of man, the hour is come,
To manifest thy name;
Call a world of sinners home
Thy goodness to proclaim:
Is not this thy proper praise,
The dead to wake, the lost to find?
Jesus, glorify thy grace
By saving all mankind.

"Except a corn of wheat fall into the ground (Gr., Earth) and die, it abideth alone: but if it die, it bringeth forth much fruit."—John 12, v. 24.

I.

1. The Father's Fellow and his Son
On his everlasting throne
Did long alone abide;
But fell, when God became a man,
Into our earth, an heavenly grain,
And here the Saviour died.

2. The church's Principle and Seed,
Jesus, for a season dead,
Sprung up out of the grave:
He did thro' his own virtue rise,
And re-ascended to the skies,
Our sinful world to save.

3. He yields the infinite increase,
Millions of his witnesses
Out of his passion shoot,
Thro' Jesus quickning power believe,
Life from their Saviour's death receive,
And fill the world with fruit.

4. In them th' immortal Seed remains,
Them the Bread of life sustains,
And feeds and multiplies,
Till that eternal harvest come,
And raise their bodies from the tomb,

And store them in the skies.

"Except a corn of wheat fall into the ground (Gr. earth) and die, it abideth alone, but if it die, it bringeth forth much fruit."—John 12, v. 24.

II.

1. The members must their Head pursue,
One with Him they suffer too,
Or barren still abide:
Dies every consecrated grain,
Dies every re-begotten man
With Jesus crucified.

2. As banish'd long from human thought,
Lord, thy follower is forgot,
Is buried out of sight,
Till Thou his dear Redeemer come,
And call his soul out of thy tomb,
And bring him forth to light.

3. Who now participates thy death,
Shall thy living Spirit breathe,
Bring forth the fruits of grace,
Thy gifts abundantly improve,
Attaining in the fear of love
The perfect holiness.

"He that loveth his life, shall lose it."—John 12, v. 25.

Th' inordinate, excessive love
Of life, and the vain things below
Damps the belief of joys above,
Of joys which few desire to know;
Regardless of that bliss unseen
Their portion here the worldlings chuse,
And for a moment's pleasure mean
Consent th' eternal life to lose.

"He that hateth his life in this world shall keep it unto life eternal."—John 12, v. 25.

Saviour, to Thee our hearts we give,
While here our short abode we make,
Submit the present life to live
Not for its own, but thy dear sake;
Ready we would each moment be
At thy command to lay it down,
And bear on earth thy cross with Thee,
With Thee to share thy heavenly crown.

"If any man serve me, let him follow me."—John 12, v. 26.

Thy servant, Lord, I fain would be,
Would fain thy faithful follower prove,
Abhor the things abhor'd by Thee,
Love all the objects of thy love,
Myself renounce, my life despise,
To gain thy life which never dies.

"And where I am, there shall also my servant be."—John 12, v. 26.

1. Jesus, while yet a Man of woe,
On earth Thou said'st, in heaven I am!
And all who in thy footsteps go,
Thy place above by promise claim,
Feeble, and faint, yet following on,
Thy servant shall ascend thy throne.

2. The least of thy disciples I,
Of all that ever knew thy love,
On thy most faithful word rely,
And wait till Thou my soul remove,
To see the house Thou hast prepared,
To win thro' grace thy own reward.

"If any man serve me, him will my Father honour."—John 12, v. 26.

Jesus, how great thy servants are!
What dignity on man bestow'd!
We, who rejoice thy yoke to share,
Are honour'd with th' esteem of God,
Thy praise, thy glory we obtain,
And kings we in thy kingdom reign.

"Now is my soul troubled; and what shall I say? Father, save me from this hour: but for this cause came I unto this hour."—John 12, v. 27.

1. In trouble I dare not complain,
When Jesus himself is distrest,
O'rewhelm'd by a sight of his pain,
With grief above measure opprest!
He seems at a loss what to say:
But rescue he will not desire,
Consum'd by the wrath of that day,
Baptis'd with a torrent of fire!

2. Who all our infirmities knows
Doth all our infirmities feel,
And when the fierce cup overflows,
Submitting his innocent will,
The cup from his Father receives,
That I my vocation may see:
To me an ensample he leaves,
He leaves of his patience to me.

3. Supernally strengthen'd to bear
The sight of the terrible hour,
My weakness I humbly declare,
My Lord in the furnace adore;
Thy cross I accept and embrace,
Thy death I no longer decline,
So Thou who hast died in my place,
Preserve me eternally thine.

"Father, glorify thy name."—John 12, v. 28.

The lasting peace of mind
The true tranquillity,
In trouble's lowest deep I find
By leaving all to Thee:
Father, thy will be done:
In thy blest hands I am,
And live and die for this alone,
To glorify thy name.

"Then there came a voice from heaven, saying, I have both glorified it, and will glorify it again."—John 12, v. 28.

Thou hast in me display'd
The glory of thy power
And wilt again reveal thine aid
In thine appointed hour;
Returning from the sky
My fears and sins remove,
And save my soul, to magnify
Thine own Almighty love.

"The people that stood by, and heard it, said, that it thundred: others said, An angel spake to him."—John 12, v. 29.

Amidst the worldly noise
And hurrying strife below,
How few the comfortable voice
Of their Creator know!
But all his voice may hear
Who still his Son imparts,
And sends the heavenly Comforter
To teach within our hearts.

"This voice came not because of me, but for your sakes."—John 12, v. 30.

For me the answer came,
Thou wilt to me make known
Thy nature, attributes, and name
Thro' thine incarnate Son,
Wilt for his sake forgive,
In honour of thy grace,
And bid a pardon'd sinner live
To thine eternal praise.

"Now is the judgment of this world: now shall the prince of this world be cast out."—John 12, v. 31.

Now, that the world our God arraign,
The world are tried themselves, and cast,
Now, that the Lord of life is slain,
The tyranny of hell is past:
Jesus by his expiring breath
Doth Satan's earthly throne o'rethrow,
Destroys who had the power of death,
And drives him to the realms below.

"And I, if I be lifted up from the earth, will draw all men unto Me."—John 12, v. 32.

The promise made our fallen race,
And by the blood of Jesus seal'd,
The word of all-attracting grace

I find ten thousand times fulfil'd:
But, Lord, I want the sight above,
The grace to saints triumphant given:
Draw by the cords of perfect love,
And draw me to thyself in heaven.

"This he said, signifying what death he should die."—John 12, v. 33.

From the tribunal of thy cross,
Satan and sin Thou dost condemn,
But vindicate thy people's cause,
And merit saving grace for them:
Thy cross to us a gracious throne
The instrument of good we find,
The source of every blessing own
And life procur'd for all mankind.

"We have heard out of the law, that Christ abideth forever: and how sayest thou, The Son of man must be lifted up?"—John 12, v. 34.

1. Seeming contrarieties
Faith with readiness receives:
Lifted up from earth He is,
Dies; and yet forever lives!
Thus his suffering saints beneath
Shame their way to glory see,
Find, in the cold arms of death,
Death is immortality.

2. Can we, Lord, the path decline
Which Thou didst vouchsafe to tread,
Followers of the Lamb Divine
Members of our patient Head?
No: our Master's joy to win,
Bear we now the lingring pain,
After Thee we enter in,
Endless life thro' death obtain.

"Walk while ye have the light, lest darkness come upon you."—John 12, v. 35.

Trav'eler, see thy gracious day,
Swiftly drawing to an end!
Mend thy pace, pursue thy way,
Ere the shades of night descend;
Fear to lose a moment's space,
Walk, advance, and hasten on,
And when death concludes thy race,
Dying shout, The work is done!

"He that walketh in darkness, knoweth not whither he goeth."—John 12, v. 35.

Void of Christ, the real Light,
God who neither fears nor loves,
Wanders on, a child of night,
In the paths of ruin roves;
On the brink of hell he stands,
Down the threatning precipice
Tumbles into Satan's hands,
Falls into the dark abyss.

"While ye have the light, believe in the light, that ye may be the children of light."—John 12, v. 36.

While with us his Spirit stays,

Jesus would salvation give,
Doth not mock our helpless race,
While he bids us all believe:
All the saving light may see,
Cast away the works of night,
Rise from sin's obscurity
Rise the children of the light.

"These things spake Jesus, and departed, and did hide himself from them."—John 12, v. 36.

1. Who himself to babes reveals,
Justly from the proud departs,
Leaves the stubborn infidels
To the blindness of their hearts,
Quite withdraws his light and power,
Since they neither would receive:
Then their gracious day is o're,
Then they never can believe.

2. Jesus, Light of life divine,
Do not hide thyself from me,
Me who would be wholly thine,
Would be always led by Thee,
Me who trust thy only love,
Who thy Spirit's law obey,
In thy face unveil'd above,
Shew me that eternal Day!

"Who hath believed our report? and to whom hath the arm of the Lord been revealed?"—John 12, v. 38.

1. The messengers rejected
May cry in every nation
How few embrace The word of grace,
The gospel of salvation!
Not all his outward wonders
Can force us to believe him
Till Jesus' love The veil remove;
And then our hearts receive him.

2. The Arm of the Almighty
We plainly then discover,
And Christ the Power Of God adore
Our souls' eternal Lover;
Who manifests the Father,
Restores us to his favour,
To end our sin, His mind brings in,
And lives in man forever.

"He hath blinded their eyes, and hardened their hearts; that they should not see &c."—John 12, v. 40.

He offer'd them sufficient light,
Which when they could, but would not see,
He left them in their nature's night,
Their unbelief's obscurity:
He offer'd them his softning grace,
And when its power they scorn'd to feel,
Forsook the sick, self-harden'd race
Who would not suffer him to heal.

"These things said Isaiah, when he saw his glory."—John 12, v. 41.

Jesus, the everlasting Son,

Thou reign'st above the sky,
Jehovah sitting on thy throne
The Lord and God most high!
Thee very God, and very Man
We see to sinners given:
And soon the glories of thy train
Shall fill both earth and heaven.

"Among the chief rulers also many believed on him, but &c."—John 12, v. 42, 43.

1. Are there not still, who would receive
Thy truth and witnesses,
Who Thee their pardning Lord believe,
But tremble to confess?
Rulers themselves with faith and fear
Thy works of wonder see,
But dare not in thy cause appear,
Or give up all for Thee.

2. Their horror of assur'd disgrace,
Of man's forbidding frown,
Their love of wealth, and pomp, and praise
Detains and keeps them down:
So much to sell for Thee they have,
They will not quit their sins,
What but thine utmost power can save
A prelate, or a prince!

"Jesus cried, and said, He that believeth on me, believeth not on me, but on him that sent me."—John 12, v. 44.

His public ministry to close,
He lifts his voice, amidst his foes,
By neither earth nor hell dismay'd;
Virtue He with his voice exerts
To reach his weak disciples hearts,
And thus their cowardise upbraid:
Sent from Jehovah in the skies,
Jesus his office magnifies:
The dignity of faith displays,
Which makes the depths of Godhead known,
Discerns the Father in the Son
With all his majesty and grace.

"He that seeth me, seeth him that sent me."—John 12, v. 45.

Inseparably one with Thee,
The Sender in the Sent we see,
Th' express Similitude Divine,
His Power and Wisdom from above,
His Truth, and Holiness, and Love
Throughout thy life and doctrine shine:
Beholding as with open face,
In Thee we on thy Father gaze
Transform'd by the transporting sight,
We praise the Godhead visible,
Come down with sinful men to

dwell,
And triumph in thy glorious light.

"I am come a light into the world, that whosoever believeth on me, should not abide in darkness."—John 12, v. 46.

The Light into the world is come,
And darts into our nature's gloom
The first divine inlivening ray:
Happy who in the Light believes,
And with that glimmering ray receives
The promise of eternal day!
He shall not long in sin abide,
The Light will bring him forth, and guide
His feet into the way of peace,
With still-increasing lustre shine,
And fill his soul with love Divine,
With all the life of heavenly grace.

"If any man hear my words and believe not, I judge him not: for I came not to judge the world, but to save the world. He that rejecteth &c."—John 12, v. 47, 48.

1. What profits it alas, to hear
Thy sayings with a careless ear,
Unless thy sayings I obey,
In vain I call thee God, or Lord;
Neglecting to perform thy word,
Thy word shall cast me in that day:
Thy gospel which I now despise,
Against me shall in judgment rise,
And aggravate my fearful doom:
Unless I feel my guilty load,
A sinner dying in my blood,
And to the Friend of sinners come.

2. A sinner now I come to Thee,
For pardon, life, and liberty,
Thy reconciling word receive:
Thou cam'st at first to shew thy grace,
Not to condemn our sinful race,
And died'st that all mankind might live.
In Thee an Advocate I have,
And answering thy design to save,
My humble confidence hold fast;
Blest with the faith that works by love,
Henceforth in all thy paths I move,
And reach my Father's house at last.

"For I have not spoken of myself: but the Father which sent me, he gave me a commandment, what I should say, and how I should speak."—John 12, v. 49.

Thy great commission to fulfil
And answer all thy Father's will,
His word Thou hast declar'd to man,
His word is not distinct from

thine,
But Father, Son, and Spirit join
To make the hidden myst'ry plain:
The whole Divine oeconomy
Appointed and prescrib'd to Thee
Saviour, Thou hast display'd below:
And still Thou dost thy grace impart,
And still in every faithful heart
The way to heavenly glory shew.

"And I know that his commandment is life everlasting: whatsoever I speak therefore, even as the Father said unto me, so I speak."—John 12, v. 50.

Thou in the gospel hast made known
The way by thy great Father shewn,
And thither thy commandments tend,
The sum of all thy teachings this,
Obedience leads to perfect bliss,
Obedience shall in glory end.
Jesus, thy promise I embrace,
Fulness of evangelic grace,
Sufficient strength derive from Thee;
My soul upon thy word is stay'd;
Thy word believ'd, belov'd, obey'd,
Is life, eternal life, to me.

JOHN CHAPTER THIRTEEN

"Having loved his own which were in the world, he loved them unto the end."—John 13, v. 1.

1. Objects of his constant care,
The Shepherd of the sheep,
Them as in his arms did bear,
And in his bosom keep:
Them with persevering love
He died from suffering to redeem,
Then resum'd his place above,
And claim'd their thrones for them.

2. Saviour, am not I thine own?
Throughout my evil days
Surely Thou on me hast shewn
The riches of thy grace:
Thee the sinner's heavenly Friend,
In life and death I trust on Thee:
Love me, Lord, when time shall end,
Thro' all eternity.

"The devil having now put it into the heart of Judas to betray him."—John 13, v. 2.

1. Judas did first himself betray,
Or with his utmost power and art
Satan had never forc'd his way
Into the perjur'd traitor's heart:
The miser sold himself to sin,
And avarice let the murtherer in.

2. Money! the direful love of

thee,
The root of every evil still,
Springs up in deeds of perfidy;
For thee we fawn, betray, and kill,
And churchmen sell, like him of old,
Their Master and their souls for gold.

"Jesus knowing that the Father had given all things into his hands, and that he was come from God, and went to God. He riseth from supper &c."—John 13, v. 3, 4, 5.

1. My God, my God, was ever love,
Was ever lowliness like thine!
Conscious of what Thou art above
Supreme in majesty Divine,
Thy Father, ere the world began
Into thy hands had all things given,
And sanctified the Son of man
The sovereign Lord of earth and heaven.

2. Who didst from Him thy mission know
Returning to thy Father's breast,
How could thy greatness stoop so low,
God over all by all confest!
Contemplating thy glorious state
Which mortal eye had never seen,
Thou didst on thy own creatures wait,
And serve the sinful sons of men.

3. See then, ye haughty worms of earth,
The strange humility unknown!
Who boast your power, or pomp, or birth
Behold Jehovah's only Son!
The sight might kings themselves convert:
God only could so far submit:
Satan is in the traitor's heart,
The Lord most high is at his feet!

"He laid aside his garments, and took a towel, and girded himself. After that he poureth water into a bason, and began to wash his disciples feet, and to wipe them with the towel wherewith he was girded."—John 13, v. 4, 5.

1. But stranger far, and more profound
That first abasement of our God,
When with eternal glory crown'd
A Man to men himself he shew'd!
He laid his dazling robes aside,
His greatness and majestic grace,
And pleas'd with sinners to abide,
Put on our nature's sordid dress.

2. Jehovah in our form appears
With frail humanity endued,
Washes his servants in his tears,
And purifies us by his blood;
Our souls immerst in guilt and clay

Are by his sacred flesh made clean,
He wipes our earthly minds away,
And all the filth of inbred sin.

"Simon saith unto him, Lord, dost thou wash my feet?"—John 13, v. 6.

1. Incomprehensible to man
The strange humility Divine
Till Jesus doth himself explain
His own mysterious love's design:
Wondring we ask, how can it be
That God should wait on man below,
That the Most-high should stoop to me,
And wash the sinner white as snow!

2. When Jesus at his feet he saw,
Peter might well repeat the word
"From a vile sinful man withdraw,
"Holy, and just, and heavenly Lord!"
But therefore will the Saviour stay,
For this in human likeness born,
To purge our guilty stains away,
And to a saint a sinner turn.

"What I do, thou knowest not now, but thou shalt know hereafter."—John 13, v. 7.

Do what Thou wilt; it should be so;
If now I cannot sound thy mind,
Thy work I shall hereafter know
The meaning of thy conduct find:
Death shall e'erlong unwind the maze
Th' inpenetrable cloud remove,
And then I see, that all thy ways
Were wisdom, faithfulness, and love.

"If I wash thee not, thou hast no part with me."—John 13, v. 8.

We have no benefit from Thee,
Unless thy blood, by faith applied,
Redeem from all iniquity,
And throughly cleanse thy ransom'd bride:
But if thy blood to flesh convert
This unbelieving heart of stone,
Mine own assuredly Thou art,
Thou art eternally mine own.

"Peter saith unto him, Lord, not my feet only, but also my hands and my head."—John 13, v. 9.

Fountain of purity Divine,
No longer I refuse thy grace,
But give up my own will to thine,
But waive my own unworthiness:
Since Thou so freely dost forgive,
And wash, and seal me for thine own,
My pardon I with joy receive,
And share the blessings of thy throne.

"He that is washed, needeth not, save to wash his feet, but is clean every whit."—John 13, v. 10.

1. If bath'd in thine atoning blood
Am I not every whit made clean,
Compleatly justified with God,
Redeem'd from all the filth of sin?
My conscience is no more defil'd,
Sprinkled and purified my heart,
I know my Father reconcil'd
I know that Thou my Saviour art.

2. Thy Spirit, Lord, the water pure
Together with thy blood applied,
Hath made my peace and pardon sure
Hath plung'd me in the mingled tide:
My care is now to wash my feet,
And if I humbly walk in Thee,
Sin I need never more repeat,
Or lose my faith and purity.

"And ye are clean."—John 13, v. 10.

Didst Thou not leave thy Father's throne
To save thy people from their sin?
Assure our hearts, the work is done,
And tell us, Lord, we now are clean;
Cleans'd by the Spirit and the word
Give us in all thy steps to tread,
As followers of our holy Lord,
As members of our sinless Head.

"But not all."—John 13, v. 10.

Not all who saving faith profess
Are wash'd in thy all-cleansing blood;
There lurks among thy witnesses
Some Judas, false to man and God!
Searcher of hearts, Thou seest alone
Our unperceiv'd hypocrisy:
Make the perfidious traitor known
And shew me, Lord, if I am he!

"Know ye what I have done to you?"—John 13, v. 12.

No: without thy farther light,
My ignorance I own
Cannot understand aright
The things which Thou hast done:
Give mine inmost soul to know
The depth of thy humility,
What thy love hath wrought below,
And daily doth for me.

"Ye call me Master, and Lord: and ye say well; for so I am."—John 13, v. 13.

Master Thee, we call and Lord,
Performing what we say
When our lives fulfil thy word,

And when our hearts obey:
O that thus we always might
Ourselves thy true disciples prove
Find, like Thee, our whole delight
In works of humble love.

"If I then your Lord and Master, have washed your feet, ye also ought to wash one another's feet."—John 13, v. 14.

1. No; the letter profits nought
And few could that fulfil;
But we all by Jesus taught
May know and do his will,
All to all may helpful prove,
To meanest offices submit:
Thus we humbly serve in love
And wash each others feet.

2. Chiefly we thy word should keep
Thy labouring messengers,
O're polluted sinners weep
And wash them with our tears:
But our tears must flow in vain,
Unless we pray them back to God:
Jesus, stoop to worms again,
And wash them in thy blood.

"I have given you an example, that ye should do as I have done to you."—John 13, v. 15.

Jesus, Lord, I fain would stoop
With thy humility
Take thy sacred burthen up,
And meekly follow Thee:
Lowly both in mind and deed
Thou hast a perfect pattern given:
Give me in thy steps to tread,
And bear thy cross to heaven.

"The servant is not greater than his Lord, neither he that is sent, greater than he that sent him."—John 13, v. 16.

Ye who minister the word
You did from Christ receive,
More respected than your Lord
Can you desire to live?
Sent by him, with humble grace
The portion of your Master meet,
Find with joy your highest place
At every sinner's feet.

"If ye know these things, happy are ye if ye do them."—John 13, v. 17.

What avails it, Lord, to know,
And not to do thy will?
This my chief delight below
Thy pleasure to fulfil:
Till I join the church above,
This only happiness by mine
Thee with all my heart to love,
And have no will but thine.

"I speak not of you all; I know whom I have chosen: but that the scripture may be fulfilled. He that eateth bread with me hath lift up his heel against me."—John 13, v. 18.

1. With such tranquillity of mind,

So mild, dispassionate, and meek,
So calm, and perfectly resign'd
I would of my betrayers speak:
And what Thou in thyself hast done,
Thou wilt repeat in all thy own.

2. Thou David after God's own heart,
Strengthen me with thy Spirit's aid,
Thy lowliness of love impart,
And lo, by bosom-friends betray'd,
I come, thy portion here to find
Rejected, spurn'd by all mankind.

"Now I tell you before it come, that when it is come to pass, ye may believe that I am He."—John 13, v. 19.

A pastor should his flock prepare,
And arm against the trying hour:
Forewarn'd the rude assault they bear,
Their Lord's Divinity and power
With stronger confidence confess
With fuller joy their Saviour bless.

"He that receiveth whomsoever I send, receiveth me: and he that receiveth me, receiveth him that sent me."—John 13, v. 20.

1. The body and the Head are one,
One Spirit in all the members lives,
And whatsoe'er to them is done
Jesus as done to Him receives,
Strangely partakes of their distress,
And suffers with his witnesses

2. But stricter still the union is
'Twixt Christ, and those He doth ordain:
Their mission is a part of his,
His place and office they sustain,
With his authority indued,
As envoys from the living God!

"Jesus was troubled in spirit, and said, Verily verily I say unto you, that one of you shall betray me."—John 13, v. 21.

1. Troubled at heart, and grieved within
The Lord of all vouchsafes to be,
He mourns his own disciple's sin,
His own disciple's perfidy,
And feels with voluntary pain
The misery of ungrateful man.

2. Pastors and priests to avarice sold
Who Jesus and his truth betray,
Basely intrude into the fold
To make immortal souls their prey,
They to the fiend admittance give,
And still the soul of Jesus grieve.

"Then the disciples looked one on another, doubting of whom he spake."—John 13, v. 22.

Sinners redeem'd, yet still inclin'd
To sin, should tremble at the name:
The evils we in others find
Ourselves may soon commit the same;
And I shall act the traitor's part,
If e'er I trust my treacherous heart.

"Now there was leaning on Jesus bosom, one of his disciples whom Jesus loved."—John 13, v. 23.

1. On his Redeemer's breast reclin'd,
And taken up with Christ alone,
No more he calls himself to mind,
By nought but Jesus kindness known:
Regardless of reproach and praise,
If blam'd by mortals or approv'd;
His name, his talents, and his grace
Lost in—the Man by Jesus lov'd!

2. The modest man, the meek in heart
May still be dignified and blest
With the belov'd disciple's part,
May with his dear Redeemer rest:
And those, that their own name forget,
Cast their ambitious pride away,
And lay themselves at Jesus feet,
Jesus will in his bosom lay.

"Peter beckoned to him, that he should ask who it should be of whom he spake."—John 13, v. 24.

The secret of the Lord is known
To saints whose hearts are kept above
Who cleave by faith to Christ alone,
And humbly fear, because they love;
Jesus on whom their souls rely,
Their every prayer and sigh receives;
Nothing he can to such deny,
And more than all they ask he gives.

"He then lying on Jesus breast, saith unto him, Lord, who is it?"—John 13, v. 25.

1. My most indulgent Saviour,
I long thy love to find,
To triumph in thy favor,
And know thy Spirit's mind:
This grace to me be given,
I nothing more request,
I want no other heaven
Than leaning on thy breast.

2. The place of John I covet
More than a Seraph's throne,
To rest in my Beloved
And breathe my final groan;

On Thee alone relying
To lose my sin and pain,
And on thy bosom dying
My life eternal gain.

"It is he to whom I shall give a sop. And when he had dipped the sop, he gave it to Judas."—John 13, v. 26.

Jesus his benefits bestows
On open friends and secret foes,
Or these to those prefers,
The sop, the outward gift, he gives
To traitors, hypocrites, and thieves,
To Satan's ministers.
Gifts will not evidence our grace,
Or riches in their shining face
The marks of goodness show;
We can by no external sign
Discern the favourites divine,
Or John from Judas know.

"And after the sop Satan entred into him."—John 13, v. 27.

1. The wretch profane who without dread
That sacred, sacramental bread
Unworthily receives,
Constrains the Saviour to depart,
And full possession of his heart
To the destroyer gives.

2. The slaves of lust and avarice
Satan demands as lawful prize,
The god whom they adore,
Invited by the world and sin
After the sop he enters in,
And never leaves them more.

"Then said Jesus unto him, That thou dost, do quickly."—John 13, v. 27.

1. How hopeless is a sinner's case,
No more restrain'd by Jesus grace,
Left to the fiend alone!
The reprobate by God abhor'd,
The slave with his indwelling lord
Is now forever one.

2. Conscience, and fear, and shame are o're,
Obstructed in his sins no more,
The soul insensible
His tyrant's last commands fulfils,
In haste his own damnation seals,
And rushes into hell.

3. Least this my dreadful end should be,
My Saviour go not far from me;
Who hast my rescue been,
Still with thy tempted servant stay
And hedge about with thorns my way,
And hold me back from sin.

4. I know, if Thou thy hand withdraw,
Without restraint, remorse, or awe
I into sin shall run,

Caught in the hellish fowler's snare,
Abandon'd to extreme dispair
Eternally undone.

"Now no man at the table knew for what intent he spake this unto him."—John 13, v. 28.

1. Doth Jesus still the traitor spare,
And patient to the end forbear
T' expose his basest foe?
O may I thus behave to mine,
And all the tenderness Divine
To harden'd sinners show.

2. O that, like his disciples, I
Might to myself his word apply;
With candid charity
The traitor undisclos'd receive,
Nor evil of the worst believe,
Till forc'd by what I see!

"Some of them thought, Jesus had said unto him, that he should give something to the poor."—John 13, v. 29.

Christ and his friends the poor relieve,
Alms from their little stock they give;
And shall not I afford
My love in poverty to show,
And gladly the last mite bestow
To feed my hungry Lord!

"He then having received the sop, went immediately out."—John 13, v. 30.

1. Who hears his warnings with disdain,
And Jesus gifts receives in vain
Must fall from sin to sin,
No time in Satan's service lose,
No hellish drudgery refuse,
Till Tophet takes him in.

2. Satan admits of no delay,
But governs with despotic sway
Whoe'er his yoke receives,
His slave he drives, and urges on,
But never ventures him, alone,
Or time for thinking gives.

3. But O! how desperate he and blind,
Who Jesus leaves so good and kind,
For an infernal lord!
The frantic, base, ungrateful fool
Plung'd headlong in the burning pool
Must share the fiend's reward.

"And it was night."—John 13, v. 30.

1. Horrible night, for murther made!
Beneath whose execrable shade
Demons their treason hide!
Betray'd was God's eternal Son:
The darkest deed that e'er was done,
The blackest parricide!

2. Most lovely night, with blessings crown'd,
When Jesus sold, the ransom found,
Consenting to be slain!
The brightest deed that e'er was done!
He made our foulest sins his own,
He gave his life for man!

3. He left on this auspicious night
The death-commemorating rite
Which life divine imparts,
The feast which all our wants relieves,
And Christ with all his fulness gives
Into our longing hearts.

"Now is the Son of man glorified, and God is glorified in him."—John 13, v. 31.

1. Entred upon his final scene
He sees the joy before him set,
O'relooks the shame and pain between,
And hastes his great reward to meet;
The vict'ory is already won,
Already of the prize possest
He reigns as on his Father's throne,
He triumphs in his Father's breast!

2. Redemption's wondrous work is wrought,
(The Lamb from earth's foundation died)
The debt is paid, the pardon bought,
The righteous God is satisfied:
His wrongs repair'd, his law fulfil'd,
His Power, and Wisdom from above,
His Truth shines forth in Christ reveal'd,
His perfect Holiness and Love!

"If God be glorified in him, God shall also glorify him with himself, and shall straightway glorify him."—John 13, v. 32.

Who gave his life mankind to save,
And the great God to glorify,
In forty hours he left the grave,
In forty days regain'd the sky:
When Jesus from the dead He rais'd,
The Father glorified the Son,
Jehovah by Jehovah plac'd,
Th' eternal Partner of his throne.

"Little children, yet a little while I am with you: Ye shall seek me: and as I said unto the Jews, Whither I go ye cannot come; so now I say unto you."—John 13, v. 33.

1. O the strength of Jesus' zeal!
What is ours, compar'd to thine?
What can fondest mothers feel
Like that tenderness Divine?
Yet, unless our Lord depart,
Wean'd, alas, we cannot be:
When the loss hath broke my

heart,
Draw my broken heart to Thee.

2. Jesus vanish'd from my sight,
Of thine absence I complain,
Seek that sensible delight
That extatic joy in vain:
Where Thou art, I cannot come;
Yet I after Thee shall rise,
Soon emerging from the tomb,
Meet my Saviour in the skies.

"A new commandment I give unto you, that ye love one another; as I have loved you, that ye also love one another."—John 13, v. 34.

1. O put it in our inward parts,
Write the new precept on our hearts
In characters divine;
Inspire us with thy Spirit's love;
Stronger than death it then shall prove,
A copy, Lord, of thine.

2. That strange excess of love unknown
Bestow'd on those Thou call'st thine own,
Bestow it now on me,
And rendring back what I receive,
My life a sacrifice I give
For all thy saints and Thee.

"By this shall all men know that ye are my disciples, if ye have love one to another."—John 13, v. 35.

1. The love impartial and sincere
Th' inimitable character
On genuine saints imprest,
O that I in myself could find,
Indow'd with my Redeemer's mind,
With his affection blest!

2. Inlarg'd beyond the narrow space
Of those that their own sect embrace,
And none besides approve,
I would, to liberty restor'd
Love all the lovers of my Lord,
And all who seek his love.

3. Jesus, the gospel-grace impart
To mine, and every longing heart,
Take us into thy fold,
The truth of pure religion give,
That all who bear thy name may live,
And love like those of old.

4. The mark on every face impress,
That like thy first-born witnesses
We hand in hand may move,
And ready each for each to die,
Constrain the world again to cry
"See, how these Christians love!"

"Whither I go, thou canst not follow me now, but thou shalt follow me afterwards."—John 13, v. 36.

The times and seasons when to give
His grace, are in my Saviour's power;
And what I cannot now receive,
I shall, in his appointed hour:
His great salvation is for me,
The moment when I need not know;
Suffice that I my Lord shall see,
And walk as Jesus walk'd below.

"Lord, why cannot I follow thee now? I will lay down my life for thy sake."—John 13, v. 37.

1. He cannot now his Pattern trace,
Because he fondly thinks he can,
Nor knows the desperate wickedness,
The evil heart that is in man:
He should to Jesus word submit,
But doth on his own strength rely;
He cannot his own judgment quit,
Yet promises for Christ to die.

2. A fancied strength presumption gives,
And stops our praying for the true:
But who his own weak heart believes,
His foolish confidence shall rue:
Full of himself, the swelling worm
Is of a martyr's zeal possest,
Can might things for God perform,
Yet fails, and stumbles in the least.

"Jesus answered him, Wilt thou lay down thy life for my sake?"—John 13, v. 38.

Jesus must first for Peter die,
And purchase the courageous grace,
Must his own Godhead testify,
That Peter may his Lord confess:
The Son of God, the martyrs Head
Doth power for his disciples claim,
And gives us, dying in our stead,
The strength to suffer for his name.

"Verily, verily I say unto thee, The cock shall not crow, till thou hast denied me thrice."—John 13, v. 38.

How deep and unperceiv'd in man
The wound of self-presuming pride!
Only the great Physician can
Reveal what nature strives to hide:
Righteous, and wise, and gracious too,
He lets his lov'd Apostle fall,

Lays the wound open to our view,
And thus provides a cure for all.

JOHN CHAPTER FOURTEEN

"Let not your heart be troubled: ye believe in God, believe also in Me."—John 14, v. 1.

Calmer of the troubled heart,
Bid my unbelief depart;
Speak, and all my sorrows cease,
Speak, and all my soul is peace:
With the hope of thy return,
Comfort me, whene'er I mourn,
And till I thy glory see,
Bid me still believe in Thee.

"In my Father's house are many mansions: I go to prepare a place for you."—John 14, v. 2.

1. Can we mourn, as broken-hearted,
We who hang upon thy love,
Jesus, for our sake departed
To thy Father's house above?
Source of all our consolations,
There we our Forerunner see:
In those lasting habitations
Thou hast found a place for me.

2. All our hopes and souls we venture
On thy never-failing word,
Sure into thy joy to enter,
Sure to triumph with our Lord;
Though we fall into distresses,
Into countless trials fall,
When thy love in death releases,
Heaven shall make amends for all.

"And if I go and prepare a place for you I will come again, and receive you unto myself, that where I am, there ye may be also."—John 14, v. 3.

1. Thou who hast undertook our cause,
Art fitting up the house of God:
The house was purchas'd on thy cross,
And cost thee all thy sacred blood:
Our Head Thou didst arise again,
Our Harbinger go up on high,
And gifts receive for sinful men,
And pour thy Spirit from the sky.

2. Thou hast inroll'd our names above,
Hast in our names possession took,
Who thy Divine appearing love,
And for thy final coming look:
Sure as Thou dost our place prepare,
Thou wilt with majesty come down,
And take us in that day to share
Thy joy, thy glory, and thy crown.

"I will come again."—John 14, v. 3.

Comfort of all believing hearts,
Support of suffering saints below,
This is the word which life imparts,
And bears us thro' the vale of woe;
And trusting in their faithful Lord,
To come again, and fetch his bride,
Millions have liv'd upon this word,
And for this precious promise died.

"Whither I go ye know, and the way ye know."—John 14, v. 4.

Imperfectly they knew
Who but in part believ'd,
And Christ the living Way and true
Implicitly receiv'd;
Till Christ explain'd, increas'd
The faith himself had given:
And then they openly confess'd,
And follow'd Him to heaven.

"Thomas saith unto him, Lord, we know not whither thou goest, and how can we know the way?"—John 14, v. 5.

We grosly misconceive
The oracles Divine,
Till Thou an understanding give,
And in our darkness shine,
The gospel faith bestow
Which doth thy face display,
And then, dear Lord, in Thee we know
The Life, the Truth, the Way.

"I am the way, and the truth, and the life."—John 14, v. 6.

I.

1. By thy example, Lord,
Shew us Thyself the Way;
The Truth by thy own word
Into our hearts convey;
The Life by thy own grace bestow,
And then in Thee our God we know.

2. The Way to God Thou art;
O might I walk in Thee:
The Truth, thy light impart,
And make thy servant free:
The Life of grace, Thyself reveal,
And then my soul with glory fill.

"I am the way, and the truth, and the life."—John 14, v. 6.

II.

1. By faith we walk in Thee
The Way: the Truth of grace
And full felicity
By stedfast hope embrace;
And Thee th' eternal Life approve,
The only Object of our love.

2. We out of Thee the Way

No end of wandring find:
Without the Truth, we stray,
In sin and error blind:
Without the Life as dead appear,
And hell must be our sepulchre.

"I am the way, and the truth, and the life."—John 14, v. 6.

III.

1. Our heart hath lost by sin
The life of righteousness,
Our mind is dark within,
And wants the light of grace,
Our senses miss the creature-road,
Which should conduct us back to God.

2. But lo, in Christ alone
Again the Way we see
To God and heaven made known
Thro' his humanity,
Again the Truth his light imparts,
And Christ the Life revives our hearts.

"I am the way, and the truth, and the life."—John 14, v. 6.

IV.

1. Thee Jesus we confess
Our Advocate and Friend,
Truth of the promises,
And joys which ne'er shall end,
Our Principle and Head receive,
By whom alone thy members live.

2. Who wilfully refuse
The Life, the Truth, the Way,
Deserve themselves to lose,
And in delusion stray,
Depriv'd of grace, while here they breathe,
And then to die the endless death.

3. But O! the Way came down
Our wandring souls to seek,
The Truth of light unknown
Did in our darkness speak,
And lest we should in death abide,
The Life himself for sinners died.

4. Now in the Way we go
Who Christ by faith receive,
By faith the Truth we know,
By faith the Life we live,
On Jesus cross to heaven ascend,
Where faith in Jesus sight shall end.

"No man cometh unto the Father, but by me."—John 14, v. 6.

1. The great Invisible, unknown
In darkness inaccessible,
Jehovah's co-eternal Son,
Thou only dost to man reveal,
And thro' the fountain of thy blood
Bring back a rebel world to God.

2. Author of our salvation Thee,
Author of faith our hearts confess,
Thro' thy atonement on the tree

Bold we approach the throne of grace,
And find, thy Name to sinners given
Saves us from hell, and lifts to heaven.

3. Thy Father's mind thro' Thee we know,
His image with his grace retrieve,
To Him we in thy footsteps go,
His hidden life in Thee we live,
And led by thy good Spirit, remove
To see his open face above.

"Have I been so long time with you, and yet hast thou not known me, Philip?"—John 14, v. 9.

1. Me, me Thou justly mayst upbraid:
Ev'n from my earliest infancy
Thou hast with thy frail creature stay'd,
Yet still, O Lord, I know not Thee;
My Saviour unreveal'd Thou art,
Unfelt this moment in my heart.

2. With me, I find, thou still dost dwell,
For unconsum'd on earth I live,
I am not with the fiends in hell,
But wait thy Spirit to receive,
Who makes thy heavenly Father known,
And shews that God and Thou art one.

3. O woudst Thou now thy Spirit breathe,
And bid my unbelief depart,
The peace Thou didst to me bequeath,
The pardon, speak into my heart,
And let me now my Father see,
The Image of my God in Thee.

4. Sufficient is that sight alone
To answer all my wishes here:
Come then, and make the Godhead known,
As crucified for me appear,
Be Thou set forth before mine eyes,
I ask no other paradise.

"Believest thou not that I am in the Father, and the Father in me?"—John 14, v. 10.

1. Who shall make the Father known,
The absolute I AM,
One in essence with the Son,
In person not the same!
Reason at the myst'ery reels
Which faith presumes not to declare:
Each in each forever dwells,
And yet distinct they are.

2. Every thing the Son receives
With being from the Sire,
All He is the Father gives,
Yet is not chief, or prior;
What he gives he still retains,
And with his unbeginning Son
Consubstantial God he reigns
Thro' endless ages one!

"Believe me that I am in the Father and the Father in me: or else believe me for the very works sake."—John 14, v. 11.

1. That Thou art God Most-high,
Thy actions testify,
Proof Divine thy wonders give;
Lives the Father in the Son,
Thou dost in the Father live,
Both inexplicably one.

2. Yet must I more desire,
And different proof require:
Sovereign, everlasting Lord,
If almighty Love Thou art,
Speak the soul-convincing word,
Fix the Witness in my heart.

3. Then shall my actions show
That God resides below,
In his genuine children seen,
By his Spirit's traits display'd,
Him who seals the sons of men,
Makes the members like their Head.

"He that believeth on me, the works that I do, shall he do also, and greater &c."—John 14, v. 12.

1. Jesus, to thy Father gone,
Thou hast thy suit obtain'd,
Sent th' Almighty Spirit down,
And power for man ordain'd;
Ampler power thy servants show'd
Than that Thou didst thyself display,
Thee declar'd th' eternal God,
And taught the world t' obey.

2. Thou didst by thy garment's hem
The body's plague expel,
The believer in thy name
Could by his shadow heal:
In thy name the twelve went forth,
To work the works by Thee design'd,
Spake with tongues, proclaim'd thy worth,
And conquer'd all mankind.

3. Still Thou dost thine arm reveal,
Thy power and goodness spread,
Sinsick souls the faithful heal,
And daily raise the dead,
Still in every age and place
The men whom Thou art pleas'd to send,
Work the greater works of grace,
And work, till time shall end.

"And whatsoever ye shall ask in my name, that will I do, that the Father may be glorified in the Son."—John 14, v. 13.

1. Jesus, I thy merits plead,
Who didst my nature take,
Whatsoe'er Thou know'st I need
I ask it for thy sake:
Do the thing my case requires;
(My helpless case to Thee is known)
Satisfy thine own desires,
And take me to thy throne.

2. All this mountain-load remove
Of guilt and misery,
That thy Father's power and love
May shine display'd in Thee:
Fit my soul with Thee to live,
Who hast for my salvation died;
Then Thou shalt the praise receive,
And God be glorified.

"If ye shall ask any thing in my name, I will do it."—John 14, v. 14.

Lord, I ask it in thy name
To be preserv'd from sin,
Keep me free from actual blame,
Till I am pure within:
Lord, I ask a farther grace,
A kingdom in thy realms above;
Bring me to that heavenly place
And crown me with thy love.

"If ye love me, keep my commandments."—John 14, v. 15.

I.

Strangers to thy love are they,
Who call it bondage to obey:
Be it our delight to prove
Obedience is the truth of love:
Love which no compulsion knows,
But freely from the Fountain flows,
Returns spontaneous to the skies,
Pure as the streams of paradise.

"If ye love me, keep my commandments."—John 14, v. 15.

II.

1. But if I love Thee not,
How can I, Lord, obey?
Who hast my soul so dearly bought,
Thy precious blood display:
O let thy wounds impart
To me the loving power,
And I shall serve with all my heart,
And never grieve thee more.

2. Inspire me with the grace,
And lo, my grateful love,
By walking in thy righteous ways,
I gladly come to prove,
Thy counsel to fulfil,
To live for God alone,
And do on earth thy blisful will,
Like those around thy throne.

"And I will pray the Father, and he shall give you another Comforter, that he may abide with you forever."—John 14, v. 16.

I.

1. Jesus, thy weakest followers hear,
On whom thou kindly hast bestow'd
A principle of pious fear,
An heart to seek our joy in God:

This smallest seed of love unfeign'd
We surely have receiv'd from Thee,
And tempted with our Lord remain'd,
And hoped thine utmost word to see.

2. While feebly in thy paths we tread,
And most imperfectly obey,
Thy goodness and thy truth we plead,
And for the promis'd Blessing pray:
Our day of Pentecost is nigh,
Yet still it is not fully come,
Till thy good Spirit descend from high
To make us his eternal home.

3. Upon thy faithful mercies stay'd,
We hold the general Promise fast
To us and to our children made,
To all, as long as time shall last:
That Spirit purchas'd by thy blood,
That Spirit granted to thy prayer,
Is daily on thy church bestow'd,
The saints abiding Comforter.

4. Father who always hearst our Friend,
And Advocate before thy throne,
Vouchsafe that Paraclete to send,
That Spirit of thy spotless Son;
Ah, give him in our hearts to dwell,
To fill with life, and love, and peace,
To constitute, and fix, and seal
Our present and eternal bliss.

"And I will pray the Father, and he shall give you another Comforter, that he may abide with you forever."—John 14, v. 16.

II.

1. Jesus, we hang upon the word
Our faithful souls have heard of Thee:
Be mindful of thy promise, Lord,
Thy promise made to all, and me,
Thy followers who thy steps pursue,
And dare believe that God is true.

2. The truth of Deity reveal,
And let the promise now take place;
Be it according to thy will,
According to thy word of grace,
Thy sorrowful disciples chear,
And send us down the Comforter.

3. He visits now the troubled breast,
And oft relieves our sad complaint,
But soon we lose the transient Guest,
But soon we droop again, and faint,
Repeat the melancholy moan,
Our joy is fled, our comfort gone.

4. Hasten him, Lord, into our heart,
Our sure inseparable Guide:
O might we meet, and never part,
O might He in our hearts abide,
And keep his house of praise and prayer,
And rest, and reign forever there!

"Even the Spirit of truth, whom the world cannot receive, because it seeth him not, neither knoweth him; but ye know him, for he dwelleth with you, and shall be in you."—John 14, v. 17.

1. Father, glorify thy Son;
Answering his all-powerful prayer,
Send that Intercessor down,
Send that other Comforter,
Whom believingly we claim,
Whom we ask in Jesus Name.

2. Him the world cannot receive,
Him they neither see nor know,
Blind in unbelief they live,
All his gracious work below
All his inspirations deem
Foolish as a madman's dream.

3. But by faith we know and feel
Him, the Spirit of truth and grace:
With us He vouchsafes to dwell,
With us while unseen he stays:
All our help and good, we own,
Freely flows from Him alone.

4. Yet, Thou know'st, we cannot rest
Help'd by an external Guide,
Till the transitory Guest
Enter, and in us abide:
Give him, Lord, thy Spirit give,
In us constantly to live.

5. Wilt Thou not the Promise seal,
Good and faithful as Thou art,
Send the Comforter to dwell,
Every moment in our heart?
Yes, Thou must the grace bestow:
Truth hath said it shall be so!

"I will not leave you comfortless; I will come to you &c."—John 14, v. 18, 19, 20.

1. Saviour, and Prince of peace,
Thy saying we receive;
Thou wilt not leave us comfortless,
Thine own Thou wilt not leave:
Poor, helpless orphans we
A while thine absence mourn,
But we thy face again shall see,
And bless thy swift return.

2. No longer visible
To eyes of flesh and blood,
Come, Lord, in us Thyself reveal,
O come, and shew us God:
Because Thou liv'st above,
Let us thy Spirit know,
And in the blisful knowledge prove
Eternal life below.

3. Hasten the day, when we
Shall surely know and feel

Thou art in God, and God in Thee,
And Thou in us dost dwell:
To us who keep thy word
Thou with thy Father come,
And love, and make us, dearest Lord,
Thine everlasting home.

"Because I live, ye shall live also."—John 14, v. 19.

1. Be it according to thy word;
Jesus, our living, quickning Lord,
To Thee our all we owe:
Thy rising is the cause of ours,
And fills our souls with heavenly powers,
When Thee we truly know.

2. Fountain of life, I gasp for Thee!
Thy streams of immortality
Into my heart derive:
Now let me live the life of grace,
And when compleat in holiness,
The life of angels live.

"At that day ye shall know, that I am in my Father, and you in me, and I in you."—John 14, v. 20.

1. That happiest day I long to see,
To fathom the great mystery,
And by thy Spirit know
That Thou dost in thy Father dwell,
One God incomprehensible
But by the Church below.

2. Thy members with Thyself are one,
Flesh of our flesh, bone of our bone,
Who didst our nature take;
And when Thou hast thy Spirit shed,
Assur'd that Thou art Man indeed,
We here thy body make.

3. In Thee we then are creatures new,
And testify that Thou art true,
And dost thy Spirit give,
Thy nature, image, mind impart,
And still in every faithful heart
Our Hope of glory live.

4. Conscious of the indwelling God,
We feel thy love diffus'd abroad,
Thy perfect love reveal'd;
Come is our day of Pentecost,
And Father, Son, and Holy Ghost
His spotless Church hath fill'd.

"He that hath my commandments, and keepeth them, he it is that loveth me: and he that loveth me shall be loved of my Father, and I will love him, and will manifest myself to him."—John 14, v. 21.

1. Happy soul, whom Jesus chuses,
Loving servant of his Lord!
Love obedience true produces,
Love shall bring its own reward:

To his most imperfect lover,
Him who just begins to know,
Jesus will himself discover,
All the depths of Godhead show.

2. For that farther revelation
Humbly, Lord, I wait on Thee:
Visit with thy great salvation,
Shew thine utmost love to me,
Make thy goodness pass before me,
With thy heavenly Father one,
In my heart display thy glory,
Then translate me to thy throne.

"If any man love me, he will keep my words: and my Father will love him, and we will come unto him, and make our abode with him."—John 14, v. 23.

1. O happy state of grace
In which by faith we stand!
Who Jesus' word obeys,
And keeps his kind command,
Communion closer still shall know,
And dwell with God in him, below.

2. The man whose heart approves
The precepts of his Lord,
The path of duty loves,
And practises the word,
To Jesus, and his Father dear,
Shall entertain the Godhead here.

3. Not to those earliest days,
The promise was confin'd,
The Spirit of his grace
Is bought for all mankind,
And all who love the Lord receive
The Lord within their hearts to live.

4. O Son of God, to Thee
We make our bold appeal,
Wou'dst Thou the Deity
To all the world reveal?
Thou, Lord, the faithful Witness art:
Return the answer in our heart.

5. Come quickly from above,
And bring the Father down,
Infuse the perfect love,
Make all the Godhead known,
Come, Father, Son, and Spirit come,
And seal us thine eternal home.

"These things have I spoken unto you, being yet present with you. But the Comforter, which is the holy Ghost, whom the Father will send in my name, he shall teach you all things, and bring all things to your remembrance, whatsoever I have said unto you. Peace I leave with you &c."—John 14, v. 25, 26, 27.

1. Jesus, we on the word depend
Spoken by Thee while present here,
"The Father in my name will send
"The holy Ghost, the Comforter."

2. That Promise made to Adam's

race
Now, Lord, to us, ev'n us fulfil,
And give the Spirit of thy grace,
To teach us all thy welcome will.

3. That heavenly Teacher of mankind
That Guide infallible impart,
To bring thy sayings to our mind,
And write them on our willing heart.

4. He only can the words apply
Thro' which we endless life possess,
And deal to each his legacy,
His Lord's unutterable peace.

5. That peace of God, that peace of thine
O might he now to us bring in,
And fill our souls with power divine,
And make an end of fear and sin!

6. The length, and breadth of love reveal,
The height and depth of Deity,
The heirs of sure salvation seal,
And change, and make us all like Thee!

"He shall teach you all things."—John 14, v. 26.

O that we might the Spirit find
By Jesus grace bestow'd,
Which leads us into all the mind,
And all the things of God!
Come, holy Ghost, thy power display,
And teach us all in one,
Teach us in Christ the living Way
To God's eternal throne.

"Peace I leave with you, my peace I give unto you: not as the world giveth, give I unto you. Let not your heart be troubled, neither let it be afraid."—John 14, v. 27.

1. Saviour, Lord, who at thy death
Peace didst to thy church bequeath,
Now confer the peace on me,
Bring me now my legacy.

2. Give me (not as mortals give,
Hoping better to receive)
That for which I sigh and mourn,
Give, and look for no return.

3. Grant me for thy mercy sake,
Me, who no return can make,
That which I can never buy;
Save, and freely justify.

4. Grant me (not as childish men
Grant, and ask their gifts again,)
Peace which none can take away,
Peace which shall forever stay.

5. Now the benefit impart,
Speak it to my troubled heart,
Comfort, and Thyself restore,
Come, and bid me sin no more.

6. Come, and wipe away my tears,
Come, and scatter all my fears,

Take me to thy loving breast,
Lull me to eternal rest.

"Ye have heard how I said unto you, I go away, and come again unto you. If ye loved me, ye would rejoice, because I said, I go unto the Father."—John 14, v. 28.

This is our rejoicing here,
That Thou to heaven art gone,
Dost at God's right hand appear,
And seated on his throne:
Object of our faithful love
Thou wilt, who hast for sinners died,
Leave again thy place above,
And come to fetch thy bride.

"For my Father is greater than I."—John 14, v. 28.

Greater than the Son, as man,
The Father we confess;
Neither Son nor Father can,
As God, be more or less:
From eternity, the Word,
The God supreme, we worship Thee
Jesus, with thy Sire ador'd
To all eternity.

"And now I have told you before it come to pass, that when it is come to pass, ye might believe."—John 14, v. 29.

Faith we surely know and feel
The end of prophecies,
Trusting Thee, who didst foretell
Thine own triumphant rise,
Confident, the hour will come
When we the promis'd life shall gain,
After Thee forsake the tomb,
And in thy kingdom reign.

"The prince of this world cometh."—John 14, v. 30.

Ye who madly love your sins,
By the worldly spirit led,
Know, that Satan is your prince,
Know, the devil is your head:
Ye that your own will pursue,
Only move as he inspires,
His designs ye blindly do,
Gratify the fiend's desires.

"But he hath nothing in me."—John 14, v. 30.

1. Jesus fill'd with sanctity,
Sanctity itself Thou art!
Nought of evil is in Thee,
Nought that takes the tempter's part:
Satan came in vain to find,
Aught in Thee he call'd his own;
Pure in life, and heart, and mind,
Sinless Thou, and Thou alone.

2. Saviour, take my sins away,
All my sinfulness remove,
Bid me always watch and pray,
Fill'd with faith and purest love;
Keep possession of my breast,
Thou my true Perfection be;
Satan then may still molest,
Nothing shall he find in me.

"But that the world may know that I love the Father; and as the Father gave me commandment, even so I do."—John 14, v. 31.

Anointed, sent from Him,
Saviour, Thou didst fulfil
Thy great commission to redeem,
And do the Father's will;
Hereby thy heart we know,
Who didst our griefs sustain,
And unto death obedient, show
Thy love for God, and man.

"Arise, let us go hence."—John 14, v. 31.

At thy command we rise,
And hence depart with Thee,
Strong in the strength thy cross supplies
We walk to Calvary;
With thy obedience meet
The summons from above,
And, like our Lord, by death compleat
Our sacrifice of love.

JOHN CHAPTER FIFTEEN

"Every branch that beareth fruit, he purifieth it, that it may bring forth more fruit."—John 15, v. 2.

1. If grafted into Thee, the Vine,
I bring forth fruit, the praise is thine:
But use thy sin-retrenching power,
Prune me, that I may bring forth more,
That thro' thy Spirit's grace I may
The truth with all my heart obey.

2. Kindly Thou dost chastize, reprove
The objects of thy choicest love,
That thus we may thy mind express,
Partakers of thy holiness,
May meekly all thy sufferings share,
And fruit unto perfection bear.

"Now ye are clean through the word which I have spoken unto you."—John 15, v. 3.

1. The word of pardning grace
If I have heard from Thee,
And did by faith embrace,
And am from sin set free;
The word did then my change begin,
True holiness impart;
And still thy Spirit works within,
And purifies my heart.

2. The reconciling word
Thy cleansing blood applied,
And trusting in my Lord
My soul is sanctified:
And if I still abide in Thee,
Thou wilt my faith increase,
And bless with spotless purity,
With perfect holiness.

"Abide in Me."—John 15, v. 4.

I will abide in thee, my Lord,
Till life's extremest hour,
For thou who gav'st the gracious word,
Shalt give the gracious power:
And summon'd, with my friends above,
Thine open face to see,
An age of everlasting love
I shall abide in thee.

"Abide in Me, and I in you."—John 15, v. 4.

In Christ the holy One
We dwell by faith alone,
The holy One, we feel
By faith, in us doth dwell:
Communion doth from union flow,
Till God as we are known we know.

"As the branch cannot bear fruit of itself, except it abide in the vine: no more can ye, except ye abide in me."—John 15, v. 4.

1. Unless we faith receive
And still to Jesus cleave
Our God we cannot please
By fruits of righteousness,
Or work a work, or speak a word,
Or think a thought—without the Lord.

2. But freely justified
In Christ if we abide,
The Spirit's fruits we show,
In true experience grow,
Daily the sap of grace receive,
And more, and more like Jesus live.

"I am the Vine: ye are the branches."—John 15, v. 5.

Branches we could not be,
Unless we were in Thee,
But grafted in the Vine,
By faith, we now are thine:
O may we still our faith retain,
And thine eternally remain.

"He that abideth in me, and I in him, the same bringeth forth much fruit: for without me ye can do nothing."—John 15, v. 5.

I.

1. Sin, unimpower'd by grace,
I never can confess;
Till Thou repentance give,
Sin I can never leave;
Till Thou the contrite wish inspire,
I never can Thyself desire.

2. Thee, Lord, and Thee alone
Author of faith I own,
Thee, Saviour I confess
Giver of holiness,
Who only dost on man confer
Our souls' eternal Comforter.

3. While sever'd from the Root
I cannot bring forth fruit;

But to my Saviour join'd,
The same in heart and mind,
I wait in impotence to prove
The whole omnipotence of love.

"He that abideth in me, and I in him, the same bringeth forth much fruit: for without me ye can do nothing."—John 15, v. 5.

II.

1. Stupendous mystery!
Thy people, Lord, with Thee,
The members with the Head
Throughout the earth dispread,
In mind, and will, and Spirit join,
One church, one body, and one Vine.

2. Thy grace our souls revives,
And animates our lives,
The Spirit from Thee proceeds,
And sanctifies our deeds,
Prevents, and with his power attends,
And all in thy great glory ends.

3. By virtue from the Root
Thy branches bring forth fruit,
The hundred-fold increase
Of solid righteousness,
Till with thy humbling Spirit fill'd
The pure, the perfect love we yield.

"Without me, ye can do nothing."—John 15, v. 5.

1. Join'd no longer to the Tree,
I nothing good can do,
Broken off, O Christ, from Thee
Can nothing ill eschew,
Sever'd now thro' unbelief
The double impotence I feel,
Overwhelm'd with sin and grief,
And sinking into hell.

2. Pity, Lord, thy creature's pain,
And challenging for thine,
Graft me in on Thee again
The true immortal Vine;
Graft me in to part no more,
Till love's maturest fruit I bear;
Then I reach the heavenly shore,
And bloom eternal there.

"If a man abide not in me, he is cast forth as a branch, and is withered; and men gather them, and cast them into the fire, and they are burned."—John 15, v. 6.

1. Ah! wretched souls, who once in grace,
Who one in Thee, were truly thine,
But left for sin thy righteous ways,
And shipwreck made of faith divine,
By unbelief broke off from Thee,
They die in their apostacy!

2. Among the branches found no more,

Depriv'd of faith, and life, and love,
Abandon'd to the tempter's power
Vilest of all th' apostates prove,
The sorest punishment require,
Cast into that eternal fire.

3. Saviour, reverse my righteous doom
Fallen alas, from pardning grace,
Yet do not in thy wrath consume,
But give me still a longer space,
And graft again into the Vine,
And keep my soul forever thine.

"If ye abide in me, and my words abide in you, ye shall ask what ye will, and it shall be done unto you."—John 15, v. 7.

I.

1. While the power of faith I prove,
I still abide in Thee,
While thy words, O Lord, I love,
Thy words abide in me:
Strongly on my mind impress,
That thence they never may depart;
Grave the truth of righteousness
Forever on my heart.

2. Fruit of faith and charity,
The prevalence of prayer,
Prayer, which all obtains from Thee,
Abundant fruit shall bear:
Prayer its principle maintains,
The faith by which our spirit lives,
All thy promises it gains,
And all thy life receives.

3. Praying on for faith's increase,
In every grace we grow,
Reach the finish'd holiness,
And to perfection go;
One with Thee by faith and love,
We ask, and have whate'er we will,
Till we from the vale remove,
And find thee on the hill.

"If ye abide in me, and my words abide in you, ye shall ask what ye will, and it shall be done unto you."—John 15, v. 7.

II.

What shall I ask but Thee?
Thou, Lord, art all in one:
In time and in eternity
I ask my God alone.

"Herein is my Father glorified, that ye bear much fruit, so shall ye be my disciples."—John 15, v. 8.

1. Father, thy name be sanctified!
Thy nature to my soul declare,
So shall I in the Vine abide,
And fruit unto thy glory bear:
A witness of redeeming grace,
O might I in thy Spirit live,
Abound in works of righteousness;
And Thou shalt all the praise receive.

2. One only work on earth I have,
One only means thy praise to show,
My own and others souls to save
Is all my business here below:
I live thy mercy's minister
Myself to second life restor'd,
A genuine child of God appear,
A true disciple of my Lord.

3. So let my light to others shine,
That they my works of faith may see,
With wonder own they are not mine,
But wrought by thy great power in me,
Th' effects of thy triumphant grace
O might they all adore and prove,
And born again my Father praise,
Th' almighty God of faithful love.

"As my Father hath loved me, so have I loved you."—John 15, v. 9.

1. He for thy sake approves us,
With grace divinely free,
And still thy Father loves us
As members, Lord, of Thee:
The cause of his election
Unsearchable we own,
And all our God's affection
Receive thro' Thee alone.

2. Thy love's an emanation
Of his to Thee above:
Before the world's foundation
Thou didst thy people love:
And whom Thou mak'st thy dwelling
Thou surely wilt defend,
And by thy Spirit's sealing
Preserve us to the end.

"Continue ye in my love."—John 15, v. 9.

Thee, Jesus, I adore,
Whose word doth strength ordain,
And trusting in thy power
I shall thy love retain,
Continue in thy favour
Till soul and body part,
If Thou my dearest Saviour,
Continue in my heart.

"If ye keep my commandments, ye shall abide in my love: even as I have kept my Father's commandments, and abide in his love."—John 15, v. 10.

1. Obedience to our Lord must prove
The truth and constancy of love,
By this our faithfulness is tried,
By this we in his love abide:
Submissive to the Father's will
He bids us his commands fulfil,
And joins in all he owns for his
Obedience and eternal bliss.

2. Jesus, the true fidelity
The Spirit's fruits produce in me,
O let my life and heart confess
Th' effects of thine almighty grace,

That fill'd with faith which works by love,
And serving like thy saints above,
My soul may gain the joy prepar'd
The fulness of thine own reward.

"These things have I spoken unto you, that my joy might remain in you, and that your joy might be full."—John 15, v. 11.

1. Thou didst rejoice t' obey
Thy Father's utmost will:
Thy joy, dear Lord, in us shall stay
Who thy commands fulfil:
And when thy will is done
By us, like those above,
We find our heaven on earth begun
In pure obedient love.

2. The more like Thee we live,
The fuller joy is given,
We more abundant bliss receive,
And larger draughts of heaven:
Our confidence fill up,
Till faith improves to sight;
And then we lose both faith and hope
In love's supreme delight.

"This is my commandment, that ye love one another, as I have loved you."—John 15, v. 12.

Jesus, that new command of thine
I languish to obey:
The zeal of charity divine
Into my heart convey,
That in and for my God alone
I may embrace, esteem,
And after Thee my life lay down,
The brethren to redeem.

"Greater love hath no man than this, that a man lay down his life for his friends."—John 15, v. 13.

Greater love is not in man,
But greater is in God;
Life for sinners to regain
Jehovah sheds his blood,
Gives himself a sacrifice,
His own most precious blood expends,
Freely for his foes he dies
And turns them into friends.

"Ye are my friends, if ye do whatsoever I command you."—John 15, v. 14.

Who can the grace explain?
My God doth condescend
To call a worm, a man,
A sinful man, his friend;
If answering his designs
With a true heart and free,
I do what He injoins,
And doth himself in me.

"Henceforth I call you not servants; for the servant knoweth not what his Lord doth."—John 15, v. 15.

No longer held by servile fear,
Thy pleasure we fulfil,
And principled with love sincere
Delight to do thy will:
Thy will concerning us we know
That daily crucified
Blameless we in thy steps should go
To triumph at thy side.

"But I have called you friends."—John 15, v. 15.

To be thy ministers above
Seraphic flames aspire,
But we by thy redeeming love
We are exalted higher:
Our thoughts and praises it transcends
The love on men bestow'd;
Men are the favourites and friends,
The bosom-friends of God!

"All things that I have heard of my Father, I have made known unto you."—John 15, v. 15.

Thy friends instructed are by Thee,
Jehovah's only Son,
The secrets of eternity
Are to thy church made known;
The Unction doth in us abide,
In all thro' grace forgiven,
The Spirit is our inward Guide
And leads our souls to heaven.

"Ye have not chosen me, but I have chosen you."—John 15, v. 16.

Thee we never could have chose,
Dead in sins and trespasses:
But Thou hast redeem'd thy foes,
Bought the universal peace,
That our whole apostate kind
Might receive thee from above,
Call'd our common Lord to find,
Sav'd by free, electing love.

"I have ordained you, that you should go, and bring forth fruit, and that your fruit should remain."—John 15, v. 16.

Jesus, dost thou not ordain
Us to go, and fruit to bear,
Fruit that always shall remain,
Souls that may thy praise declare?
Sinners whom for Thee we win
Rescue then, and still defend,
From the world, and hell and sin
Save: and save them to the end.

"That whatsoever ye shall ask the Father in my name, he may give it you."—John 15, v. 16.

Father, in the powerful name
Of thy wel-beloved Son
Hear us, who the promise claim,
Keep us, till our work is done,
Give the faith to persevere,
Give the patience to endure,

Hide our life till Christ appear;
Then our full reward is sure.

"These things I command you, that ye love one another."—John 15, v. 17.

1. Obedient to our Lord's command,
Join every heart and every hand
Of those who Jesus know
T' advance the kingdom of his grace,
To publish our Redeemer's praise,
And spread his love below.

2. O were we in thy Spirit join'd!
One heart, one judgment, and one mind
To all the labourers give,
Unite us closer, Lord, to Thee,
That all may in thy name agree,
And to thy glory live:

3. That all may think, and speak the same,
Jointly our common Lord proclaim,
Our mission fully prove,
Determined Thee alone to know,
And to thy church the pattern show
Of pure primeval love.

"If the world hate you, ye know that it hated me before it hated you."—John 15, v. 18.

This is our consolation, Lord,
The world's fierce enmity
We bear, assur'd it first abhor'd
And persecuted Thee:
Thy friends in every age and place
Are hated by thy foe:
But if the scandal we embrace,
We shall the glory know.

"If ye were of the world, the world would love its own: but because ye are not of the world, but I have chosen you out of the world, therefore the world hateth you."—John 15, v. 19.

1. The hatred of our ancient foe
Contentedly who bear,
We are not of the world, we know,
And this themselves declare:
Their maxims we no more receive
As by their spirit led,
But faithfully to Jesus cleave,
And suffer with our Head.

2. As evil when they cast us out
And shun our company,
They will not suffer us to doubt
If we belong to Thee:
Saviour, whom they reject, disdain,
We find Thou dost approve,
And thus another mark obtain
Of thine electing love.

"Remember the word that I said unto you, The servant is not greater than the Lord. If they have persecuted me, they will also persecute you: if they have kept my saying, they will keep yours also."—John 15, v. 20.

1. Reason and sense would fain forget
The cross-imposing word,
"The servant is not more discreet,
"Or greater than the Lord:"
If Christ they persecuted here,
Their malice will pursue
His every saint and minister,
As sure as God is true.

2. "In pagan times it might be so,"
The prudent world allow,
"But all the true religion know,
"But all are Christians now."
Christians in name, they vex and grieve,
They persecute and kill
The men that would in Jesus live;
And all his word fulfil.

3. Because the truth they cannot bear
They hate its witnesses,
And all who live the gospel, share
The sanctified distress:
They will not, Lord, to Thine agree,
Who Satan's works approve,
And till they cease from hating Thee
Thy church they cannot love.

"But all these things will they do unto you for my names sake, because they know not him that sent me."—John 15, v. 21.

1. The world, our unrelenting foe,
May false pretences make,
But persecute thy flock, we know,
And hate us for thy sake
Because our God they have not known,
They treat us with despite,
And by their cruel judgments own
Our lives are in the right.

2. Yet will we not the world upbraid,
The infidels condemn:
Grace only hath the difference made
Betwixt our souls and them:
The grace which we may lose by pride,
May be on them bestow'd,
And when they feel thy blood applied,
They know the pardning God.

"If I had not come, and spoken unto them, they had not had sin: but now they have no cloak for their sin."—John 15, v. 22.

1. Hadst Thou not come to Adam's race,

And call'd them all to turn and live,
Offer'd thy free, sufficient grace
With power the pardon to receive,
They might have charg'd their death on Thee,
As reprobate by thy decree.

2. But who thy heavenly doctrine hear,
And view the wonders of thy power,
Yet will not their Creator fear,
Or Thee their Saviour-God adore,
They must their wilful folly own,
Undone; but by themselves undone.

3. No colour for their sin they have,
Their stubborn infidelity:
Thou dost declare thy will to save,
They will not thy salvation see,
But from thine arms of mercy fly,
And die, because resolv'd to die.

"If I had not done among them, the works which none other man did, they had not had sin."—John 15, v. 24.

1. Who to those gracious words of thine
Might sinless their assent refuse,
Soon as they saw the works Divine,
Condemn'd, and left without excuse,
Their wilful unbelief they shew'd,
And justly perish'd in their blood.

2. The world may thus our words deny
Who pardon and his Spirit claim,
But when our actions testify,
When all our lives declare the same,
They must th' authentic truth receive,
Thy real witnesses believe.

"They hated me without a cause."—John 15, v. 25.

1. Is there such dire malignity
And black ingratitude in man?
Such sin Satanical in me?
With grief and shame I own, I can
Vilest of fiends incarnate prove,
And hate a God whose name is love.

2. My mind is hatred against God,
My life rebellion and despite
To Thee, who hast on me bestow'd
Thy Son, thy soul's supream delight,
Thus to remove my enmity
As causeless, as thy love for me.

"But when the Comforter is come, whom I will send unto you from the Father, even the Spirit of truth, which proceedeth from the Father, he shall testify of me."—John 15, v. 26.

I.

Spirit of truth, the Comforter,
Proceeding from the Father's throne,
Come, and thine inward witness bear
Of Jesus, his eternal Son;
Him, the great uncreated Word,
Give me the God supreme to call,
Essence, I am, Jehovah, Lord,
My God who made, and died for all.

"But when the Comforter is come, whom I will send unto you from the Father, even the Spirit of truth, which proceedeth from the Father, he shall testify of me."—John 15, v. 26.

II.

1. Jesus, our exalted Head,
Regard thy people's prayer,
Send us in thy body's stead
Th' abiding Comforter,
From thy dazling throne above,
From thy Father's glorious seat
Send the Spirit of truth and love,
The' eternal PARACLETE.

2. Issuing forth from Him and Thee
O let the Blessing flow,
Pour the streaming Deity
On all thy church below:
Him to testify thy grace,
Him to teach how good Thou art,
Him to vouch thy Godhead, place
In every faithful heart.

3. God of God, and Light of Light,
Thee let him now reveal,
Justify us by thy right,
And stamp us with thy seal,
Fill our souls with joy and peace,
Wisdom, grace, and utterance give,
Constitute thy witnesses,
And in thy members live.

4. By the Holy Ghost we wait
To say, Thou art the Lord,
Sav'd, and to our first estate
In perfect love restor'd;
Then we shall in every breath
Testify the power we prove,
Publish thee in life and death
The God of truth and love.

"And ye also shall bear witness of Me, because ye have been with me from the beginning."—John 15, v. 27.

Thy weak disciple I,
Jesus, for years have been:
Thee let me testify
The Truth that frees from sin,
The Wisdom from above,
The Life to mortals given,

The Power of perfect love,
The Way to God in heaven.

JOHN CHAPTER SIXTEEN

"These things have I spoken unto you, that ye should not be offended."—John 16, v. 1.

1. Ye of the Christian sect,
By faith to Jesus join'd,
No mercy, or remorse expect,
No justice from mankind:
The world in every age
Their hate of Christ express,
And vent their antichristian rage
Against his witnesses.

2. But nothing shall offend
Or turn out of the way
You that on Jesus word depend,
And on his promise stay;
Forewarn'd, without surprize
Without concern or fear
Ye see the threatning storm arise,
Ye see your Saviour near.

3. Ye scorn the tyrants frown,
And to their wrongs submit,
And let them spurn, and tread you down,
As clay beneath their feet:
Beneath their rage ye fall
The victory to obtain,
All things endure, to conquer all,
And die with Christ to reign.

"They shall put you out of the synagogues: yea, the time cometh that whosoever killeth you will think that he doth God service."—John 16, v. 2.

1. Saviour the time is come,
And lo, as Thou hast said
The Spirit of persecuting Rome
Throughout the earth is spread!
With blind, religious zeal
The Formalists agree
Out of their churches to expel
The men that cleave to Thee.

2. Yet while Thou dost restrain
Their anger's last excess:
They dare not light their fires again,
Our numbers to increase:
Aware, that by our death
Thy church would growth receive,
They gnaw their tongues, and gnash their teeth,
And suffer us to live.

"These things will they do unto you, because they have not known the Father, nor me."—John 16, v. 3.

1. The world, who know not God,
Must hate the men that do,
That live by faith in Jesus' blood,
And Jesus tempers shew:
And if the sons of night
Usurp the Christian name,
They still abhor the sons of light,
In every age the same.

2. Their ignorance we find
The ground of enmity,
That hatred of the carnal mind
Against thy church and Thee:
But caution'd by our Lord,
We suffer all their ill
Who every day deny thy word,
And every day fulfil.

"But these things have I told you, that when the time shall come, ye may remember that I told you of them."—John 16, v. 4.

1. The long-predicted things
Fulfil'd we daily find,
And bless th' accomplishment which brings
Thy sayings to our mind:
We thus our strength renew,
And more than conquerors prove,
Assur'd, O God, that Thou art true,
That Thou art Power and Love.

2. Oppos'd by earth and hell
Their impotence we see,
Th' infernal gates cannot prevail
Against thy church and Thee:
The world we see o'rethrown,
Th' accusing fiend subdued,
Triumphant thro' thy word alone
Thy Spirit and thy blood.

"And these things I said not unto you at the beginning, because I was with you."—John 16, v. 4.

1. Christ the times and seasons knows
His counsels wise to give;
Grace he then on us bestows
His sayings to receive:
First his Godhead he reveals,
The Man who suffer'd in our stead,
Then our sympathy foretells,
Our dying with our Head.

2. Followers of the Crucified,
His grace almighty prove,
First believe for you He died
And trust his faithful love:
Then expect the great distress,
Crush'd by the persecutor's power,
Jesus patient mind possess,
And face the fiery hour.

"But now I go my way to him that sent me, and none of you asketh me, Whither goest thou?"—John 16, v. 5.

1. With the goods and ills below
Intirely occupied,
Nothing we desire to know,
We nothing seek beside;
Till Thou kindly dost rebuke
Our careless infidelity:
Then to things unseen we look,
And ask, O Lord, for Thee.

2. Present with thy people still,
And in thy word Thou art,
Dost thy precious Self reveal
To every praying heart;
While we faithfully inquire,
Thou dost our doubts and griefs remove,

God that answerest by fire,
The fire of heavenly love!

"But because I have said these things unto you, sorrow hath filled your heart."—John 16, v. 6.

1. The love of Jesus cross how rare!
We sadden its approach to see,
Afraid his sacred load to bear,
And trace his steps to Calvary:
Our dread to lose the goods below,
With fame, or friends, or ease, to part,
O'rewhelms the faithless soul with woe,
And fills with grief the selfish heart.

2. Sorrow may enter and remain;
A Christian heart it should not fill:
Saviour, in us it cannot reign,
Who bow submissive to thy will:
Our faith and hope superior rise,
And keep the struling evil down,
Till fully sav'd, we grasp the prize,
And thro' thy cross obtain thy crown.

"It is expedient for you that I go away."—John 16, v. 7.

Can I gain by losing Thee?
Yes; if so my state require,
If mine own infirmity
Force Thee, Saviour, to retire:
For when I thine absence mourn
Poor with poverty divine,
Soon the Comforter's return
Speaks my Lord forever mine.

"If I go not away, the Comforter will not come unto you."—John 16, v. 7.

1. Son of God, for Thee we languish,
Still thine absence we bemoan,
Overwhelm'd with grief and anguish,
Poor, forsaken, and alone:
Thou art to thine heaven departed;
See us thence, with pity see,
Comfortless and broken-hearted,
Drooping, dead for want of Thee.

2. Once thy blisful love we tasted,
Chear'd by Thee with living bread:
O how short a time it lasted,
O how soon the joy is fled!
Where is now our boasted Saviour,
Where our rapture of delight?
Thou hast, Lord, withdrawn thy favor,
Thou art vanish'd from our sight.

3. Yet Thou hast the cause unfolded,
Could we but the truth receive,
Thou in humbling love hast told it,
Needful 'tis for us to grieve:

Stript of that excessive pleasure,
Fondly we the loss deplore,
Till we find again our treasure,
Find, and never lose thee more.

4. That we may Thyself inherit,
Us Thou dost a while forsake,
That we may receive thy Spirit,
Thou hast took his comforts back;
After a short night of mourning
We again shall see thy face,
Triumph in thy full returning,
Glory in thy perfect grace.

5. For thy transient outward presence
We thine endless love shall feel,
Seated in our inmost essence
Thou shalt by thy Spirit dwell:
Jesus come; Thyself the Giver
Let us for the gift receive,
Let us live in God forever,
God in us forever live!

"But if I depart, I will send him unto you."—John 16, v. 7.

1. O Thou who by thy blood
Hast brought a world to God,
Thou who to thy Father gone
Dost in our behalf appear,
Hear thy desolate servants groan,
Send us down the Comforter.

2. Hadst Thou not purg'd our stain,
And gone to God again,
None of Adam's helpless race
Could that blessed Spirit find:
But Thou hast obtain'd the grace,
Purchas'd him for all mankind.

3. Didst Thou not plead above
For us thy dying love,
Never could we hope thine aid,
Never for thy Spirit call:
But Thou hast the Father pray'd,
Hast receiv'd the Gift for all.

4. "And if I go away,"
(By faith we hear thee say)
"I the Comforter will send,
"Comforter of you that grieve,
"All your goings to attend,
"Ever in your hearts to live."

5. Amen our hearts reply
Uplifted to the sky,
Pant to be thy blest abode,
Swell to be possest by Thee,
Fill'd with our indwelling God,
Fill'd to all eternity.

"When He is come, He will convince the world of sin, and of righteousness, and of judgment."—John 16, v. 8.

I.

1. Spirit of truth, from Jesus come,
Accomplishing his word,
Smite the sinners that presume
In vain to call him Lord:
Thou who only canst convince
The world and me of unbelief,
Shew the root of all my sins,
And fill my heart with grief.

2. Give me now myself to know

An helpless infidel,
Stranger to that God below
Who did my sorrows feel:
Not one grain of faith have I,
Till Thou reveal the gasping God,
Jesus' death for me apply,
And wash me in his blood.

"When He is come, He will convince the world of sin, and of righteousness, and of judgment."—John 16, v. 8.

II.

1. Holy Ghost, convince my heart
Of Jesus righteousness,
Counted just thro' his desert,
If I am sav'd by grace:
God appeas'd in Christ declare,
Our righteous Advocate above,
Speak in me his answer'd prayer,
And seal his dying love.

2. Open now my spirit's eyes
Th' Invisible to see,
Christ the just, above the skies
Demanding life for me:
While his righteousness I claim,
Thyself demonstrate me forgiven,
Justified in Jesus name,
And register'd in heaven.

"When He is come, He will convince the world of sin, and of righteousness, and of judgment."—John 16, v. 8.

III.

1. Spirit of true holiness,
Thy last, great work fulfil,
In my sinless soul express
The Father's righteous will;
With thy heavenly nature come,
And witness Christ in me reveal'd,
Satan and his works to doom,
And speak their ruin seal'd.

2. Cast th' usurper from his throne,
And utterly destroy,
Let thy kingdom stand alone
In holy peace and joy,
Joy which none can take away,
Peace that never shall remove,
Holiness without alloy,
And pure, millennial love.

"He shall convince the world of sin, because they believe not on me."—John 16, v. 9.

I.

1. Eternal Paraclete, descend,
Thou Gift and Promise of our Lord,
To every soul, till time shall end,
Thy succour, and Thyself afford,
Convince, convert us, and inspire;
Come, and baptize the world with fire.

2. Come, and display thy power below,
And work thy threefold work of

grace:
Compel mankind themselves to know,
Convince of sin th' apostate race,
Brood o're the deep of nature's night,
And speak again, Let there be light!

3. Thou only know'st the fallen man,
Thou only canst his fall reveal,
The monster to himself explain,
And make his darkness visible,
Pierce all the folds of hellish art,
And rent the covering from his heart.

4. Come then, thou soul-dividing Sword,
That dost from Jesus mouth proceed,
The foes and haters of their Lord
Find out, o'return, and strike them dead,
Destroy the sin that keeps them blind,
And slay the pride of all mankind.

5. Spirit of truth in all begin
That work of thine awakening power,
Convince the Christian world of sin,
Who Satan, and not Christ adore;
Who Jesus slight, reject, disclaim,
And never knew his saving name.

6. Shew them they never yet receiv'd
The Truth, whom they in words profess,
They never yet in Christ believ'd,
Or own'd the Lord their Righteousness:
Still in the damning sin they lie,
As pleas'd in unbelief to die.

7. People, and priest are doubly dead,
Are aliens from the life divine,
Gross darkness o're the earth is spread,
Till Thou into the conscience shine,
The powerful quick, conviction dart,
And sound the unbelieving heart.

8. O wou'dst Thou now in all reveal
The righteous wrath of hostile heaven,
Because the blood they will not feel,
The blood that shews their sins forgiven,
They will not Him their Lord receive,
They will not come to Christ, and live.

"He shall convince the world of sin, because they believe not on me."—John 16, v. 9.

II.

1. Arm of the Lord, awake,

awake,
The terrors of the Lord display,
Out of their sins the nations shake,
Tear their vain confidence away,
Conclude them all in unbelief,
And fill their hearts with sacred grief.

2. Impart the salutary pain,
The sudden soul-condemning power,
Blow on the goodliness of man,
Wither the grass, and blast the flower,
That when their works are all o'rethrown,
The word of God may stand alone.

3. Trouble the souls that know not God,
Their careless christ-less spirits wound,
O'rewhelm with their own sinful load,
And all their virtuous pride confound,
Their depth of wickedness reveal,
And shake them o're the mouth of hell.

4. Naked, and destitute, and blind
Themselves let the poor wretches see,
Their total fall lament to find,
Till every mouth is stopt by Thee,
And all the world with conscious fear
Guilty before their God appear.

5. Guilty, because they know not Him
Who liv'd, and died, their souls to save,
Who came, his people to redeem:
No part, or lot in Christ they have,
Till Thou the painful veil remove,
And shew their hearts his dying love.

"He shall convince the world of righteousness, because I go to my Father, and ye see me no more."—John 16, v. 10.

I.

1. Come then to those who want thine aid,
Who now beneath their burthen groan,
Bind up the wound Thyself hast made,
The righteousness of faith make known,
Offer'd to all of Adam's line,
The perfect righteousness Divine.

2. Convince the souls who feel their sin,
There is, there is a ransom found,
A better righteousness brought in,
And grace doth more than sin abound;
Pardon to all is freely given,
For Jesus is return'd to heaven.

3. He died to purge our guilty stain,
He rose the world to justify,
And while the heavens our Lord contain,
No longer seen by mortal eye,
He reigns our Advocate above,
And pleads for all his bleeding love.

4. His bleeding love tis Thine to seal
With pardon on the contrite heart:
To us, to us the grace reveal,
The righteousness impute, impart,
Discharge thy second function here,
And now descend the Comforter.

5. The righteousness of Christ our Lord
For pardon of our sins, declare,
Inspeak the everlasting word,
That freely justified we are,
By grace receiv'd, and brought to God,
And sav'd thro' faith in Jesus blood.

"He shall convince the world of righteousness, because I go to my Father, and ye see me no more."—John 16, v. 10.

II.

1. Spirit of faith, on Thee we call,
The merits of our Lord t' apply;
Convince, and then convert us all,
Condemn, and freely justify,
Set forth the all-atoning Lamb,
And spread the powers of Jesus name.

2. Jesus the merciful and just
To every heart of man reveal,
In Him enable us to trust,
Forgiveness in his blood to feel,
Let all in Him redemption find;
Sprinkle the blood on all mankind.

3. Is He not to his Father gone,
That we his righteousness might share?
And art not Thou on earth sent down,
The fruit of his prevailing prayer,
The Witness of his grace, and Seal,
The heavenly Gift unspeakable?

4. O might we each receive the grace
By Thee to call the Saviour mine!
Come, holy Ghost, to all our race
Bring in the righteousness Divine,
Inspire the sense of sin forgiven,
And give our earth a taste of heaven.

"He shall convince the world of judgment, because the prince of this world is judged."—John 16, v. 11.

1. Again, Thou Spirit of burning,

come,
Thy last great office to fulfil,
To shew the hellish tyrant's doom,
The hellish tyrant's doom to seal,
To drive him from thy sacred shrine,
And fill our souls with life divine.

2. Of judgment now the world convince,
The end of Jesus coming show,
To sentence their usurping prince,
Him, and his works destroy below,
To finish and abolish sin,
And bring the heavenly nature in.

3. Who gauls the nations with his yoke,
And bruises with an iron rod,
And smites with a continual stroke,
The world's fierce ruler and its god,
Wilt Thou not, Lord, from earth expel,
And chase the fiend to his own hell?

4. Yes, Thou shalt soon pronounce his doom,
Who rules in wrath the realms below,
That wicked One reveal, consume,
Avenge the nations of their foe,
In bright, vindictive lightning shine,
And slay him with the Breath Divine.

5. Then the whole earth again shall rest,
And see its paradise restor'd,
Then every soul in Jesus blest
Shall bear the Image of its Lord,
In finish'd holiness renew'd,
Immeasurably fill'd with God.

6. Spirit of sanctifying grace,
Hasten that happy gospel-day,
Come, and restore the fallen race,
Purge all our filth and blood away,
Our inmost souls redeem, repair,
And fix thy seat of judgment there.

7. Judgment to execute is thine,
To kill and save is thine alone;
Exert that energy Divine,
Set up thine everlasting throne,
The inward kingdom from above,
The boundless power of perfect love.

8. O wou'dst Thou bring the final scene,
Accomplish thy redeeming plan,
Thy great millennial reign begin,
That every ransom'd child of man
That every soul may bow the knee,
And rise, to reign with God in Thee!

"I have yet many things to say unto you, but ye cannot bear them now."—John 16, v. 12.

1. With milk Thou dost the infants feed,
Meat to the strong believers give,
In season due, as each hath need,
As each is able to receive;
Thou sow'st the seeds of truth sublime
In the dark heart of feeble man,
Thou know'st thine own appointed time
Thine own mysterious work t' explain.

2. Those many things at first unknown,
Thy Spirit shews us where to find,
Not by tradition handed down,
By men corrupt, deceitful, blind:
The acts by thine Apostles wrought
Repeating on our hearts He seals,
The truths in their Epistles taught,
And in the mystic book reveals.

"Howbeit, when He the Spirit of truth is come, he will guide you into all truth &c."—John 16, v. 13, 14, 15.

1. Spirit of truth descend,
And with thy church abide,
Our Guardian to the end,
Our sure, unerring Guide,
Us into the whole counsel lead
Of God reveal'd below,
And teach us all the truth we need
To life eternal know.

2. Whate'er Thou hear'st above
To us with power impart,
And shed abroad the love
Of Jesus in our heart:
One with the Father and the Son
Thy record is the same;
O make in us the Godhead known
Thro' faith in Jesus name.

3. To all our souls apply
The doctrine of our Lord,
Our conscience certify,
And witness with the word,
Thy realizing light display,
And shew us things to come,
The after-state, the final day,
And man's eternal doom.

4. The Judge of quick and dead,
The God of truth and love,
Who doth for sinners plead
Our Advocate above:
Exalted by his Father there
Thou dost exalt below,
And all his grace on earth declare,
And all his glory shew.

5. Sent in his name Thou art,
His work to carry on,
His Godhead to assert,
And make his mercy known:
Thou searchest the deep things of God,
Thou know'st the Saviour's mind,

And tak'st of his atoning blood
To sprinkle all mankind.

6. Now then of his receive,
And shew to us the grace,
And all his fulness give
To all the ransom'd race;
Whate'er he did for sinners buy
With his expiring groan,
By faith in us reveal, apply,
And make it all our own.

7. Descending from above,
Into our souls convey
His comfort, joy, and love,
Which none can take away,
His merit, and his righteousness
Which makes an end of sin;
Apply to every heart his peace,
And bring his kingdom in.

8. The plenitude of God
That doth in Jesus dwell,
On us thro' Him bestow'd
To us secure and seal:
Now let us taste our Master's bliss,
The glorious heavenly powers,
For all the Father hath is His,
And all He hath is ours.

"He shall take of mine, and shall shew it unto you."—John 16, v. 15.

Holy Ghost, by Him bestow'd
Who suffer'd on the tree,
Take of my Redeemer's blood,
And shew it unto me:
Witness with the blood Thou art;
Apply it to this soul of mine,
Now assure my sprinkled heart
It is the blood Divine.

"Ye shall weep and lament, but the world shall rejoice &c."—John 16, v. 20, 21, 22.

1. Jesus, dear departed Lord,
True and gracious is thy word;
We in part have found it true;
All thy faithful mercies shew.

2. Thou art to thy Father gone,
Thou hast left us here alone,
Left us a long fast to keep,
Left us for thy loss to weep.

3. Laugh the world, secure and glad,
They rejoice, but we are sad,
We alas, lament and grieve,
Comfortless, till Thou relieve.

4. As a woman in her throes
Sinks o'rewhelm'd with fears and woes,
Sinks our soul thro' grief and pain,
Strugling to be born again:

5. As she soon forgets to mourn,
Glad that a man-child is born,
Let us, lighten'd of our load,
Find deliverance in our God.

6. Jesus, visit us again,
Look us out of grief and pain,
Kindly comfort us that mourn,
Into joy our sorrow turn.

7. Thy own joy to us impart,

Root it deeply in our heart,
Joy which none can take away,
Joy which shall forever stay.

8. All the kingdom from above,
All the happiness of love,
Be it to thy mourners given,
Pardon, holiness, and heaven.

"Ye now have sorrow &c."—John 16, v. 22.

1. Come, holy, celestial Dove,
To visit a sorrowful breast,
My burthen of guilt to remove,
And bring me assurance and rest:
Thou only hast power to relieve
A sinner o'rewhelm'd with his load,
The sense of acceptance to give,
And sprinkle his heart with the blood.

2. With me if of old Thou hast strove,
And strangely with-held from my sin,
And tried by the lure of thy love
My worthless affections to win;
The work of thy mercy revive,
Thine uttermost mercy exert,
And kindly continue to strive,
And keep, till I yield thee my heart.

3. Thy call if I ever have known,
And sigh'd from myself to get free,
And groan'd the unspeakable groan,
And long'd to be happy in Thee;
Fulfil the imperfect desire,
Thy peace to my conscience reveal,
The sense of thy favour inspire,
And give me my pardon to feel.

4. If, when I had put thee to grief,
And madly to folly return'd,
Thy pity hath been my relief,
And lifted me up as I mourn'd;
Most pitiful Spirit of grace,
Relieve me again, and restore,
My spirit in holiness raise,
To fall, and to suffer no more.

5. If now I lament after God,
And gasp for a drop of thy love,
If Jesus hath bought thee with blood,
For me to receive from above;
Come heavenly Comforter, come,
True Witness of mercy divine,
And make me thy permanent home,
And seal me eternally thine.

"But I will see you again."—John 16, v. 22.

Return, most gracious Lord, return
Our souls' supreme delight:
Our hearts that in thine absence mourn
Shall triumph in thy sight;
With Thee we shall a joy obtain
Which none can take away,
For when Thou shew'st Thyself again,
Thou wilt forever stay.

"Whatsoever ye shall ask the Father in my name, he will give it you."—John 16, v. 23.

1. Father, I ask in Jesus name,
Most unworthy as I am
Thy blessing to receive,
Yet for my Saviour's sake alone
Thine only well-beloved Son
Thou wilt thy Spirit give.

2. I have no right to ask thy love,
But thro' Him who prays above
My Advocate with Thee,
Whose Spirit breathes into my breast
Desires which cannot be exprest,
And groans for grace, in me;

3. Thou knowst my Mediator's mind,
Hearst the Friend of all mankind
Who pleads before thy throne,
The thing deserv'd by Jesus grant,
The only thing on earth I want,
And make thy goodness known.

4. The Gift unspeakable Thou art;
Give Thyself into my heart
Mysterious One in Three,
And speak me by thy presence seal'd,
With Father, Son, and Spirit fill'd
Thro' all eternity.

"Hitherto ye have asked nothing in my name: ask, and ye shall receive, that your joy may be full."—John 16, v. 24.

1. Nothing have we ask'd of Thee,
Compar'd with what we want,
With thy large benignity,
And readiness to grant:
Thou hast promis'd to bestow
Whate'er we in thy name require:
Give us then Thyself to know,
Fulfil thine own desire.

2. Power to pray and never cease
We in thy name request,
Peace, inviolable peace,
And everlasting rest,
Plenitude of joy and love,
Till faith fill'd up can hold no more:
Then we join the hosts above,
And face to face adore.

"At that day ye shall ask in my name, and I say not unto you, that I will pray the Father for you."—John 16, v. 26.

1. Saviour, Thou needst not say
Thou wilt the Father pray:
More than words thy kindness prove,
Showers of never-ceasing grace
Shew, that Thou art heard above,
Advocate for all our race.

2. Thy prayer the world sustains,
And keeps from hellish pains;
Blessings on the saints it sheds,

Living streams of righteousness,
Answers all thy people's needs,
Fills their hearts with power and peace.

3. Thy prayer I daily feel
Seal'd with thy Spirit's seal:
Yes, the Comforter I find
Helping mine infirmity,
Bringing all thy words to mind,
Witnessing thy love for me.

4. Thro' Him impower'd I am
To ask in Jesus name,
Father, save, for Jesus sake,
Thine, who would continue thine,
Till I yield my spirit back,
Purchase dear of blood Divine.

"For the Father himself loveth you, because ye have loved me, and have believed that I came out from God."—John 16, v. 27.

1. Father of Christ our Saviour,
Thou hast thy mercy shew'd,
Receiv'd us into favor,
And shed thy love abroad:
Thou only didst discover
Jehovah from above;
And Him our heavenly Lover
We in thy Spirit love.

2. Before the world's foundation,
He from thy bosom came;
Th' eternal generation
Of Jesus we proclaim:
And every true believer,
Thou for thy child dost own,
And lovest us forever,
As members of thy Son.

"I came forth from the Father, and am come into the world: again, I leave the world, and go to the Father."—John 16, v. 28.

1. O Jesus, we adore Thee!
From all eternity,
There was no God before Thee:
There is no God but Thee:
Thee by thine incarnation,
Made manifest below
The God of our salvation
The Son of man we know.

2. Thy days of flesh are ended,
And to thy Father's breast
Thou art again ascended,
In thy own joy to rest:
Thy sanctifying Spirit
Thou wilt to us send down,
And we shall soon inherit
Thine everlasting throne.

"Lo, now speakest Thou plainly, and speakest no proverb &c."—John 16, v. 29, 30.

1. When Jesus imparts
The truth to our hearts,
And his sayings explains,
Not a shadow of doubt in our spirit remains;
The truth we confess,
The Interpreter bless,
And walk in his sight
And dwell with our Lord in a region of light.

2. The Omniscient Lord
Thou unfoldest thy word,
And preventing my prayer
Thou art pleas'd thy unsearchable grace to declare:
Thy grace I receive,
And with comfort believe,
And am sure Thou art He
Who from heaven came down, to inhabit in me.

"Jesus answered them, Ye do now believe. Behold the hour cometh, yea, is now come, that ye shall be scattered every man to his own, and shall leave me lone."—John 16, v. 31, 32.

1. Who doth indeed believe,
And now in Christ stands fast,
May fondly his own soul deceive,
And dream the danger past,
May ignorantly think
He now has conquer'd all,
And boast, secure on ruin's brink,
That he can never fall.

2. His consolation sweet
If Christ bestows on me,
It makes me ready to forget
My own infirmity;
Unless my Saviour near
A second grace impart,
And give me constantly to fear
This base unfaithful heart.

3. Ungrateful as I am
Thy favours I receive,
But call'd to suffer for thy name
My gracious Master leave:
I dread to drink thy cup,
When shame and pain are nigh,
Refuse to take thy burthen up,
And on thy cross to die.

4. Rejecting thy distress,
I oft have Thee forsook:
But all my past unfaithfulness
Thou on thyself hast took,
Hast bought for me the power
The humble constancy
To stand in every future hour
And live and die with Thee.

"Yet I am not alone, because the Father is with me."—John 16, v. 32.

1. A soul by man forsaken
May hang upon thy cross,
For Thou hast undertaken
The friendless sinner's cause;
His comfort in affliction
That Thou regard'st thine own,
And thro' thy dereliction
He dwells with God alone.

2. My Lord by all deserted
Remembers the forelorn,
Binds up the broken-hearted,
And blesses those that mourn:
And if in my temptation
Thou dost my soul attend,
I'l bear the tribulation
Which but with life shall end.

"These things have I spoken unto you, that in me ye might have peace. In the world ye shall have tribulation: but be of good chear, I have overcome the world."—John 16, v. 33.

I.

1. Yes, the promis'd tribulation,
Saviour, in the world we find,
Find the pledge of sure salvation
In a patient, chearful mind:
Thou the gracious word hast spoken;
Thy companions in distress,
Thankful we accept the token
Of our everlasting peace.

2. Peace surpassing all expression,
Heavenly bliss begun below,
Now, ev'n now in the possession
Of our loving Lord we know;
Peace the seal of sins forgiven,
Peace which Thou my Saviour art,
Fills with antedated heaven
Mine, and every faithful heart.

3. With an hostile world surrounded,
Us Thou dost at parting chear:
We shall never be confounded,
Conscious that Thou still art here,
We on all our foes shall trample,
Sharers of thy victory,
Followers of thy great example,
Conquerors of the world thro' Thee.

"These things have I spoken unto you, that in me ye might have peace. In the world ye shall have tribulation: but be of good chear, I have overcome the world."—John 16, v. 33.

II.

1. Away with our fears!
The Almighty appears
Our Captain and Head!
We are all to infallible victory led:
He hath singly subdued
The world with their god,
And he bids us "Pursue,"
And He speaks to our hearts "I have conquer'd for you!"

2. In his Spirit alone,
We are bold to go on,
His victory share,
And by patience o'recome the afflictions we bear:
No storms of distress
Can ruffle our peace,
While we aim at the prize,
And on Jesus his cross to his kingdom arise.

3. Our implacable foe
We daily o'rethrow,
To the evils submit,
And the goods upon earth we tread under our feet;
With Jesus endure,
Till for glory mature
Our souls we resign,
And ascend, to partake of the triumph Divine.

JOHN CHAPTER SEVENTEEN

"These things spake Jesus; and lift up his eyes, and said."—John 17, v. 1.

Himself, with lifted hands and eyes,
The great, vicarious Sacrifice
He offers up for all our race,
Our faithful, merciful High-priest
To God presenting his request,
For every child of Adam prays:
First for the twelve He interceeds,
And then for all believers pleads,
And then for all the ransom'd kind,
That seeing how the Christians live,
The world may faithfully receive
And every soul his Saviour find.

"Glorify thy Son, that thy Son also may glorify thee."—John 17, v. 1.

1. When full four thousand years are past,
The destin'd hour arrives at last
For God to glorify his Son:
Again the Father's arms receive
With Him in his own joy to live
The Partner of his heavenly throne!
Again th' angelic hosts adore
Their Maker-God, who was before
Angel or man began to be;
Who now resumes his sovereign right,
Brightness of uncreated Light,
I AM from all eternity!

2. Saviour and Prince inthron'd on high,
Thou dost thy Father glorify,
His majesty on earth display,
Who sent thee from his bosom down,
To make his love and justice known,
The universal debt to pay:
Thou dost his Name to man declare,
And stamp us with the character,
The truth and holiness divine,
The depths of deity reveal,
Thy members with thy Spirit seal,
That God in all his saints may shine.

"As Thou hast given him power over all flesh, that he should give eternal life to all whom thou hast given him."—John 17, v. 2.

Full power to Thee thy Father gave,
Supreme authority to save
Whoe'er their proffer'd Lord embrace:
All flesh is now by purchase thine,
Who didst thy precious life resign
To ransom the whole fallen race:
Thou woudst on every soul bestow

The faith thro' which thy people know
Eternal life on earth reveal'd:
Thou dost thy quickning Spirit give
To all who lovingly believe,
And find their blood-bought pardon seal'd.

John 17, v. 2, 3.

Fulness of power the world to save
Thy Father hath confer'd on Thee,
All flesh He to thy merit gave,
And Thou hast prov'd thy power on me;
Thou hast to me the Father shew'd,
Thine everlasting Spirit given:
And lo, I live the life of God,
I live on earth the life of heaven!

"This is eternal life, that they might know thee the only true God, and Jesus Christ whom thou hast sent."—John 17, v. 3.

In peace divine unspeakable
Th' angelic happiness we feel,
The life enjoy'd by saints above,
If Thou, his co-eternal Son,
The Father in thyself make known,
And tell our hearts, that God is Love:
Soon as Thou dost thy Spirit impart,
The one true God, we know Thou art,
Our Prophet, Priest, and King receive,
Sent to restore our paradise,
With Thee we mount above the skies,
With Thee ev'n now in heaven we live.

"I have glorified thee on earth: I have finished the work which thou gavest me to do."—John 17, v. 4.

Thou laidst on earth the stedfast base,
On which Thou dost thy kingdom raise,
Thy church to fill the realms above;
Thou hast with all his will complied,
And thro' thy passion glorified
The righteous God of truth and love:
Thou hast thy ministry fulfill'd,
Thy faithful testimony seal'd,
Finish'd the work thy Father gave,
Then, when Thou didst incline thine head,
A voluntary Victim bleed,
And die Thyself the world to save.

"And now, O Father, glorify thou me with thine own self, with the glory which I had with thee before the world was."—John 17, v. 5.

Jesus, thy prayer is answer'd

now,
The Man, Jehovah's Fellow Thou Art seated on thy Father's throne,
Bright Effluence of the Light Divine,
Thou dost in thy own glory shine
From all eternity thy own:
The Man who did our world redeem
Is cloath'd with Majesty supreme,
Thy body now is glorified,
Thou wear'st the mediator's crown,
That we may in thy right sit down,
And reign exalted at thy side.

"I have manifested thy name unto the men which thou gavest me out of the world: thine they were, and thou gavest them me; and they have kept thy word."—John 17, v. 6.

Whom first to Thee thy Father gave
On them thy present power to save
Jesus, Thou didst in mercy show;
His name, his nature, and his mind
Benevolent to all mankind
Thou bad'st thy twelve Apostles know:
His own and Abraham's progeny
The men whom He bestow'd on Thee
Redeeming from the world and sin,
With thine adopting Spirit blest,
Their gracious Father they confest,
And kept thy word which spoke them clean.

John 17, v. 6.

Redeem'd by thine electing love,
And separate from the world I am,
Endow'd with wisdom from above
I know the great Jehovah's name;
Thou hast the Deity declar'd,
His nature to my soul reveal'd:
And soon in me, thy death's reward,
Thy sayings shall be all fulfill'd.

John 17, v. 7.

Good in myself whereon to ground
My hopes of bliss, I seek no more,
Cause of all good in creatures found
Thy grace, O Father, I adore:
Instructed by thy humble Son,
(Thy Son from all eternity)
The Fountain of perfection own,
The whole of Excellence in Thee.

"Now they have known that all things whatsoever thou hast given me are of thee &c."—John 17, v. 7, 8.

In order foremost of the Three,
Fountain of Life and Deity,
Thy Father, with the twelve, we

own,
Jesus by highest heaven ador'd,
Thy mission, miracles, and word,
Thy Godhead is from Him alone:
Thy all Thou didst from God receive:
Thou didst to thine Apostles give
His words thro' thy internal grace:
They knew thee then his only Son,
Sent from the everlasting throne
To save our whole apostate race.

John 17, v. 8.

Jesus, in whom I now believe,
The Author of my faith Thou art,
The words Thou didst from God receive
Thy Spirit hath spoke them to my heart:
By these convinc'd I surely know
Thou art his co-eternal Son,
Who sent thee down to die below,
And bring his rebels to his throne.

"I pray for them: I pray not for the world, but for them which thou hast given me, for they are thine."—John 17, v. 9.

Not for the world of sinners dead,
Not for the living faithful seed,
As yet the common Saviour prays:
The Twelve, his most peculiar care,
First mention'd in his final prayer,
Are first establish'd by his grace:
Them for their office high design'd,
Elected out of all mankind,
To Thee by Love Paternal given,
Jesus, thy prayer doth first secure,
And make thy church's pillars sure,
And seal them, favourites of heaven.

John 17, v. 9.

Inspiring me with faith divine
Thou, Lord, out of the world hast took,
Hast pray'd for this weak soul of mine:
And for thy prayer's return I look:
Thy prayer's return I daily find,
Unlike the world of sinners live,
To Thee and to thy people join'd,
Till all thy fulness I receive.

"And all mine are thine, and thine are mine, and I am glorified in them."—John 17, v. 10.

Jesus, Jehovah's equal Son,
Thou and thy Father are but one,
Thine interests are with his the same,
Distinction none of thine and mine;
And hence the messengers divine
Were all Apostles of the Lamb,

Thy power throughout their lives was seen;
Superior to the power of men,
It prov'd the Source from which it flow'd,
When in thy name the sick they heal'd,
The dead they rais'd, the fiends expel'd,
And thus thy sovereign Godhead shew'd.

John 17, v. 10.

Jesus, thy Father's child I am,
Who made me by thy powerful word:
Me for thine own vouchsafe to claim,
The work, the purchase of my Lord:
Thou didst redeem me by thy blood,
That Thee my soul may glorify,
And triumph in a dying God,
And spread thy praise thro' earth and sky.

"And now I am no more in the world, but these are in the world, and I come to thee. Holy Father, keep &c."—John 17, v. 11.

While Jesus doth to heaven ascend,
He asks his Father to defend
The little flock he leaves below;
Dependant upon God He prays,
As man; as God confers the grace,
His own eternal birth to show;
The constant need of prayer t' explain,
Thro' which we sure support obtain
In every conflict and distress;
And blest with final victory,
Holy, and true, and good, to Thee
Ascribe the everlasting praise.

"Holy Father, keep through thine own name those whom thou hast given me, that they may be one as we are."—John 17, v. 11.

God heard the acceptable prayer
When Jesus to his Father's care
Did his first family bequeath:
Jehovah's name became their tower,
He magnified his saving power,
And made them faithful unto death:
His holiness did theirs secure,
And kept from all pollution pure;
His unity preserv'd them one,
Till conquerors thro' his faithful love
They found their place prepar'd above,
And join'd their Saviour on his throne.

John 17, v. 11.

1. Thy painful days of flesh are o're,
Redeemer of our fallen race,
We see thee, Lord, on earth no more,

Nor hear thy words of truth and grace:
But we, thy followers, are constrain'd
As in the midst of wolves to dwell,
Still in an evil world detain'd,
And urg'd by all the hosts of hell.

2. Jesus our Head to heaven is gone,
But we are in the world, distrest:
Father, respect thy praying Son,
And grant his prevalent request;
Preserve us pure from sinful blame,
From every spot and wrinkle free,
And keep thro' thine almighty Name
United each to each in Thee.

"While I was with them in the world, I kept them in thy name: those that thou gavest me I have kept, and none of them is lost, but the son of perdition."—John 17, v. 12.

1. The Shepherd good rejoic'd to keep,
While in the world, his numbred sheep,
The sheep his Father had bestow'd:
He kept them in his Father's name,
The power and goodness to proclaim,
The truth and faithfulness of God:
Jesus to Thee the twelve were given,
Their names were all inscrib'd in heaven;
Yet Judas by transgression fell;
His name was blotted from thy book,
When his own mercies he forsook,
And challeng'd his own place in hell.

2. That none of thine elect may boast,
One of the chosen twelve was lost,
He made himself perdition's son;
For whom Thou hadst a throne design'd,
He sold the Saviour of mankind,
And forfeited his promised crown:
Faithful he might have prov'd to thee,
But fell from his integrity
By no decree of thine compel'd;
He cast thy slighted grace away,
Gave himself up, the tempter's prey,
And thus his own destruction seal'd.

"And now I come to thee, and these things I speak in the world, that they might have my joy fulfilled in themselves."—John 17, v. 13.

While yet Thou liv'dst a Man of woe,
Thy latest words of grace below,

Thou didst to thy disciples leave,
That soon recalling them to mind,
They might thy power and Spirit find,
And consolation strong receive:
Thee when they saw no longer here,
They felt th' indwelling Comforter
Accomplishing thy whole design,
Granted they found thy prayer and seal'd,
With all thy joy and Spirit fill'd,
With all the plenitude Divine.

"I have given them thy word; and the world hath hated them, because they are not of the world, even as I am not of the world."—John 17, v. 14.

Who first receiv'd th' ingrafted word,
Thy followers by the world abhor'd,
By patience and obedience shew'd
The faith which thro' thy sayings came,
And gloried in their Master's shame
Undaunted confessors of God:
Thy marks were in their bodies seen:
The filth and offscouring of men
Thy badge and daily cross they bore:
And still whoe'er belong to Thee
Detested by the world must be,
Till time and sin shall be no more.

"I pray not that thou shouldest take them out of the world, but that thou shouldest keep them from evil."—John 17, v. 15.

Thy members must their trial take,
And suffer, Saviour, for thy sake,
And to thy will submit their own,
The general scorn and hate abide,
Dead to the world and crucified,
Till all their work on earth is done:
The earliest preachers of thy love
Thou woudst not, Lord, from earth remove;
Thy presence from the evil pure
Preserv'd, and kept them in the flame,
Till out of great distress they came,
And made their crown by sufferings sure.

John 17, v. 15.

Taught by our Lord we will not pray
To be out of the world remov'd,
But keep us in our evil day
Till patient faith is fully prov'd;
From sin, the world, and Satan's snare
The members of thy Son defend,
Till all thy character we bear,
And grace matur'd in glory end.

"They are not of the world, even as I am not of the world."—John 17, v. 16.

Partakers of thy ministry,
The men who still are sent by Thee
Are men, not of the world but God;
They all its vain desires deny,
Against its evils testify,
And tread the path their Pattern trod:
Thy mind and Spirit they possess,
The tempers of their Lord express,
Acquainted with thy sorrows live,
Themselves of no repute they make,
And poor becoming for thy sake
Thy cup in life and death receive.

"Sanctify them through thy truth: thy word is truth."—John 17, v. 17.

That Spirit pure of truth and love,
That sacred Unction from above
Did thy first messengers ordain;
It set them for Thyself apart,
Reveal'd thy word to every heart,
And cleans'd their lives from every stain:
Still by the gospel word applied
Thy ministers are sanctified,
The truth they lovingly receive,
It saves their souls and sets them free;
And consecrated, Lord, to Thee
Thy holy word they preach and live.

John 17, v. 17.

Thro' the pure evangelic word
Thine image, Lord, on us impress,
And speak us after God restor'd
In true internal holiness:
Thy word the channel of thy love
Thro' meek and patient faith apply,
And fit us for the joys above,
And take us spotless to the sky.

"As thou hast sent me into the world, even so have I also sent them into the world."—John 17, v. 18.

Ambassador of the Most-high,
Thy Father sent thee from the sky
To make his truth and mercy known;
And every chosen instrument
By thee into the world is sent,
To carry thy great business on:
They of thy work obtain a part,
And labouring sinners to convert,
Their ministerial task fulfil,
Ready their lives to sacrifice,
(That precious souls may reach the skies)
And with their blood the record seal.

"And for their sakes I sanctify myself, that they may be sanctified through the truth."—John 17, v. 19.

Jesus, was ever love like thine!
Victim immaculate, Divine,
Self-offer'd in the sinner's place,
For thine elect Apostles slain,
For all who their commission gain,
For every child of Adam's race!
We thro' thy death the power receive,
The sanctifying truth believe,
Partakers of thy sacrifice
Bodies and souls present to God,
With thine all-patient mind endow'd,
And to thy heavenly kingdom rise.

"Neither pray I for these alone, but for them also which shall believe on me through their word."—John 17, v. 20.

1. Faithful and merciful High-priest,
Supreme in power and love Divine,
While underneath thy wings we rest,
We in thine intercession join:
Saviour, Thou dost thy dying care
To every age alike extend,
And by the virtue of thy prayer
Thy church is kept, till time shall end.

2. Faith thro' the Apostolic word
The faith of thine elect we feel;
The Holy Ghost, my God and Lord
Thee in my heart doth now reveal;
I know my interest in thy blood,
My pardon seal'd I now receive,
Thy death hath brought my soul to God,
And trusting in thy death, I live.

"That they all may be one, as thou Father art in me and I in thee, that they also may be one in us: that &c."—John 17, v. 21.

1. Jesus, Thee the Head we own,
The Saviour of mankind:
Thou of twain hast made us one,
Hast Jews and Gentiles join'd:
Both thy mystic body are,
In Thee the scatter'd members meet:
Thro' thine all-prevailing prayer
Our harmony compleat.

2. By one Spirit inspir'd and led
We to each other cleave,
Nourish'd with immortal Bread
The life of faith we live;
Call'd to purity and peace,
The fellowship of saints we prove
In the bond of perfectness,
And unity of love.

3. In thy heavenly Father one,
We all his children are,
Of thy flesh and of thy bone

Thy holy nature share;
All into thy Spirit drink,
All baptis'd into thy name,
One in heart and mind, we think,
And act, and speak the same.

4. Closer knit to God and Thee
Jesus, in us make known
All the hidden mystery,
The holy Three in One:
Thus convinc'd the world shall feel
Thy Father's gracious will and mind,
Know He sent thee down to dwell
In us, and all mankind.

"And the glory which thou gavest me, I have given them: that they may be one, even as we are one."—John 17, v. 22.

1. What to Thee thy Father gave
Thou dost on man bestow,
Souls re-born thy Spirit have,
Thy glorious image show,
Stampt with real holiness,
Partakers of thy life, they shine,
All thy members, Lord, express
The Unity Divine.

2. One, though not the same, with Thee,
And each with each they are,
The Divine plurality,
And simple nature share:
In thy permanent abode
When Father, Son, and Spirit meet,
Transcript of the tri-une God
Thy Church is all compleat.

"I in them, and they in me, that they may be made perfect in one, and that the world may know that thou hast sent me, and hast loved them, as thou hast loved me."—John 17, v. 23.

1. Jesus, with thy Father come,
And bring our inward Guide,
Make our hearts thy humble home,
And in thine house abide,
Shew us with thy presence fill'd,
Fill'd with glory from thy throne,
Wholly sanctified, and seal'd,
And perfected in one.

2. Thus thy Father's kind intent
Let the whole world perceive,
Know He from his bosom sent
His Son, that all may live,
Sent Thee every soul to bless,
That in thy loving Spirit join'd
All may with one mouth confess
The Saviour of mankind.

3. By the miracle of grace
Bring every outcast in,
Shew to all our ransom'd race
The power that saves from sin;
All our ransom'd race convert,
That every child of man may prove
Thee residing in his heart,
And know that God is Love.

4. God in Christ is Love to me,
He loves me for thy sake,

Loves us all, as part of Thee
Who didst our nature take:
Wills our God that all should live,
Thro' faith in Thee his favourite Son,
Should thy proffer'd joy receive,
And triumph on thy throne.

"Father, I will that they also whom Thou hast given me, be with me where I am; that they may behold my glory which thou hast given me: for thou lovedst me before the foundation of the world."—John 17, v. 24.

1. Lord, thy Testamental Will
Is ratified by God,
Seal'd by thy own Spirit's seal,
And written in thy blood:
Trusting, sharing in thy death
To us thy life shall all be given,
Us to whom thou dost bequeath
Th' inheritance of heaven.

2. As his only Son and Heir
Thou challengest thine own,
Askest that thy church may share
Thine everlasting throne,
Praying in thy proper right,
Thou dost for us demand the grace,
The beatifying Sight
Of thy own glorious face.

3. Head and members, Christ intire
We must together be,
In the bosom of thy Sire,
And glorified with Thee:
Thee, before the world began,
And us He did as thine approve,
Chosen in the Son of man
By his eternal love.

"O righteous Father, the world hath not known thee; but I have known thee, and these have known that thou hast sent me."—John 17, v. 25.

1. Father of our gracious Lord,
Thy righteousness we own;
By th' angelic host ador'd,
And by thy children known,
Hidden from the world Thou art,
Till humbly they thy Son receive;
Then they find him in their heart,
And one with God they live.

2. We have surely found him here,
Sent in his saints to dwell,
Faith's Almighty Finisher
Thy justice to reveal:
Justice now confers the prize,
Deserv'd, and purchas'd by thy Son:
Justice wills that we should rise,
His members, to his throne.

"And I have declared unto them thy name, and will declare it: that the love wherewith thou hast loved me, may be in them, and I in them."—John 17, v. 26.

1. Christ our Head, and heavenly Lord,

Thou only canst proclaim
By thine own inspoken word
Thy heavenly Father's name:
Thou to us hast made it known,
His Power, and Wisdom from above,
Thee his Righteousness we own,
His Truth, and Life, and Love.

2. Thou his name unspeakable
Wilt farther yet declare,
Till we all his nature feel,
And all his impress bear,
Till compleat in holiness
We comprehend the mystery,
Fill'd with all his love and grace,
Forever fill'd with Thee.

3. Come, thou Holy one of God,
And by that Spirit Divine
Shed in all our hearts abroad
Thy Father's love and thine:
Fit us for the blisful Sight,
And when Thou hast thy saints prepar'd,
Glory on our foreheads write,
Thyself our full Reward!

JOHN CHAPTER EIGHTEEN

"Jesus went forth with his disciples over the brook Cedron."—John 18, v. 1.

The Emblem had in trembling haste
The brook with his companions past,
Mournful, disconsolate, dismay'd,
When David from his rebel fled:
But calm the Son of David goes
To meet his fierce, ungrateful foes,
The life of Absalom to buy,
And for a world of rebels die.

"Where was a garden, into the which he entred and his disciples."—John 18, v. 1.

For evil in a garden done
Christ in a garden must atone:
Freely he comes, by suffering there,
Our loss of Eden to repair,
Bears in the memorable place
The sins of our devoted race,
Takes on himself the wrath of God,
To quench it with his tears and blood.

"And Judas also which betrayed him, knew the place: for Jesus ofttimes resorted thither with his disciples."—John 18, v. 2.

The place apostates know,
And never can forget,
Where Jesus and his church below
In solemn worship meet:
Yet Him in vain they claim
Who to his foes desert:
Disciples, confessors in name,
But traitors false in heart.

"Judas having received a band of men ... cometh &c."—John 18, v. 3.

With sorrow, Lord, and fear
We thine Apostle see
Renounce his sacred character,
And hell prefer to Thee;
For we who fiercely blame
The wretch with Satan fraught,
Left to ourselves, should do the same,
Should sell our God for nought.

"Judas cometh thither with lanterns, and torches, and weapons."—John 18, v. 3.

When Satan rules and urges on
The blindfold slaves of wickedness,
Lanterns they bring, to seek the Sun,
And arms, th' Omnipotent to seize.

"Jesus therefore, knowing all things that should come upon him, went forth, and said unto them, Whom seek ye?"—John 18, v. 4, 5, 6.

Freely He lays the ransom down,
The life which none could take away,
Goes forth to meet the ills foreknown,
Yields himself up an easy prey;
His foes by miracle struck blind,
Struck down by one resistless word

Their Lord instructs himself to find,
And gives them power to seize their Lord.

"They answered him, Jesus of Nazareth. Jesus saith unto them, I am he. And Judas also which betrayed him stood with them."—John 18, v. 5.

Sinners to seek and save He came,
They seek, that they their God may slay:
And I of the dire number am,
And Jesus with a kiss betray:
But let the season past suffice,
That with the ruffian-band I stood;
I see thee now with open'd eyes,
And prostrate own My Lord, my God!

"As soon then as he had said unto them, I am He, they went backward, and fell to the ground."—John 18, v. 6.

1. That irresistible I AM
Declares the present Deity,
Yet none convinc'd their God proclaim,
Whose power and love they feel and see:
Who struck their bodies to the ground,
He might have struck their souls to hell,
In chains of penal darkness bound,

And plung'd in flames unquenchable.

2. Ah, what can outward wonders do,
T' o'recome the stubbornness of man?
Unless Thou bind our spirits too,
Thy judgments cast us down in vain:
My hopes, designs, or health o'rethrow,
Yet will I not to Thee submit;
But give my heart thy love to know,
And then I worship at thy feet.

"Then asked he them again, Whom seek ye? and they said Jesus of Nazareth."—John 18, v. 7.

1. Jesus the oft-repeated call
Doth to obdurate sinners give,
Time to recover from their fall,
To weigh their ways, repent, and live:
He turns us to our hearts again,
He asks me, whom I seek below,
Would I the world, or Christ obtain,
The joy of grace or nature know?

2. Him do I seek, by faith t' adore,
Or by my sins to crucify?
Jesus, Thou dost my thoughts explore,
My soul is naked to thine eye:
I seek, or think I seek my Lord,
That when I find thy precious grace,
Thy name may be confess'd, ador'd,
And hallow'd with eternal praise.

"If therefore ye seek me, let these go their way."—John 18, v. 8.

1. Anxious thy followers' lives alone
To save, forgetful of thine own,
Thou dost by thy command
Strike down whoe'er their God oppose,
Or secretly restrain thy foes,
And rule the ruffian band.

2. Thy servants, Lord, they must dismiss,
They cannot thine Apostles seize
Prohibited by Thee,
Who freely dost thy life resign
A bleeding sacrifice divine
For all mankind, and me.

"That the saying might be fulfilled which he spake, Of them which thou gavest me have I lost none."—John 18, v. 9.

1. Shepherd of souls, the lambs and sheep
Thy tender love delights to keep
In every dangerous hour,
Thou hid'st us by thy guardian love
Beyond the reach of sin, above
The world, and Satan's power.

2. Safety and strength in Thee we have,
Thou wilt our souls and bodies save,
Who on thine arm depend:
That arm omnipotent, divine,
Which holds this feeble soul of mine,
Shall keep me to the end.

3. Me by thy Father's love bestow'd
Thou wilt preserve, the gift of God,
Nor with thy purchase part,
(Ready so oft to leave the fold;)
Thou wilt not quit thy mercy's hold,
Or lose me from thy heart.

2. Let heathens force by force repel,
Let bigots boast their fiery zeal,
The cup which God to Christ did give,
Ye followers of the Lamb, receive,
(The cup to all his members given)
And die on earth, to reign in heaven.

3. Jesus, I would with joy embrace
Thy portion here, thy patient grace,
Meekly my nature's will resign,
Accept the precious gift divine,
Thy sacred cup of grief unknown,
Thy cross, which mounts me to thy throne.

"Then the band, and the captain, and the officers of the Jews took Jesus, and bound him."—John 18, v. 12.

I.

Adorable captivity
Which sets a world of prisoners free
From sin and Satan's iron chain!
Our souls Thou offer'st to release;
Pardon, and liberty, and peace
We all may thro' thy bonds obtain.
Jesus, thy dear redeeming grace
By faith we thankfully embrace,
Injoy our perfect freedom here,
Servants of righteousness we rise,
As sons of God regain the skies,
As heirs at thy right hand appear.

"Then the band, and the captain, and the officers of the Jews took Jesus, and bound him."—John 18, v. 12.

II.

Happy the highly-favour'd man
Who wears thine honourable chain,
To inward liberty restor'd!
Jesus, with thee in Spirit join'd,
He triumphs, for thy cause confin'd,
The joyful prisoner of the Lord:

Who thy captivity partake,
And calmly suffer for thy sake,
Our bonds are sanctified by thine:
And when we have endur'd with Thee
Thy death of pain and infamy,
We shall in all thy glories shine.

"Now Caiaphas was he which gave counsel to the Jews, that it was expedient that one man should die for the people."—John 18, v. 14.

The world exult to see pursued
Their counsel to destroy the good,
And God permits them to oppress,
And curses with their own success:
When priests against his church conspire,
Accomplishing the fiend's desire,
Their triumph doth their fall portend,
Their joys in endless sorrows end.

"Simon Peter followed Jesus."—John 18, v. 15.

I.

With nature for his guide,
The self-presuming man,
Who follows in the strength of pride,
He follows Christ in vain:
He cannot persevere,
Or stand a threatning word,
But struck with misbelieving fear
Basely disowns his Lord.

"Simon Peter followed Jesus."—John 18, v. 15.

II.

"Let my disciples go,"
The warning Saviour said;
But Peter must his courage show,
And stay, while others fled,
Single in Jesus cause
He dares a troop defy,
But dares not follow to the cross,
Or with his Master die.

"Simon Peter followed Jesus."—John 18, v. 15.

III.

Trusting his own weak heart
He could not God believe,
Who vow'd, though all beside depart,
He will to Jesus cleave:
"Thy persecuted Lord
"Thou canst not now pursue:"
He tries, but finds the slighted word,
By sad experience true.

"That disciple went in with Jesus into the palace of the high priest."—John 18, v. 15.

Occasions sure to meet
Of sin and sad disgrace
To the proud mansions of the

great
Our Lord we will not trace:
The houses of his foes
Unfit for Christians are;
And Jesus by compulsion goes,
Goes to be humbled there.

"Then went out that other disciple, and brought in Peter."—John 18, v. 16.

Thou never wilt forget
His fatal courtesy
Who to the houses of the great
Admittance gains for thee:
Expos'd to shame and pain,
Thou must take up thy cross,
Or suffer, if the world thou gain,
Thy soul's eternal loss.

"Then said the damsel Art thou also one of this man's disciples? He saith, I am not."—John 18, v. 17.

I.

The man that on himself relies
By blind presumption led,
Strong as a rock in his own eyes,
Is weaker than a reed:
With fainting heart and feeble mind
He fears his Lord to own:
And lo, by the first breath of wind
The pillar is o'rethrown!

"Then said the damsel, Art thou also one of this man's disciples? He saith, I am not."—John 18, v. 17.

II.

Urg'd by the hostile world, unless
The truth I testify,
And one of his, myself confess,
My Master I deny:
I still renounce my Lord in deed,
Unless I serve his will,
Obedient in his footsteps tread,
And all his mind fulfil.

"And Peter stood with them, and warmed himself."—John 18, v. 18.

1. The weak with prudent fear should shun
Th' inquisitive and idle croud,
Far from th' infectious converse run
Of men who blush to mention God,
Assemblies where the fiend presides,
And all their tongues and counsels guides.

2. The fools' companion is not wise,
Nor can his innocence maintain,
His virtue with the slaves of vice,
Or touch the world without a stain;
That pitch which makes the conscience foul,

And ruins, and destroys the soul.

"The high priest then asked Jesus of his disciples, and of his doctrine."—John 18, v. 19.

1. If men the Sovereign Priest arraign,
If men th' eternal Truth decry,
Shall thy disciples, Lord, complain?
Or meekly to the charge reply
Suspected, or accus'd, like Thee,
Of error and conspiracy?

2. Still let the world their charge repeat,
As factious innovators brand,
The servants like the Master treat;
At their unrighteous bar we stand,
We stand, their utmost wrath t' abide,
We stand—with Jesus at our side!

"In secret have I said nothing."—John 18, v. 20.

1. O might I, like Jesus, be
Foe to guile and secrecy,
Walk as always in his sight,
Free and open as the light,
Boldly to mankind appeal,
All the truth of God reveal!

2. Lord, that I to friend and foe
May thy utmost counsel show,
To thy messenger impart
The true nobleness of heart,
The unfeign'd simplicity
The pure mind, which was in Thee.

"Why askest thou me? ask them which heard me, what I have said unto them: behold they know what I said."—John 18, v. 21.

1. Join we, Lord, as taught by Thee,
Stedfastness and modesty,
Patiently our souls possess,
Resolute the truth confess,
Speak it, when accus'd by men,
Firmly to the last maintain.

2. Challenge we the world to show
What they of thy servants know:
Walk we not in open day?
Let the most malicious say,
Real testimony give
How we speak, and how we live!

"One of the officers struck Jesus with the palm of his hand."—John 18, v. 22.

1. O'rewhelm'd with grief and shame I see
My Saviour buffetted for me;
For faults which I have done,
Meekly He doth th' affront sustain,
T' abase the loftiness of man,
And for my pride atone.

2. Confounded in the dust I wou'd

The sufferings of an humbled God
With meekest awe adore,
Insulted as my Pattern be,
And never feel the injury,
And never murmur more.

"Jesus answered him, If I have spoken evil, bear witness of the evil: but if well, why smitest thou me?"—John 18, v. 23.

Silent we turn the other cheek,
The private injury pass by;
Yet when requir'd for God to speak,
From crimes ourselves to justify,
Submissive to the powers that be
We dare not obstinate appear,
But speak with mild sincerity,
Our office, not ourselves, to clear.

"Now Annas had sent him bound unto Caiaphas."—John 18, v. 24.

1. Thou, Saviour, by thy sacred bands
Didst expiate man's audaciousness,
Who rashly dared extend his hands
The interdicted fruit to seize:
Thy hands are tied to loosen ours,
The instruments of sin set free,
Redeem our captivated powers,
And give us hearts to die for Thee.

2. Those voluntary bonds of thine
Break all the bonds my will has made,
And fill with confidence divine
My soul on my Redeemer stay'd:
In perfect liberty from sin
I serve thee as thy hosts above
When Thou hast made me free within,
Free to obey, and praise, and love.

"Art thou one of his disciples? He denied, and said, I am not."—John 18, v. 25.

See the strength that is in man!
Peter by a word o'rethrown
Checks our self-presumption vain,
Makes our utter weakness known:
Thus we feel our helplesness,
Tremble at temptation nigh,
Own our constant need of grace,
From ourselves to Jesus fly.

"Peter then denied again, and immediately the cock crew."—John 18, v. 27.

I.

Thrice he promis'd to confess,
Thrice his suffering Lord denies,
Thus performs his promises,
Bonds and death he thus defies!
But let Jesus' look convert;
Then the reed a rock shall prove,
Thrice express his faithful heart,
Thrice protest his humble love.

"Peter then denied again, and immediately the cock crew."—John 18, v. 27.

II.

1. Saviour, till thine eye recalls,
Till thou dost thy work begin,
Lower still the sinner falls,
Harden'd falls from sin to sin:
O that now the cock might crow!
Griev'd at my apostasy,
Jesus, thy compassion show,
Turn, and look me back to Thee.

2. Though I have thy Spirit griev'd,
Have so oft relaps'd again,
In thy mercy's arms receiv'd,
Favour I may still obtain:
Peter gives me back my hope;
After frequent falls restor'd,
I shall soon be lifted up,
Praise again my pardning Lord.

"They themselves went not into the judgment-hall, lest they should be defiled."—John 18, v. 28.

1. Legal impurity they dread
Who innocence oppress,
Nor fear the guiltless blood they shed
Should stain their consciences:
And thus our formalists maintain
Their sanctity's renown,
While gnats out of the cup they strain,
And swallow camels down.

2. Bitter, implacable, and proud
They in externals trust,
Abhor the genuine sons of God,
And persecute the just;
Heathens profane far off they see,
At open sinners start,
With eyes full of adultery,
And murther in their heart.

"If he were not a malefactor, we would not have delivered him up unto thee."—John 18, v. 30.

'Tis thus our fierce, unrighteous foes
Their enmity declare,
Guilty of blackest crimes suppose,
And drag us to the bar:
The tedious forms of justice vain
They furiously pass by,
Pronounce us impious and profane,
And judge, before they try.

"The Jews said unto him, It is not lawful for us to put any man to death. That the saying of Jesus might be fulfilled, which he spake, signifying what death he should die."—John 18, v. 31, 32.

1. A criminal they could not doom,
They might an innocent release,
Permitted by imperious Rome
To hear and try the witnesses:
But lo, the rage of Jewish zeal

Conspires with Roman policy,
Thy sure prediction to fulfil
And nail thee, Saviour, to the tree.

2. And shall thy followers complain,
Who in thy steps profess to go,
Condemn'd by rash, oppressive man,
Entreated like Thyself below?
Or rather patiently receive
The treatment which confirms us thine,
And when pronounc'd unfit to live,
Our spirits on thy cross resign!

"Art thou the king of the Jews?"—John 18, v. 33.

1. King of the Jews and Gentiles too,
Born from above, and form'd anew
By thy creating power,
Thee, Jesus, we with joy confess,
And prostrate at thy throne of grace
Thy majesty adore.

2. O wouldst thou to my heart explain
The nature of thy Spirit's reign
The hidden mystery,
That fill'd with peace and love unknown
My pure, self-emptied soul may own
Thou art a King in me.

"What hast thou done?"—John 18, v. 35.

Jesus, what hast Thou done?
No evil was in thee;
But thou hast made my deed thine own,
A criminal for me:
For Adam's sinful race
Thou art condemn'd to die,
That thro' thy blood and righteousness
We all may reach the sky.

"My kingdom is not of this world &c."—John 18, v. 36.

1. Not by force of arms upheld
The kingdom of thy grace
Stands invisible, conceal'd
In the peculiar race,
Ruling over all it stands,
A kingdom that can never move,
Stablish'd by Almighty hands,
The Hierarchy of Love!

2. Not with worldly pomp and power
Thou dost thy sway maintain,
Righteousness and peace restore
And happiness to man:
All thy joyful subjects own,
Thy Spirit in thy kingdom given
Makes our hearts thy humble throne,
And turns our earth to heaven.

"Thou sayest, I am a king. To this end was I born, and for this cause came I into the world, that I might bear witness unto the truth."—John 18, v. 37.

1. Jesus, King of righteousness,
Thy people taught by Thee,
Bold before the world confess
Thy royal dignity:
Born for this alone we are,
And in thy testimony join,
By our words and lives declare
The power of truth Divine.

2. Thee, the Truth we testify
Which makes us free from sin,
God descended from the sky
And manifest within;
Thee our Life in life and death
Our real Holiness we praise,
Publish with our latest breath
The Truth of love and grace.

"Every one that is of the truth heareth my voice."—John 18, v. 37.

1. All that to the Truth belong
The Saviour's word believe,
Manna dropping from thy tongue
With humble joy receive,
Listening to thy voice fulfil
The law of liberty and love,
Serve thy good and perfect will
As angels do above.

2. Be it all my business, Lord,
While here on earth I stay,
Gladly to attend thy word,
And faithfully obey:
Thou to me thy Spirit give
And taught by his anointing, I
Witness of the truth shall live,
And in its service die.

"Pilate saith unto him, What is truth?"—John 18, v. 38.

1. The men who human praise desire,
Who set their heart on things below,
Like Pilate, carelesly inquire,
But will not wait the truth to know,
But soon their slighted Lord forsake,
And cast his words behind their back.

2. Not with a cold or double heart,
But faith's sincerity unfeign'd
We ask thee, Saviour, to impart
The knowledge in Thyself contain'd,
And give our newborn souls to prove
The Truth the Life of perfect Love.

"I find in him no fault at all."—John 18, v. 38.

1. His innocence we daily find
Acknowledg'd, and abandon'd too
By men, who favourably inclin'd
To Truth, yet tremble to pursue
The narrow path by Jesus trod,

And suffer with a patient God.

2. Jesus, the only faultless Man,
Thee would I constantly confess,
Thy sovereign Deity maintain,
Stand by thy hated witnesses,
Undaunted for thy cause contend,
And Thee in life and death defend.

"But ye have a custom that I should release unto you one at the passover: will ye therefore that I release unto you the king of the Jews?"—John 18, v. 39.

I.

Arm'd with authority the man
Who for an innocent intreats,
He loses all his efforts vain,
His own high dignity forgets:
He should the clam'rous croud command,
Declare for truth and equity,
Th' oppressors to their face withstand,
And set the injur'd captive free.

"But ye have a custom that I should release unto you one at the passover: will ye therefore that I release unto you the king of the Jews?"—John 18, v. 39.

II.

1. Father, how great thy love to man,
Love inconceivable, unknown!
Thy bowels toward thy foes restrain
Their bowels toward thy favrite Son:
Had Jesus been from sufferings freed,
Releas'd we never could have been:
But dying in the sinner's stead,
He saves a world from death, and sin.

2. The criminal prefer'd to Thee,
Saviour, myself amaz'd I find!
At the true Passover set free
The criminal is all mankind:
Deliver'd by the Paschal Lamb
We all our pardon may receive:
And lo, a sinner sav'd I am,
And ransom'd by thy death I live!

"Then cried they all again, saying, Not this man, but Barabbas. Now Barabbas was a robber."—John 18, v. 40.

1. Who blame the sin of Jews abhor'd,
Of Jews that once renounc'd their Lord,
We blindly every day
Our own corrupt desires fulfil,
To save the life of nature's will,
The life of Jesus slay.

2. Our carnal joys and pleasures here
We to this Man of grief prefer,
This self-denying Man:
We will not suffer in his cause,
But hate his poverty and cross,

The scandal and the pain.

3. By wild impetuous passion led
We still repeat the direful deed,
With one consent we cry
(While to the world our hearts we give,)
In us let the first Adam, live,
And let the Second die.

4. But let the season past suffice:
Jesus, we now unite our cries
And ask the death of sin:
Nail this Barabbas to the tree,
These lusts which steal our hearts from Thee;
And spread thy life within.

5. The cruel murtherers of our God
Which shed so oft thy precious blood
No longer, Lord, reprieve,
But slay them by the Spirit of grace,
And with thy vital holiness
In all thy members live.

JOHN CHAPTER NINETEEN

"Then Pilate therefore took Jesus, and scourged him."—John 19, v. 1.

1. The Man of griefs, by all despis'd,
Loaded with pain and infamy,
Like a rebellious slave chastiz'd,
We mourn, but wonder not, to see:
He stands in the first Adam's place,
Beneath our penalties and pains,
Of all our disobedient race
The sin and chastisement sustains.

2. His sacred flesh the scourges tear,
While to the bloody pillar bound,
The ploughers make long furrows there,
Till all his body is one wound:
The sins we in our flesh have done,
For these He doth the torture feel,
He sheds his blood for these t' atone,
And by his stripes our souls4 to heal.

"And the soldiers platted a crown of thorns, and put it on his head, and they put on him a purple robe."—John 19, v. 2.

I.

Inrobed and crown'd in mockery
Thou dost for Adam's sin atone,
Who fain would independent be,
And live like God, supreme, alone:
With pride intail'd on all the kind,
We too would reign admir'd, ador'd:
But here the remedy we find
The meekness of our humbled Lord.

"And the soldiers platted a crown of thorns, and put it on his head, and they put on him a purple robe."—John 19, v. 2.

II.

Thou wou'dst not from the people take
A crown without reproach or pain,
But scoff'd, and wounded for our sake
Thou dost the grief and shame sustain;
Thou dost the crown of thorns receive,
To make thy patient kingdom known
And lo, with Thee we die, and live,
We suffer, and ascend thy throne.

"And said, Hail King of the Jews: and they smote him with their hands."—John 19, v. 3.

1. They crown with prickly thorn,
With purple rags adorn,
Mock him in his tatter'd robe,
Smite with sacrilegious hands,
Him whose power supports the globe,
Him who earth and heaven commands.

2. But Thee thy saints revere
With loyalty sincere:
Dignified by thy disgrace,
Hail derided Majesty!
Every tongue shall soon confess,
Every soul bow down to Thee.

3. Omnipotently great
Ev'n in thy low estate,
Cloth'd again with all thy power
Israel's King, thy sway we own;
Prostrate Seraphim adore,
Cast their crowns before thy throne.

4. Yet still thy saints attend
To see their King descend:
Hasten, Lord, the destin'd time,
Sovereign Potentate appear,
On thy cloudy car sublime,
Come, and fix thy kingdom here.

"Behold, I bring him forth to you, that ye may know that I find no fault in him."—John 19, v. 4.

1. If the just God himself consent
That thou shou'dst be entreated so,
Thou must deserve the punishment
For crimes which Pilate doth not know,
The crimes which only God can find,
The crimes of me, and all mankind.

2. Thee, innocent in deed and thought,
Th' unrighteous judge is forc'd to clear;
Yet burthen'd with another's fault,

Thou bear'st the sinner's character,
And suffer'st, guiltless, on the tree,
That God may find no fault in me.

"Then came Jesus forth, wearing the crown of thorns, and the purple robe. And Pilate saith unto them, Behold the man!"—John 19, v. 5.

I.

1. Sinner, behold what thou hast done!
Expos'd thy King to grief unknown,
To anguish and disgrace:
Thy sins have cover'd him with scorn,
Thy sins have crown'd his head with thorn,
And marr'd his heavenly face.

2. Yet in that Man deform'd for thee
The fulness of the Godhead see,
That Man of grief and love
The Lord, thy Lord and God confess,
Who by his blood and righteousness
Hath bought thy crown above.

"Then came Jesus forth, wearing the crown of thorns, and the purple robe. And Pilate saith unto them, Behold the man!"—John 19, v. 5.

II.

1. More pretious than the gold and gems
That shine in earthly diadems,
The thorns of Jesus crown,
Stain'd with the blood of God, they pay
The debt of all mankind, and lay
The general ransom down.

2. A rich inheritance they buy,
Eternal mansions in the sky
For Adam's favour'd race:
And every ransom'd soul with me
By faith thy mangled form may see,
And then thy glorious face.

"They cried out, saying, Crucify him, crucify him."—John 19, v. 6.

1. Angry at th' ungrateful Jews
Them we ignorantly blame,
Them who did their King refuse,
Every day we do the same,
Still, away with him, we cry,
Still require that He should die!

2. Sin for vengence calls aloud,
'Gainst his innocence prevails,
Clamouring for his guiltless blood,

Jesus to the cross it nails;
Sin which I alas, have done,
Murthering God's eternal Son.

"We have a law, and by that law he ought to die, because he made himself the Son of God."—John 19, v. 7.

The Son of God himself he made,
Himself he prov'd the Son of God,
The law of love divine obey'd,
Of justice, which requir'd his blood:
His blood must purge our sinful stain,
Jehovah's vengence satisfy,
Salvation for the world obtain;
And by this law he ought to die.

"When Pilate therefore heard that saying, he was the more afraid."—John 19, v. 8.

How wretched is the man,
How sure of ill success,
Who fondly seeks with effort vain
God and the world to please!
He soon thro' servile fear
Gives up the injur'd side,
And Jesus in his members here
Again is crucified.

"He saith unto Jesus, Whence art thou? But Jesus gave him no answer."—John 19, v. 9.

I.

1. When He could himself defend,
The Saviour holds his peace,
Our apologies to end,
And clamours to suppress:
Hear we then the speechless Lamb
Who doth our eagerness reprove,
Silence and forever shame
Our self-excusing love.

2. Charg'd with crimes we never knew
Answer we not a word,
Quietly the steps pursue
Of our most patient Lord,
Wrongs without emotion bear,
Rest in thy humility:
Whence, and whose, and what we are,
Is known, O God, to Thee.

"He saith unto Jesus, Whence art thou? But Jesus gave him no answer."—John 19, v. 9.

II.

Yes, thou silent Man of woe,
Thy mind we comprehend,
Thankfully rejoice to know
Thy love's mysterious end:
Death unmerited to shun,
Thyself if Thou hadst justified,
All mankind condemn'd, undone

The second death had died.

"Speakest thou not unto me? knowest thou not, that I have power to crucify thee, and have power to release thee?"—John 19, v. 10.

I.

By Pilate urg'd in vain to speak,
Jesus with all his humbled powers
In silence and submission meek
His Judge invisible adores,
Disposing all the acts of men
The sovereign Arbiter he sees:
And lo, the sinner's cause to gain,
His silence doth our guilt confess!

"Speakest thou not unto me? knowest thou not, that I have power to crucify thee, and have power to release thee?"—John 19, v. 10.

II.

A righteous judge can never boast,
Or glory in his boundless power,
Can never do a deed unjust,
Or let the wolf the lamb devour:
He only from above receives
A power to make the laws take place,
The laws whose minister he lives
The laws he first himself obeys.

"Thou couldest have no power at all against me, except it were given thee from above."—John 19, v. 11.

1. Thee may I ever keep in view
Crush'd by abus'd authority,
The evil instruments look thro',
The wisdom of my Father see
Which lets the world thy church oppress,
Or kill thy passive witnesses.

2. Thy power doth now their rage confine,
Fast bound as by a secret chain:
And till thy hand the warrant sign,
Their malice threatens us in vain;
We know our hairs are numbred all,
Nor one without thy leave can fall.

3. Wherefore on Thee we fix our eyes,
And wait the counsels of thy will,
Assur'd that all in earth and skies
Shall only thy design fulfil,
To thine eternal glory tend,
And in our full salvation end.

"From thenceforth Pilate sought to release him."—John 19, v. 12.

He must the wrath Divine appease,
He must a world of sinners buy:
Man cannot rescue or release,

When God hath doom'd his Son to die.

"If thou let this man go, thou art not Cesar's friend."—John 19, v. 12, 13.

When passion in the judge prevails,
Human respect, or earthly hope,
His feeble love of justice fails,
And loth, he gives the guiltless up:
The slave of fame who would be just
Yet sooth the giddy multitude,
Sooner or late, he surely must
To interest sacrifice his God.

"Behold your king."—John 19, v. 14.

1. Jesus, while the world despise thee
We our humbled King confess,
By the marks we recognize thee,
Bleeding Prince of life and peace:
By the tokens of thy passion
Us thy faithful subjects know;
Then reveal thy great salvation,
Then our crowns of life bestow.

2. Thro' humility and patience
Here Thou dost thy sway maintain,
Out of mighty tribulations
Come thy saints with thee to reign;
King of griefs, our hearts adore thee,
Pain'd with thy afflictions, own
Suffering is thy people's glory,
Suffering leads us to thy throne.

"But they cried out, Away with him, away with him, crucify him &c."—John 19, v. 15.

1. Who yield their hearts the sordid throne
Of pride or base desire,
Jesus they for their King disown,
And still his death require:
Away with him! they will not have
This man of woe to reign,
They will not suffer him to save,
But crucify again.

2. Cesar their only king they know;
The power invisible
The kingdom of thy grace below,
Lord, they refuse to feel:
The throne they might with Thee divide,
The holy Ghost receive,
But will not suffer at thy side,
And in thy glory live.

"Then delivered he him therefore unto them to be crucified. And they took Jesus and led him away."—John 19, v. 16.

1. Who take at first the Saviour's side,
Thro' cowardly regard to men,
Thro' interest, or ambitious pride,
We soon abandon him again,

Or lead him to his cross away,
And Jesus in his members slay.

2. Thee that we may no more deny,
Appear as bleeding on the tree;
Ourselves we then shall crucify,
In close Divine conformity
Our steady faithfulness approve,
And pay thee back thy dying love.

"And he bearing his cross, went forth."—John 19, v. 17.

I.

1. Victim of an angry God,
Devoted to the skies,
Isaac-like, He bears the wood
Of his own sacrifice;
Bears with strength invincible
The arms which still the world o'rethrow,
Daily conquer sin and hell,
And our last deadly foe.

2. King of saints, He meekly bears
The sceptre of his cross
Thus his royal power declares,
And executes his laws,
Thus his government maintains,
The virtue of his death exerts,
By his bleeding passion reigns
In all his people's hearts.

"And he bearing his cross, went forth."—John 19, v. 17.

II.

1. Emblem of our sins, He groans
Beneath the cross's load,
Thus for all our guilt atones,
And heals us by his blood:
Let us on our Surety gaze,
That lovely, piteous Spectacle!
Lo, He suffers in our place
What we deserve to feel.

2. Strength for us his sufferings buy
To imitate our Head:
Let us then ourselves deny,
And in thy footsteps tread,
Go we forth to Calvary,
And bearing thy reproach and pain,
Patient of the cross with Thee
Thy crown immortal gain.

"They crucified him."—John 19, v. 18.

1. Bound to the altar see
The bleeding Sacrifice!
Uplifted on that shameful tree
He hangs 'twixt earth and skies!
Jesus the Crucified
Invites our sinful race,
And with those arms extended wide
Would all mankind embrace.

2. Was ever grief like his,
Who bears Jehovah's name!
Of all his glory stript He is,

And cover'd with our shame,
Cover'd with his own blood
Whom earth and heaven desires,
The Father's Joy, th' eternal God
In agonies expires!

3. Number'd with sinners Thee
My Saviour I confess,
Strugling in death to ransom me
And all our dying race:
My Purchaser Divine,
My rightful Lord Thou art,
And lo! I answer thy design,
And give thee all my heart!

"They crucified two other with him, on either side one, and Jesus in the midst."—John 19, v. 18.

Virtue by few embrac'd
We find in Christ alone,
Betwixt two opp'osite vices plac'd
Essential Virtue own:
And still the Truth is seen
With error by its side;
And Christians among sinful men
Are daily crucified.

"Jesus of Nazareth, the King of the Jews &c."—John 19, v. 19, 20.

1. Jesus, by the judge allow'd
Supreme in regal power,
Very and eternal God
Let all thy saints adore:
All the Israelites indeed
Their bleeding King and Saviour own,
On the cross we plainly read
Thy title to the throne.

2. King proclaim'd in different tongues,
Is our expiring God;
All mankind to Thee belongs,
The purchase of thy blood:
Universal Monarch Thou
Command the nations to submit,
Jews, and Greeks, and Heathens bow
Thy subjects at thy feet.

"Then said the chief priests to Pilate, Write not, The king of the Jews &c."—John 19, v. 21, 22.

1. Conscience, and remorse for sin,
Remembrancers severe,
After the dire act begin
To plague the wicked here:
Soon they wish the deed effac'd,
Which meets and blasts their guilty eyes,
In their view forever plac'd,
And written in the skies.

2. Written with an iron pen
My horrid crime I see,
I the Prince of life have slain,
The Saviour on that tree!
Torn by sin his sacred flesh,
Those nails into his body driven,
Crucified my Lord afresh,
The King of earth and heaven.

3. Every sinner's King, and mine

Thy Majesty I own,
Cover'd with the blood Divine
Which did for all atone:
While I at thy cross remain,
The crimson flood, the gushing tide,
Washes out my sinful stain,
And saves the regicide!

"Then the soldiers, when they had crucified Jesus, took his garments."—John 19, v. 23.

By his nakedness He owns
Man's original offence,
For our sinful shame atones,
For our loss of innocence;
Soon as we our sins confess,
Hides them from his Father's eyes,
Cloathes us with his righteousness,
Gives us back our paradise.

"They made four parts, to every soldier a part."—John 19, v. 23.

All is grace and mystery!
Lo, his spoils divided are,
(While He hangs on yonder tree)
Every soul may claim a share:
Jesus, and whate'er is his,
Let the world of sinners find;
Common his salvation is,
Parted out to all mankind.

"The coat was without seam. They said therefore, Let us not rent it &c."—John 19, v. 23, 24.

1. Heathens in every age contend
For forms of godliness,
And strictly charge us not to rend
Our Lord's external dress:
For Christ himself they nothing care,
Yet unity maintain;
The seamless coat they will not tear,
That each the whole may gain.

2. Each party calls the coat their own,
As masters of the loom,
Though neither at Geneva spun,
Nor Babylonish Rome:
Their feuds and strifes which never cease
Their fierce divisions prove,
They have not known the bond of peace,
The unity of love.

"Now there stood by the cross of Jesus, his mother, and his mother's sister, Mary the wife of Cleophas, and Mary Magdalene."—John 19, v. 25.

1. The coward Peter had denied,
The judge thro' fear had crucified,
His followers base themselves betook
To flight, and all their Lord forsook;
The weaker sex, the Marys three

Patterns of faith and constancy
By Jesus on the cross remain,
And thence their strength and courage gain.

2. Arm'd with the power of Jesus grace,
Surmounting nature's tenderness,
The sharp heart-piercing sword they feel,
The horrors of that spectacle;
Unmov'd by shame or danger near,
His only dying cries they hear,
Regardless of th' outrageous croud,
They only mark his streaming blood.

3. The martyrs thus their strength receiv'd,
While with the Man of griefs they griev'd,
And dared the fiery test abide
Partakers with the Crucified:
Thus all the followers of the Lamb
Endure the pain, despise the shame,
And power to suffer in his cause
Find at the foot of Jesus cross.

"Behold thy son: behold thy mother."—John 19, v. 26, 27.

We would thine aged followers give
The honour to a parent due,
We would the young with love receive
Purer than nature ever knew:
Saviour, bestow th' entend'ring grace,
Us in a new relation join,
So shall we all thy saints embrace,
And love them with a love like thine.

"I thirst."—John 19, v. 28.

He thirsted to redeem his foe,
And reconcile a world to God,
He long'd that all his love might know,
Sav'd by the virtue of his blood!
Be satisfied: we thirst for Thee,
We add our strong desires to thine:
See then, thy soul's hard travail see,
And die, to make us all divine.

"It is finished!"—John 19, v. 30.

1. Tis finish'd: the Messiah dies,
Cut off for sins, but not his own!
Accomplish'd is the sacrifice,
The great redeeming work is done;
Finish'd the first transgression is,
And purg'd the guilt of actual sin,
And everlasting righteousness
Is now to all the world brought in.

2. Tis finish'd, all my guilt and pain,
I want no sacrifice beside;
For me, for me the Lamb is slain,

And I am more than justified;
Sin, death, and hell are now subdued,
All grace is now to sinners given,
And lo, I plead th' atoning blood
For pardon, holiness, and heaven.

"He bowed his head, and gave up the ghost."—John 19, v. 30.

1. Jacob gather'd up his feet,
Expiring in the bed,
Jesus doth to death submit,
And freely bows his head,
Willingly the ransom pays,
Gives himself a sacrifice,
Pleas'd to suffer in our place
He bows his head, and dies.

2. All the sins of all mankind
On Jesus head were laid;
Now he hath his life resign'd,
And our whole debt is paid;
Now we may our parting breath
Into our Father's hands commend,
Live forever thro' the death
Of our expiring Friend.

"But one of the soldiers with a spear pierced his side."—John 19, v. 34.

He sleeps! and lo, his wounded side
Gives being to his spotless bride!
Out of his side the church is took:
And while we on our Saviour look,
We constitute the second Eve,
And thro' our Husband's dying live.

"And forthwith there came out blood and water."—John 19, v. 34.

1. The Rock is smote by Moses' rod,
And pours a consecrated flood:
I see the fountain open wide,
I see th' inseparable tide
Atoning blood, and water clean
To expiate, and wash out my sin.

2. Jesus, from Thee I surely know
The streams of full salvation flow,
Confiding in thy death possess
The pardon and the holiness;
The double life thy wounds impart
The peace, and purity of heart.

"He that saw it, bare record, and his record is true: and he knoweth that he saith true, that ye might believe."—John 19, v. 35.

I do believe the record true,
Thou cam'st by blood, and water too,
By blood t' atone, by water clean
To wash out all my inbred sin,
To sprinkle, and renew my heart,
To make me, Saviour, as Thou art,
And then take home thy spotless bride,

And place me glorious at thy side.

"These things were done, that the scripture should be fulfilled, A bone of him shall not be broken."—John 19, v. 36.

1. Behold Him bleeding on the tree!
The scripture, and Divine decree
His death for sin require
In weakness crucified and slain,
His strength to save doth still remain
Unbroken and entire.

2. True Paschal Lamb, to Thee I look;
To set the bones which sin hath broke,
Thy Spirit's power exert,
Mighty to save a world from sin
Thy salutiferous grace bring in,
And heal my contrite heart.

"And again another scripture saith, They shall look on him whom they pierced."—John 19, v. 37.

1. My sins have done the deed,
His sacred body torn:
I see him bow his head,
I look on him, and mourn!
The Man I pierc'd, tis He, tis He!
I feel, I feel, He dies for me!

2. O may I ever gaze
On an expiring God,
On that disfigur'd face
Deform'd with tears and blood,
Till coming in the clouds I own,
And mount to meet him on his throne!

"Joseph of Arimathea, being a disciple of Jesus, but secretly for fear of the Jews, besought Pilate that he might take away the body."—John 19, v. 38.

1. Thro' fear of the self-righteous Jews
Who Jesus secretly pursues,
And lurks a while unknown,
May out of weakness be made strong,
And bold before the worldly throng
His Lord and Saviour own.

2. Soon as his death confers the grace,
Jesus we unasham'd confess;
His weakest follower I
Appear undaunted in his cause,
Live in the spirit of his cross
Or dare for Christ to die.

"There came also Nicodemus, which at the first came to Jesus by night."—John 19, v. 39.

1. Who all our sin and weakness knows,
Strength in th' appointed time bestows,
To answer his design;
But oft in love our cure delays,
To make the virtue of his grace

With brightest lustre shine.

2. If first to Christ by night we came,
If still our stronger brethren blame
Our feeble-mindedness,
We trust at that distinguish'd hour
To claim him boldly, and with power
In life and death confess.

"Then took they the body of Jesus, and wound it in linnet clothes, with the spices."—John 19, v. 40.

1. Who our mortality put on,
Our burial-clothes vouchsafes to wear:
And when these bodies we lay down,
Drest in the wedding robe we are,
As such our burial-clothes esteem
When worn and sanctified by Him.

2. Of spices all his garments smell,
Aloes and myrrh and cassia breathe:
Our faithful souls perceive and feel
The fragrant virtue of his death;
His death doth dying sinners chear,
His death perfumes the sepulchre.

"Now in the place where he was crucified, there was a garden."—John 19, v. 41.

Death and the grave their baleful power
Their dread commission to devour
In Eden's garden first obtain'd,
And since o're all mankind have reign'd:
Disarm'd they in a garden are,
O'recome their Conqueror's strength declare,
Who doth to us the victory give,
Who died that all mankind may live.

"In the garden was a new sepulchre, wherein was never man yet laid."—John 19, v. 41.

The only sinless Man and just,
He cannot mix with common dust,
But born of a pure virgin's womb,
Must rise out of a virgin-tomb:
The tomb is new, where Christ is laid,
New is the heart for Jesus made,
And all his purity receives,
While God in man forever lives.

"There laid they Jesus."—John 19, v. 42.

II.

1. My faith with joy and wonder sees

Jesus, thy sacred obsequies,
A burial which hath power to save
From death, a burial of the grave!
It beautifies the hideous tomb,
It dissipates the frightful gloom,
Smoothly prepares my easiest bed,
The softest pillow for my head.

2. O that I now my wish might have,
And sink into my Saviour's grave,
O that this flesh, no more opprest
With pain and sin, in hope might rest!
My soul disburthen'd of its clay
On eagles wings would soar away,
Behold the Sun with eagles eyes,
And grasp my Lord in paradise.

"There laid they Jesus."—John 19, v. 42.

I.

1. Here lies of life th' immortal Prince
Under arrest for all our sins!
Our Surety hath procur'd our peace,
Discharg'd we are by his release:
The Sun is vanish'd from our sight,
But conqueror of the shades of night
He rises brighter than before,
He rises soon to set no more.

2. Prisoner of death, and silent here
He lies, till the third morn appear;
He then returns to life again,
And death is by his captive slain;
The grave is now for us o'recome,
Our bodies ransom'd from the tomb
After our Head triumphant rise,
And wear his glories in the skies.

JOHN CHAPTER TWENTY

"The first day of the week &c."—John 20, v. 1.

When vanquishing our sloth and ease
We wait at Jesus' sepulchre,
The Lord removes the hindrances,
And scatters all our grief and fear,
Himself He to his mourners shows,
His Spirit in our hearts is shed,
Life on our drooping souls bestows,
And calls, and raises from the dead.

"Then she runneth, and cometh to Simon Peter &c."—John 20, v. 2.

A soul who hath the Saviour known,
And seen him bleeding on the cross,

When Christ out of his sight is gone,
Most sensibly resents the loss,
He weeps disconsolate, and sighs,
And tells to Jesus friends his pain,
And restless every means he tries,
To find his dear-lov'd Lord again.

"Peter went forth and that other disciple, and came to the sepulchre."—John 20, v. 3.

The pastor call'd a soul to aid
In search of Him who lives, though dead,
Should rise, and run without delay,
And bring the mourners on their way;
Himself in haste his Lord to find
Should leave all earthly things behind,
But never from the tomb depart,
Till Christ is risen—in his heart.

"So they ran both together: and the other disciple did outrun Peter, and came first to the sepulchre."—John 20, v. 4.

I.

Swiftly, the man whom Jesus loves
In quest of his Redeemer moves;
Sad Peter bears a load of woe,
And clog'd with guilt and shame moves slow:
But soon he finds the Lord from heaven,
And much he loves, when much forgiven,
On Jesus cross his life lays down,
And first obtains the martyr's crown.

"So they ran both together: and the other disciple did outrun Peter, and came first to the sepulchre."—John 20, v. 4.

II.

O might I at the goal arrive,
And find the Crucified alive,
Outstrip my old companion here,
And foremost reach the sepulchre!
There let my peaceful ashes lie,
Till my Redeemer bows the sky,
And Jesus, Conqueror of the grave
Returns, my quicken'd dust to save.

"He stooping down, and looking in, saw the linnet clothes lying."—John 20, v. 5.

Only thus, by stooping low,
By divine humility,
Can I my Redeemer know,
Him who left the grave for me:
Prostrate faith with watry eyes
Looks into the sepulchre,
Sees the tokens of his rise,
Sees its living Lord appear.

"Then cometh Peter, and went into the sepulchre."—John 20, v. 6.

Can the grave a Christian scare,
Yawning like destruction's pit?
No undying worms are there:
Free from dread he enters it,
In the place where Christ was laid,
Calm he lays his body down,
Thro' the grave pursues his Head,
Thro' the cross obtains the crown.

"He seeth the linnet clothes lie, and the napkin by itself."—John 20, v. 6, 7.

1. Christ returning to the skies
Drops his mantle in his rise,
Marks of temporary death
Leaves the linnet clothes beneath,
Puts his robes of glory on,
Re-ascends his Father's throne.

2. We the linnen-garments need,
Left to sheet our softest bed,
Left in Jesus grave they are,
Ours to hallow and prepare;
There the separate napkin lies,
Left to dry the mourner's eyes.

"Then went in also that other disciple, and he saw, and believed."—John 20, v. 8.

With hasty grief and fear
Who seek the Crucified,
Visit the holy sepulchre,
And at his tomb abide,
I shall the proofs perceive,
The tokens more than see,
And quicken'd by his Spirit believe
He rose, to live in me.

"Mary stood without at the sepulchre, weeping."—John 20, v. 11 &c.

1. Expecting at Jesus's grave
The signs of his favour restor'd,
His virtue to quicken, and save,
I sigh for a sight of my Lord!
My Only-beloved is gone,
Has left me in trouble and pain;
His Spirit, alas, is withdrawn!
Ah, when shall I find him again!

2. Forgotten of God, and forsook,
Dissolv'd in an ocean of tears;
I into his sepulchre look,
And mourn till a Saviour appears:
No vision of angels I prize,
Unless He his Spirit impart,
Unless the Delight of my eyes
Discover himself to my heart.

3. Ev'n now my affliction he sees,
Unseen, yet invisibly nigh,
My Saviour observes my distress,
And marks with a merciful eye:
This burthen of sorrow and pain
A glimpse of his face shall remove:
He waits to be gracious again,
To give me a sight of his love.

4. I turn from the creature away
To Him whom alone I desire;
He hears my infirmity pray
While Him of Himself I require:
Where is the dear Lord of my heart,
Whom only I languish to see?
As sure as in heaven Thou art,
Thou art with a mourner for Thee.

"Woman, why weepest thou?"—John 20, v. 15.

1. Sinners, dismiss your fear,
The joyful tidings hear!
This the word that Jesus said,
O believe and feel it true,
Christ is risen from the dead,
Lives the Lord who died for you.

2. Haste, to his tomb repair,
And see the tokens there,
See the place where Jesus lay,
Mark the burial-clothes he wore:
Angels near his relicks stay,
Guards of Him who dies no more.

3. Why then art thou cast down,
Thou poor afflicted one?
Full of doubts, and griefs, and fears,
Look into that open grave!
Died He not to dry thy tears?
Rose He not thy soul to save?

4. Knowst thou not where to find
The Saviour of mankind?
He hath borne himself away,
He from death himself hath freed,
He on the third auspicious day,
Rose triumphant from the dead.

5. To purge thy guilty stain
He died and rose again:
Wherefore dost thou weep and mourn?
Sinner, lift thine heart and eye,
Turn thee, to thy Jesus turn,
See thy loving Saviour nigh.

6. He comes his own to claim,
He calls thee by thy name;
Drooping soul, rejoice, rejoice,
See him there to life restor'd;
Mary,—know thy Saviour's voice,
Hear it, and reply, My Lord!

"Jesus saith unto her, Mary: She turned herself, and saith unto him, Rabboni, which is to say, Master."—John 20, v. 16.

1. It is the voice of my Belov'd,
My fears are fled, my griefs remov'd;
He calls a sinner by his name,
And He is mine, and his I am!
Jesus, by a word made known,
Thee my gracious Lord I own.

2. My gracious Lord, I know, Thou art,
The lawful Master of my heart,
I feel thy resurrection's power,
And joyful at thy feet adore;
Now I only live to prove,
Thou art God, and God is Love!

"Jesus saith unto her, Touch me not; for I am not yet ascended to my Father."—John 20, v. 17.

1. While thine earthly course was ending,
Thee the Son of God and man,
To thy Father's arms ascending
Mary might not here detain:
In thy state of exaltation
Now to sense no longer known,
Glorious God of our salvation,
Hail on thy eternal throne!

2. Thee, the Theme of all their praises,
High extol'd above all height,
Seraphs see, and veil their faces,
Sinking in a flood of light:
Yet thy ransom'd worms approach thee,
See thy smiling face and live,
Still by humble faith we touch thee,
Thee into our hearts receive.

3. Faith effects the wondrous union,
Faith unfolds the mystery,
Sweetest spiritual communion,
Son of man we have with Thee;
Faith its dearest Lord embraces,
Still by faith we clasp thy feet,
Sit with Thee in heavenly places,
At thy side forever sit.

"Go to my brethren &c."—John 20, v. 17.

1. Happy Magdalene, to whom
Christ the Lord vouchsaf'd t' appear!
Newly risen from the tomb,
Would He first be seen by Her?
Her by seven devils possest,
Till his love the fiends expel'd,
Quench'd the hell within her breast,
All her sin and sickness heal'd.

2. Yes, to her the Master came,
First his welcome voice she hears:
Jesus calls her by her name,
He the weeping sinner chears,
While she would the task repeat,
While her eyes again run o're,
Eager still to wash his feet,
Kiss them, and with joy adore.

3. Highly favour'd soul, to her
Farther yet his grace extends,
Raises the glad messenger,
Sends her to his drooping friends:
Tidings of their living Lord
First in her report they find:
She shall spread the gospel-word,
Teach the teachers of mankind.

4. Who can now presume to fear,
Who despair his Lord to see?
Jesus, wilt thou not appear,
Shew thyself alive to me?
Yes my God, I dare not doubt,
Thou shalt all my sins remove;
Thou hast cast a legion out,
Thou wilt perfect me in love.

5. Surely thou hast call'd me now,

Now I hear the voice Divine,
At thy wounded feet I bow,
Wounded for whose sins but mine!
I have nail'd him to the tree,
I have sent him to the grave:
But my Lord is ris'n for me;
Hold of him by faith I have.

6. Here forever would I lie,
Didst thou not thy servant raise,
Send me forth to testify
All the wonders of thy grace:
Lo, I at thy bidding go,
Gladly to thy followers tell
They their risen God may know,
They the life of Christ may feel.

7. Hear, ye brethren of the Lord,
Such He you vouchsafes to call,
O believe the gospel-word,
Christ hath died, and rose for all:
Turn ye from your sins to God,
Haste to Galilee, and see
Him who bought thee with his blood,
Him who rose to live in thee.

"Go to my brethren, and say unto them, I ascend unto my Father &c."—John 20, v. 17.

1. Jesus, the rising Lord of all,
His love to man commends,
Poor worms he blushes not to call
His brethren and his friends:
Who basely all forsook their Lord
In his distress, and fled,
To these he sends the joyful word,
When risen from the dead.

2. Go tell the vile deserters? no;
My dearest brethren tell,
"Their Advocate to heaven I go,
"To rescue them from hell.
"Lo, to my Father I ascend:
"Your Father now is He,
"My God, and yours, whoe'er depend
"For endless life on Me."

3. Henceforth I ever live above
For you to interceed,
The merit of my dying love,
For all mankind to plead:
Sinners, I rose again to shew
Your sins are all forgiven,
And mount above the skies, that you
May follow Me to heaven.

"Then the same day at evening, being the first day of the week, when the doors were shut, where the disciples were assembled for fear of the Jews, came Jesus and stood in the midst, and saith unto them, Peace be unto you."—John 20, v. 19 &c.

1. Jesus, on this thy solemn day,
To chase our fears and sins away,
Our living Lord appear;
Meet us, assembled in thy name,
Stand in the midst, and now proclaim
That God is present here.

2. Present, we know, Thou always art;
But speak to every troubled heart
The reconciling word;
Shew us thy wounded hands and side,
And conscious of thy blood applied
We glory in the Lord.

3. Triumphant thro' thy mortal pain
Thou dost the bleeding marks retain
T' excite our grateful love;
Thou still before thy Father's eyes
Offer'st the precious Sacrifice
Which bought our thrones above.

4. The vision of those glorious scars
Our fear dispels, our strength repairs,
And makes our Saviour known,
Imboldens us to serve thy cause,
And joyfully embrace the cross
Connected with the crown.

"Peace be unto you."—John 20, v. 19.

1. The peace Thou didst to man bequeath
So dearly purchas'd by thy death
Thou freely dost bestow,
Fruit of thy blessed lips, we feel
The peace thy gracious words reveal,
And all the comfort know.

2. We thus our legacy receive,
And blest by the Testator, live
A life of faith and love,
A life, the sure effect of thine,
The life of purity Divine
Which angels live above.

"Then said Jesus to them again, Peace be unto you."—John 20, v. 21.

1. Jesus' word doth first convey
Peace into the anxious breast,
Peace which drives the fear away,
Earnest of eternal rest:
Then his wounds he plainly shows,
Then the raptur'd child of grace
Truly his Redeemer knows,
Sees his heaven in Jesus' face.

2. Peace the Saviour speaks again
Peace to curb our joy extreme,
Peace which always shall remain,
Perfect peace with God in Him:
Then the kingdom we receive
Stablish'd sure, no more to move,
Only for his glory live,
Only breathe to breathe his love.

"Peace be unto you: As my Father hath sent me, even so send I you."—John 20, v. 21.

1. Jesus, thy word, till time shall end,
The ministerial call imparts,
Thou only dost thy servants send
By speaking peace into our

hearts:
We then declare the things we know,
Ourselves assur'd of sin forgiven,
Glad tidings of salvation show,
And publish peace 'twixt earth and heaven.

2. Apostle of thy Father, Thee,
Our Peace we joyfully proclaim,
Strong in thy Spirit's energy
Divulge the wonders of thy name;
With thy divine commission sent,
Ambassadors of the Most-high,
We cry to all mankind—Repent;
Believe; obey; and mount the sky!

"He breathed on them &c."—John 20, v. 22.

1. The Breath of Christ, that Spirit is!
Saviour, to me the gift impart,
To purge my sin, and seal my peace,
Thy Spirit breathe into my heart;
Ah, give me now the chast desire,
The spotless love and purity,
With all that holiness inspire,
With all that mind which was in Thee.

2. Thou didst inspire his mortal frame,
Thou didst the breath of lives bestow,
And man a living soul became,
The portraiture of God below:
Thou dost inspire the life of grace
And as a second soul confer
The holy Ghost on all our race,
The saints eternal Comforter.

"Whose soever sins ye remit, they are remitted unto them."—John 20, v. 23.

If Thou ordain the minister,
His word doth guilty souls release,
Doth with authority declare
Th' appointed terms of gospel peace;
The poor self-desperate sinner feels
The truth we in thy name assert,
And our report thy Spirit seals
In pardon on the faithful heart.

"And whose soever sins ye retain, they are retained."—John 20, v. 23.

But how can we their guilt retain?
The sons of infidelity
We tell, that still their sins remain
Uncancel'd, till they come to thee:
The sentence we pronounce beneath
Thou dost confirm it in the skies,
The infidel abides in death,
And, unconvinc'd, forever dies.

"The other disciples said unto him, We have seen the Lord."—John 20, v. 25.

Jesus' followers all confess
That Him they have beheld,
Known the bleeding Prince of peace,
And felt his love reveal'd:
Yet I cannot trust their word,
Till folding in my faith's embrace,
Him I find to life restor'd,
Who suffer'd in my place.

"Except I shall see in his hands the print of the nails, ... I will not believe."—John 20, v. 25.

1. No, I never will believe,
Unless my Lord I see,
Proofs infallible receive
That Jesus died for me,
Meet him risen from the dead,
Thrust my hand into his side,
Mark the prints the nails have made,
And feel his blood applied.

2. Slow of heart, Thou knowst, I am;
Mine unbelief reprove,
Call me, Saviour, by my name,
In manifested love,
Condescend to my request,
My dying Lord, my pardning God,
Come in all thy wounds confest,
And wash me in thy blood.

3. Sin, and doubt to chase away,
A drooping soul to chear,
Now thy hands and feet display,
Divinely present here,
Shew thyself, as crucified,
Th' irrefragable tokens give,
Take into thine open side,
And force me to believe.

"Again his disciples were within, and Thomas with them: then came Jesus, the doors being shut, and stood in the midst, and said, Peace be unto you."—John 20, v. 26.

1. If but one faithless soul be here,
Jesus, assembled with thine own,
Wilt Thou not in the midst appear,
Thy resurrection's power make known,
Sprinkle the sinner with thy blood,
And shew thyself his Lord and God?

2. Slower of heart than Thomas I
With thy sincere disciples meet,
A conscious unbeliever sigh
For faith and pardon at thy feet:
Thy feet alas, I cannot see,
Or feel the blood that flow'd for me.

3. But nothing can obstruct thy way,
Thou omnipresent God of love:
Come, Saviour, come, thy wounds display,
My stubborn unbelief remove,

And me among thy people bless,
And fill our hearts with heavenly peace.

4. Occasion from my slowness take
Thy faithful followers to chear,
For a poor abject sinner's sake,
Jesus, the second time appear,
Increase thy saints felicity,
And bless them all by blessing me.

"Then saith he to Thomas, Reach hither thy finger ... and be not faithless, but believing."—John 20, v. 27.

1. O how kind and condescending
Is the sinners Friend to me;
Ready with his balm attending
On my soul's infirmity!
The fresh tokens of his passion
He sets forth before my eyes,
Gives me many a demonstration
Of his life above the skies.

2. Jesus, Thee my God and Saviour
By those open scars I own,
Conscious of thy love and favour,
Freely sav'd by grace alone;
Daily all my sins forgiving,
Peace divine thy words impart,
"Be not faithless but believing"
Speaks thy life into my heart.

"My Lord, and my God."—John 20, v. 28.

1. The sight without the touch compel'd
His incredulity to yield,
And by thy bleeding wounds subdued,
Thomas replied, My Lord my God!
Thy wounds alone can conquer me,
Convince of thy Divinity,
Assure that God is all my own,
And make my heart thy peaceful throne.

2. Constrain'd I do at last believe,
And Thee my Lord my God receive,
Not man made God, but God made man,
Come down from heaven on earth to reign;
The only God, and Lord most high,
Thou didst for faithless sinners die,
Didst rise to prove our sins forgiven,
And draw me after thee to heaven.

"Because thou hast seen me, thou hast believed."—John 20, v. 29.

1. Sound in the faith, though weak and slow,
My feeble faith sincere, I know

Jesus vouchsafes t' approve;
Though long my Saviour I withstood,
He hath the infidel subdued
By manifested love.

2. Consenting to my Lord and God
The grace divine by Him bestow'd
The comfort I receive,
A witness of his quickning power,
The Author of my faith adore,
And consciously believe.

"Blessed are they that have not seen, and yet have believed."—John 20, v. 29.

1. That Man among the sons of men
With eyes of flesh we have not seen,
And yet believe on Him,
That Man Jehovah's Fellow own,
The Father's co-eternal Son,
Almighty and supreme.

2. Superior happiness we prove,
While Him, not having seen, we love,
Sure of our sins forgiven,
Eternal life in faith we feel,
The extasies unspeakable
The glorious joys of heaven.

"These things are written, that ye might believe that Jesus is the Christ, the Son of God, and that believing ye might have life through his name."—John 20, v. 31.

1. Faith comes by hearing of the word,
Comes to the heart by reading too,
While searching for our heavenly Lord,
Him in the sacred page we view,
Him whom the Holy Ghost reveals,
And pardon on our conscience seals.

2. Recorded in th' authentic book
While Jesus' life and death we read,
We for the promis'd Witness look
Who speaks him risen from the dead;
Inspir'd, we then on Him rely,
That Christ, that Son of the Most-high.

3. Jehovah's Son, declar'd with power
We by his resurrection know,
Our Lord and God supreme adore,
Our Prophet, Priest, and King below,
Whose Unction light and life imparts,
And grace and glory to our hearts.

4. Jesus, believing in thy name,
We see the tree of life arise,
Thy grace removes the sword of flame,
And gives us back our paradise,
Feeds with immortalizing food,
And fills with the pure life of God.

5. Life thro' the virtue of thy love
Spiritual life divine we gain,
With Thee our Head inthron'd above
The closest fellowship maintain,
Till face to face our God we see,
Our full, eternal Life in Thee.

JOHN CHAPTER TWENTY-ONE

"After these things Jesus shewed himself again to the disciples at the sea of Tiberias."—John 21, v. 1.

The Saviour doth in various ways
Himself to his disciples show;
He meets us, when we seek his face,
Assembled in his courts below:
He oft prevents our care and thought,
And while in common works employ'd,
Comes to us unforeseen, unsought,
And shews our hearts the living God.

"Simon saith unto them, I go a fishing."—John 21, v. 3.

1. A fisher of men Will others invite,
Each sinew to strain By day and by night,
With close application, The servants of sin
The heirs of salvation For Jesus to win.

2. But without their Lord Their efforts are vain,
The net of the word Will nothing obtain;
In darkness they labour With sorrow of heart,
One soul, or one neighbour They cannot convert.

3. Yet Jesus regards Their services past,
And fully rewards His workmen at last,
Their labours he blesses With wonders of grace,
And mighty successes, And sights of his face.

"We also go with thee."—John 21, v. 3.

1. The fishers of men In love should agree
And concord maintain, Appointed by Thee
Thro' every nation Good news to proclaim
And publish salvation By faith in thy name.

2. United in heart, Together we go,
The gospel impart, Which all men may know;
And sinners receiving Our record as thine,
Obtain by believing The fulness Divine.

"They went forth, and entred into a ship &c."—John 21, v. 3.

Their successors we find
In them, and them alone
Who cast the pride of life behind,
And tread its pleasures down,
From each superfluous need,
From all ambition free,
Who love a toilsom life to lead
In patient poverty.

"But when the morning was now come, Jesus stood on the shore."—John 21, v. 4.

I.

1. Absent from those whom most He loves,
Jesus, our faith and patience proves;
And left a tedious while,
Thro' the long night of doubts and fears
We labour, (till our Lord appears,)
With unsuccesful toil.

2. But labouring on with fruitless pain
Resolv'd we in the ship remain,
Till the expected morn:
And sure as day succeeds to night,
We see the soul-reviving Light,
And joy with Christ return.

"But when the morning was now come, Jesus stood on the shore."—John 21, v. 4.

II.

1. See a rough draught of human life!
All is one continued strife,
Fatigue, and misery!
A night of perilous distress
Without relief without success
We tempt the stormy sea.

2. But when the dreary hour is o're,
Jesus on the happy shore
Shall satisfy our need,
Shall bless us with the sight of God,
And with imperishable food
Our raptur'd spirits feed.

"But when the morning was now come, Jesus stood on the shore."—John 21, v. 4.

III.

1. Ev'n now we know, tis He, tis He!
Him with eyes of faith we see,
As in the haven stand!
Jesus, our all-victorious God
Hath waded thro' a sea of blood

To that celestial land.

2. His work is done, his suffering past,
Safe arrived he rests at last
In full supreme delight:
But we alas, are still at sea,
Compel'd in toil and jeopardy
To weather out the night.

3. Yet Him we trust who went before,
Jesus waiting on the shore
Our Spirits to receive;
We soon shall reach that quiet place,
And thro' the vision of his face
In endless raptures live.

"The disciples knew not, that it was Jesus."—John 21, v. 4.

1. Jesus sometimes by slow degrees
Himself to his disciples shows;
Darkly at first the sinner sees,
Nor yet his distant Saviour knows,
Surrounded with imperfect light,
And half discover'd to the sight.

2. He speaks in tender pitying grace,
Kindly into our wants inquires,
His love's omnipotence displays,
Satiates our inlarg'd desires,
Feeds with his wonder-working word,
And then we cry, It is the Lord!

"Then Jesus saith unto them, Children, have ye any meat?"—John 21, v. 5.

1. Jesus the poor with pity sees,
He looks into our cottages,
Inquires with condescension sweet,
My children, have ye aught to eat?
He bids us our requests make known,
Our burthens cast on Him alone,
Prevents the hungry beggar's prayer,
And feeds us with a father's care.

2. He knows our depth of poverty,
But wills that we ourselves should see,
Should humbly at his feet confess
Our utter want of every grace:
Saviour, we nothing have to eat;
Thou living Bread, thou heavenly Meat,
Indulge us with a fresh supply,
Or wanting Thee, we faint, and die.

"Cast the net on the right side, and ye shall find."—John 21, v. 6.

1. Providence extends its care
To things minutely small,
Things the most contingent are
By Wisdom order'd all:
Happy they that know his mind,
Obedient to his leading grace,

God in every action find,
And own in all their ways.

2. By thy word and Spirit led,
And Providential will
Sure to prosper in our deed,
Our net at last we fill:
Fruitless pains and labours crost
Must finally succesful be;
Nothing, Lord, was ever lost
By faithfulness to Thee.

"They cast therefore, and now they were not able to draw it for the multitude of fishes."—John 21, v. 6.

I.

This comfort is for you,
Ye Gospel-fishermen,
Who patiently your work pursue,
But seem to work in vain:
Your net persist to cast,
As Jesus ministers,
And know, one happy draught at last
Will pay your toil of years.

"They cast therefore, and now they were not able to draw it for the multitude of fishes."—John 21, v. 6.

II.

When Jesus gives the word,
And doth their labours bless,
The prosperous servants of the Lord
Admire their own success:
Appointed and employ'd
By Christ, his hand they own,
And all their fruit ascribe to God,
And praise his name alone.

"They cast therefore, and now they were not able to draw it for the multitude of fishes."—John 21, v. 6.

III.

When God hath touch'd our souls, and brought
Into the Apostolic net,
A work miraculous is wrought,
But all is not effected yet:
So long, so deeply plung'd in sin,
We still are drawn by his command,
Till He who did the work begin
Compleats, and brings us all to land.

"Therefore that disciple whom Jesus loved saith unto Peter, It is the Lord. Now when Peter heard that it was the Lord ... he did cast himself into the sea."—John 21, v. 7.

1. Jesus is first perceiv'd and known
By loving and quick-sighted John
Who hasts the joyful news to tell,
And points him out to Peter's zeal;
And Peter's fervent soul is stir'd,
And springs with joy to grasp his Lord.

2. A faithful soul will never stay,
Though pain and death obstruct the way,
But venture all, his faith to prove,
And reach the Object of his love,
Rush thro' the flame, and swim the flood,
Or wade to Christ thro' seas of blood.

3. O that they both in me might meet
The zeal and love, the light and heat!
My Master dear I first would know,
To Him thro' fire and water go,
Danger and toil for Christ despise,
Or lose my life, to gain the prize.

"The other disciples came in a little ship, dragging the net with fishes."—John 21, v. 8.

1. Thy least disciple I
In this tempestuous sea
My business occupy,
And urge my way to thee,
My whole employ, till life is o're,
To drag the net, and seek the shore.

2. My partners in the ship,
Master, vouchsafe to bless,
And help us thro' the deep
Into the port of peace
Us, and whome'er our pains have won
Receive, to feast around thy throne.

"As soon as they were come to land, they saw a fire of coals there, and fish laid thereon, and bread."—John 21, v. 9.

Miracles He multiplies!
Ocean yields its hidden store,
Earth the plenteous meal supplies,
Both confess their Master's power!
Still He doth his followers feed,
Still he gives his labourers rest,
Fills our souls with living bread,
Brings us to his heavenly feast.

"Jesus saith unto them, Bring of the fish, which ye have now caught."—John 21, v. 10.

1. Should we not on our labour live,
Sufficient sustenance receive
Who minister the word?
Should we not seek the souls of men,
And whom our happy labours gain
Present unto the Lord?

2. Master, they are not ours but thine,
Caught in the net of love divine,
The captives of thy grace
A willing multitude receive;
And while their joyful hearts believe,
Their mouth shall speak thy praise.

"Peter went up, and drew the net to land."—John 21, v. 11.

1. We nothing catch with all our care,
Till He bestow the power:
And then we still unable are
To draw the net to shore:
The souls inclos'd in Jesus' net
He helps us to bring on,
And by his influence to compleat
The work his grace begun.

2. Sinners drawn forth out of the deep
Of sin and misery,
Lord, thro' thy only name we keep
Till we present to Thee;
We build them up in holiness,
In humble faith and love,
And bring them to that blisful place,
And land them safe above.

"And for all there were so many, yet was not the net broken."—John 21, v. 11.

1. When on that celestial land
Numbers without number stand,
All their differences are o're,
Satan can divide no more,
Neither strife nor sin remains,
Universal concord reigns.

2. All harmoniously combine,
One in unity Divine,
In the bond of perfectness,
Centre of eternal peace,
All compose the church above
Church of pure, consummate love.

"Jesus saith unto them, Come and dine."—John 21, v. 12.

Christ to his servants condescends,
Invites, and treats us as his friends,
Calls us to fellowship with Him
In grace and happiness supream;
Admits, us by his Father blest
Partakers of the heavenly feast,
His glorious fulness to receive
And in his blisful presence live.

"And none of the disciples durst ask him, Who art thou? knowing that it was the Lord."—John 21, v. 12.

1. Conscious of Jesus near,
Struck dumb thro' humble fear,
While we feel his power and love,
Taste unutterable peace,
Dare we in his presence move,
Need we ask him Who He is?

2. We know He is the Lord
By earth and heaven ador'd,
On his plenitude we feed,
Cannot doubt or disbelieve,
Take in Him the real Bread,
Bread which none but God can give.

"Jesus then cometh, and taketh bread, and giveth them."—John 21, v. 13.

1. Jesus, with heavenly bread
Thou dost thy people feed,
Thoughtful of thy meanest guest
Thou distributest the meat,
Master of the gospel-feast
Thou bestow'st the power to eat.

2. All, all the blessings prove
Of thy redeeming love:
Thou who didst the Spirit buy,
Dost to each the Gift impart,
Dost the purchas'd Grace apply,
Pardon write on every heart.

"This is now the third time that Jesus shewed himself to his disciples, after that he was risen from the dead."—John 21, v. 14.

1. Our crucified Head
Is risen indeed!
His witnesses we
Are daily allow'd our Redeemer to see:
His presence He shows,
His blessings bestows,
And provides us our meat,
And admits us with Him at his table to sit.

2. By his Spirit made known,
He visits his own,
Our Saviour appears,
And the needy relieves, and the comfortless chears;
To purest delights
His disciples invites,
And his flesh is our food,
And he gives us to drink of his mystical blood.

3. The Saviour we love
We expect from above
In his body to come,
And receive his elect to our permanent home:
We shall see him again
With his heavenly train,
And in triumph arise,
His companions and friends, to a feast in the skies.

"Lovest thou me more than these? Yea, Lord: thou knowest that I love thee."—John 21, v. 15.

1. He dares no more himself prefer,
Or boast his own superior grace,
But humbly doth his love declare,
His question'd love with warmth express,
Urg'd by the thrice-repeated word,
The man who thrice denied his Lord.

2. But words will not suffice alone
T' evince his love reviv'd indeed:
The lambs whom Jesus calls his own,
The sheep he learns of Christ to feed,
And thus his strong affection

proves
Who Jesus' flock sincerely loves.

"Lord, thou knowest."—John 21, v. 15.

Peter had by experience found
That Thou omniscient art,
Whose piercing eye discerns the ground
Of each deceitful heart:
To Thee for what thy grace hath done
He humbly now appeals,
And while he trusts Thyself alone,
He all his weakness feels.

"He saith unto him again the second time, Lovest thou me?"—John 21, v. 16.

I.

1. No: my sin and shame I own,
Burthen'd with an heart of stone,
Conscious of my misery,
Destitute of love to Thee.

2. But I can to Thee appeal,
Thee who lov'dst my soul so well,
Fain I would the grace obtain,
Love my loving Lord again.

3. Till the Crucified appears
Scattering all my griefs and tears,
Humbled in the dust I cry,
Give me love, or else I die.

4. Thou who freely didst resign
Thy own life to ransom mine,
Manifest the mystery,
Shew thy bleeding love for me.

5. Only thy expiring pain
Can my stubbornness constrain;
But if Thou thy death reveal,
Then the riven rock shall feel;

6. Then I shall to Thee reply
(Vanquish'd by thy passion I)
See the love thy wounds impart,
Read it, Saviour, in my heart.

"He saith unto him again the second time, Lovest thou me?"—John 21, v. 16.

II.

1. Thou knowst that now I love thee not:
Thou know'st that thee I long to love:
And Thou for me the power hast bought,
And wilt the cursed thing remove,
The sin with which I would not part,
Which keeps thy love out of my heart.

2. Thy zeal to save my ransom'd soul
This thing impossible shall do,
And all my love of sin controul
Till love Divine my heart renew,
And force my joyful lips to own
I love thee, Lord, and thee alone.

"Feed my lambs: feed my sheep."—John 21, v. 15, 16.

I.

Help me, Lord, to feed and keep
First the lambs, and then the sheep,
Lambs to make my tenderest care,
Lambs within my arms to bear:
Both my happy charge I make,
Both I cherish for thy sake,
Thus in life and death to prove
Lov'd of thee, that thee I love.

"Feed my lambs: feed my sheep."—John 21, v. 15, 16.

II.

1. Words cannot prove
That Thee I love
My soul's eternal Lover;
Actions must the doubt remove.
And all my soul discover.

2. Fill'd may I be
With charity,
And carry in my bosom
The dear lambs redeem'd by thee,
And rather die than lose 'em.

3. By pangs extreme
Thou didst redeem
The flock of thine election:
Let me give this proof supreme
Of my unfeign'd affection.

4. By thee renew'd,
Thou Shepherd good,
I can thy cross endure,
Strive resisting unto blood
With love divinely pure.

5. Arm'd with thy mind
I come resign'd
A rival of thy passion,
Lose my life with joy, to find
The God of my salvation.

6. Now, dearest Lord,
Let fire or sword
My soul and body sever,
Give me but that parting word
"I love my God forever!"

"Peter was grieved, because he said unto him the third time, Lovest thou me?"—John 21, v. 17.

1. Jesus, I long that grief to feel
Surpassing all the joys below,
That gracious grief unspeakable
Which none but thy true lovers know,
Grief inexpressible, to be
Suspected of not loving Thee.

2. Belov'd by all Thou call'st thine own,
Dear to the pardon'd soul Thou art;
But hast Thou made thy goodness known
To me, or visited my heart?
O how shall I the secret find,
Or know the loving Saviour's mind?

3. Question'd if Thee indeed I love,
Saviour, how can I answer Thee,
The truth of my affection prove,
Unless thy Spirit speaks in me,
Reveals, and sheds thy love abroad,
And fills my simple heart with God?

4. O could I to the Lord appeal
For what the Lord in me hath wrought,
And quietly myself conceal,
By man unnotic'd and forgot,
Thrice happy, that my soul is known,
My love approv'd by God alone.

"Lord, thou knowest all things, thou knowest that I love thee."—John 21, v. 17.

1. Me Thou knowst, my gracious God,
Better than myself I know:
Thou hast shed thy love abroad,
If I taste that heaven below:
If the grace I truly prove,
Ignorant of it's degree,
Whether more, or less I love,
Lord, I leave it all to Thee.

2. Me Thou knowst; let that suffice,
All my thoughts to Thee appear:
Happy, if thy glorious eyes
See with smiles my love sincere!
Only let me labour on,
Like the Shepherd good endure,
Till I lay the body down,
Witness thus My love is pure!

"When thou wast young, thou girdedst thyself, and walkedst whither thou wouldest: but when thou shalt be old, thou shalt stretch forth thy hands, and another shall gird thee, and carry thee whither thou wouldest not."—John 21, v. 18.

1. When young and full of sanguine hope,
And warm in my first love,
My spirit's loins I girded up,
And sought the things above,
Swift on the wings of active zeal
With Jesus message flew,
O'rejoy'd with all my heart and will
My Master's work to do.

2. Freely, where'er I would, I went
Thro' Wisdom's pleasant ways,
Happy to spend, and to be spent
In ministring his grace;
I found no want of will, or power,
In love's sweet task employ'd,
And put forth, every day and hour,
My utmost strength for God.

3. As strong, and glorying in my might
I drew the two-edg'd sword,
Valiant against a troop to fight
The battles of the Lord:
I scorn'd the multitude to dread,
Rush'd on with full career,

And aim'd at each opposer's head,
And smote off many an ear.

4. But now enervated by age
I feel my fierceness gone,
And nature's powers no more engage
To prop the Saviour's throne:
My total impotence I see,
For help on Jesus call,
And stretch my feeble hands to Thee
Who workest all in all.

5. Thy captive, Lord, myself I yield
As purely-passive clay;
Thy holy will be all fulfill'd
Constraining mine t' obey:
My passions by thy Spirit bind,
And govern'd by thy word,
I'l suffer all the woes design'd
To make me like my Lord.

6. Wholly at thy dispose I am,
No longer at my own,
All self-activity disclaim,
And move in God alone;
Transport, do what Thou wilt with me,
A few more evil days,
But bear me safe thro' all to see
My dear Redeemer's face.

"Verily, verily I say unto thee, When thou wast &c."—John 21, v. 18.

Every shepherd under Thee
His love by suffering shews,
Honour, ease, and liberty,
And life itself foregoes;
Life he carries in his hand,
All for Thee accounts but loss,
Ready still at thy command
To die upon thy cross.

"Another shall carry thee whither thou wouldest not."—John 21, v. 18.

Nature innocently may
The bitter cup decline,
While in Jesus words we pray
Thy will be done, not mine!
Jesus' patient Spirit breathe,
Daily bleed and suffer on,
Die the Saviour's latest death,
And win the martyr's crown.

"This spake he signifying by what death he should glorify God."—John 21, v. 19.

1. The hoary saint for heaven mature,
Strengthen'd by this prophetic word,
Those after-sufferings to endure,
In bonds and death pursues his Lord,
His Lord and God he glorifies,
And on a cross, Like Jesus, dies.

2. O for an end like his, whose sin
I have so often made my own,
Ten thousand times unfaithful been
To Christ, as One I ne'er had known,

Ten thousand times by deeds denied,
And trampled on the Crucified.

3. O could I first repent, and prove
The bitterness of Peter's woe;
By labours of intensest love
My loyalty to Jesus show,
And feed his lambs, and feed his sheep,
Yet still go on my way, and weep!

4. Then Lord—but trembling I forbear
To emulate the martyr's crown;
Yet suffer me thy cross to share,
And lay with life the burthen down,
And while Thou dost my spirit receive,
To echo thy last word Forgive!

"And when he had spoken this, he saith unto him, Follow me."—John 21, v. 19.

1. So, Lord, let it be: With my soul I agree
To take up my cross, and to imitate Thee;
My Pattern to trace, And walk in thy ways,
By the labour of love, and the patience of grace.

2. I have nothing to do, But to prove my love true,
And in every estate my Example pursue;
To continue employ'd For the glory of God,
By expending my life, or by shedding my blood.

3. On thyself I depend My steps to attend,
And my goings uphold, till I come to the end;
Till I cross the rough tide With the help of my Guide,
And am lost upon earth, and am found at thy side.

"This spake he, signifying by what death he should glorify God."—John 21, v. 19.

1. Less by action than by patience
Bring we glory to our God;
Suffering sore and strong temptations,
Sin resisting unto blood,
We the strength of grace discover,
Plainly in our weakness seen,
Magnify our heavenly Lover,
Him who gives such power to men.

2. Thus the truth of God we witness,
Thus the truth of faith we prove,
Gain, and evidence our meetness
For th' inheritance above,
Jesus perfect mind expressing,
With our Father's will comply,
Blest with all the gospel-blessing,
Followers of the Lamb, we die.

"Peter seeth the disciple whom Jesus loved, following."—John 21, v. 20.

1. He follows Christ unbidden,
With silent steps pursues,
And sees his Way to Eden,
Who Christ his Pattern views:
He makes no declaration
Of loyalty or zeal,
But feels a strength of passion
Which saints can only feel.

2. His love by action spoken
Attracts the Saviour's eye;
He follows Christ in token
Of readiness to die:
He gives no explanation
Of that he doth record,
And seeks no approbation
But from his dearest Lord.

3. O that with John's affection
I could my Master trace,
Unmov'd by man's inspection,
By man's reproach or praise!
Or if my deed I mention
In true simplicity,
Rejoice that my intention
Is only known to Thee!

"Peter seeing him, saith to Jesus, and what shall this man do?"—John 21, v. 21.

1. Oft thy weak disciple, I
Turn my wandring thought from Thee,
Oft into the future pry,
Ask, What shall tomorrow be?
What doth thy decree intend?
What shall happen to my friend?

2. But suffice the season past:
Now thy kind rebuke I hear,
All my care and thought at last
After Thee with heart sincere
Humbly, patiently to go,
Nothing save thy cross to know.

3. From the curious vain desire
Let me, Lord, this moment cease,
Only for myself inquire
How I may my Master please,
Make my Saviour's glories known,
Live, and die to God alone.

"If I will that he tarry till I come, what is that to thee? follow thou me."—John 21, v. 22.

1. Secret things belong to God,
What He will with others do,
Be it in his season shew'd:
Only Christ I now pursue,
Nothing seek, or know beside
Christ for sinners crucified.

2. What is all the world to me,
Follower of the Lamb Divine!
Closely copying after Thee,
Lord, if I am wholly thine,
Blest with love's simplicity,
What is all the world to me!

"Then went this saying abroad among the brethren that that disciple should not die: yet Jesus said not unto him, He shall not die: but, If I will that he tarry till I come, what is that to thee?"—John 21, v. 23.

1. Shall we on tradition vain
In confidence rely,
Dream with Apostolic men
That John could never die?
Error from the truth may spring,
From Jesus' own misconstrued word,
Saints in proof of falsehood bring
The sayings of their Lord.

2. But by Jesus word alone
The error we gainsay,
Truth divinely genuine own,
And legends cast away;
Thus we understand thy mind,
(Wayfaring men who need not err)
Scripture with thy Spirit find
Its own interpreter.

"This is the disciple which testifieth of these things, and wrote these things: and we know that his testimony is true."—John 21, v. 24.

1. As truth his record we receive,
And Christ the one great God believe
The uncreated Word,
The only true and living Way
Which leads us to eternal day,
The Vision of our Lord.

2. The innocent, atoning Lamb,
Who from his Father's bosom came
We faithfully embrace;
Assur'd, his blood for all he shed,
And rose victorious from the dead,
A sinful world to raise.

3. His Spirit in our hearts hath seal'd
The word on which our faith we build,
The word of truth and love,
And Christ, th' eternal Life, we know
Was manifested here below
That we may reign above.

4. Fountain of life and light Divine,
We comprehend thy love's design,
Thy confessors increase,
The truth we live to ratify,
And witnessing the truth, we die
In everlasting peace.

"And there are also many other things which Jesus did, the which if they should be written every one, I suppose that even the world itself could not contain the books that should be written."—John 21, v. 25.

1. If all were left upon record
Which Jesus spoke and did for man,
His every gracious work and

word
Not all earth's volumes would contain;
Nor could our narrow hearts receive
His mercies inexhaustible,
Nor could the faithless world believe
That Jesus lov'd their souls so well.

2. Impossible for man to read
The whole of Jesus history;
And more than this we cannot need,
Who know that Thou, O Christ, art He!
The Way, the Truth, the Life Thou art;
And when I live, of Thee possest,
Thy Spirit in my loving heart
Supplies, and teaches all the rest.

"Amen."—John 21, v. 25.

Amen! we thus our seal set to,
Our faith's intire assent subjoin
That all, and every word is true,
Inspir'd, infallible, divine:
That all doth perfectly suffice
T' obtain the end for which tis given,
Able thro' faith to make us wise,
And fit us for our thrones in heaven.

Finished April 30, 1764.
Glory to the Alpha and Omega.

Made in the USA
Columbia, SC
05 May 2024